INDIAN ECONOMIC SUPERPOWER

FICTION OR FUTURE?

World Scientific Series on 21st Century Business

ISSN: 1793-5660

Vol. 1   New Business in India: The 21st Century Opportunity
by Paul Davies

Vol. 2   Indian Economic Superpower: Fiction or Future?
edited by Jayashankar M. Swaminathan

World Scientific Series on
21st Century Business : 2

INDIAN ECONOMIC SUPERPOWER

FICTION OR FUTURE?

JAYASHANKAR M. SWAMINATHAN
University of North Carolina at Chapel Hill, USA

World Scientific

NEW JERSEY · LONDON · SINGAPORE · BEIJING · SHANGHAI · HONG KONG · TAIPEI · CHENNAI

Published by

World Scientific Publishing Co. Pte. Ltd.

5 Toh Tuck Link, Singapore 596224

USA office: 27 Warren Street, Suite 401-402, Hackensack, NJ 07601

UK office: 57 Shelton Street, Covent Garden, London WC2H 9HE

Library of Congress Cataloging-in-Publication Data
Indian economic superpower : fiction or future? / edited by Jayashankar M Swaminathan.
    p. cm. -- (World scientific series on 21st century business, ISSN 1793-5660 ; v. 2)
    Includes bibliographical references and index.
    ISBN-13: 978-981-281-465-4
    ISBN-10: 981-281-465-5
    ISBN-13: 978-981-281-466-1
    ISBN-10: 981-281-466-3
    1. India--Economic conditions--1991– 2. Industries--India.
I. Swaminathan, Jayashankar M.
    HC435.3.I62428 2009
    330.954--dc22

                                                            2008053002

British Library Cataloguing-in-Publication Data
A catalogue record for this book is available from the British Library.

Typeset by Stallion Press
Email: enquiries@stallionpress.com

Printed in Singapore by World Scientific Printers

PREFACE

The dawn of the new century has brought India to the economic forefront in the global economy, with an increased awareness of the opportunity that India presents to the rest of the world. The Indian economy has been growing at a frenetic pace of over 7% in this new century, second only to China. The largest democracy in the world, with a population of over one billion and the largest English speaking population outside of the Western hemisphere, India is an attractive destination for business and leisure. People all over the world are eager to know more about India and its growth story.

Even though I have been in the United States since the early 1990s, and am now a US citizen, I too have been curiously studying the breakthrough developments in India over the last decade. It is important to understand that although India has a very old civilization, it is a relatively young nation. India obtained its independence from the British rule in 1947 and so is just over 60 years old (or young). From 1947 to 1990, India adopted a strong form of socialistic democracy and relied heavily on a planned economy based on the Soviet model. During this period, often called the "License Raj," almost everything was tightly and centrally controlled. Planned development was focused on fixing the state of the battered economy and improving agriculture — or at least that is where India showed a lot of progress. Though a number of institutions of higher education (particularly in science, engineering, and management) were established during this period, it was not uncommon for the majority of the graduating class of these institutions to head abroad to seek better opportunities. This was called the "brain drain." I still remember a comment from a senior member of our faculty at the Indian Institute of Technology (IIT, my alma mater) that "brain drain" was far superior to having the "brain in the drain," for that is how the elite viewed the state of the Indian economy then. However, the treatment of the water in this drain had already begun, and it would soon become purified enough to attract the attention of businesses worldwide, creating an oasis of opportunity within just a few decades.

As I witnessed the revival of the state of the Indian economy in the middle and late 1990s, I got the feeling that this was a different country altogether from the one in which I had grown up. Since the beginning of this new century, I have been researching India's development closely. My investigations started with discussions with friends and relatives. I followed the news and read articles about the Indian economy. Then, four years ago, I decided to develop an MBA course on "Doing Business in India" at the Kenan-Flagler Business School, University of North Carolina at Chapel Hill. This course would take me every year for a fortnight to India and give me an opportunity to observe the top firms operating in India from close quarters.

Over the last two years, my knowledge of India has increased manyfold as I have benefited from opportunities to conduct research, consult and interact with CEOs and top managers from firms in India, listen to and discuss government policies with leading bureaucrats and ministers, and present my opinion on India's economic future at global events. Seeking more information on the 'India story,' I read a wide range of recent books on India written by entrepreneurs, academics, travelers, politicians, and journalists, which covered a wide variety of topics related to Indian culture, politics, natural beauty, socioeconomic issues, and outsourcing to India, among others. Although many of these books had interesting dimensions, they were far from what I was looking for — a book that could provide a balanced perspective about the Indian economic growth story; a book that went beyond anecdotal evidence; a book that was not trying to sell something about India, whether tourism, offshoring, or corruption (or the lack thereof); a book that was based on solid research and the experience of individuals who had interacted extensively with businesses in India; a book that could be recommended to my Western and Indian friends alike, colleagues and professors at other universities, managers at multinational firms, and any individuals who might be interested in learning about the Indian business economy's success story, the challenges and opportunities that it faces going forward, and how they could benefit from it. This has led me to create the current book. Although this book is about India and Indian firms, I believe, many of the case examples and success stories can be adopted in other parts of the world as well.

Indian Economic Superpower: Fiction or Future?

This book has three differentiating features.

- First, this book is highly focused. Centered mostly on India's businesses and economy, this book deals little with the much-publicized ancient history of India, its culture, spiritual heritage, caste system, or natural beauty.

- Second, this book has a unique style, one not traditionally found in business books. It is an *integrated collection* of thoughts and ideas from some of the most experienced experts on India. When I decided to create this book, I had the option either to write it all by myself, or to collaborate with a selective group of experts. Although the former would have been easier in terms of execution, I followed the latter approach to create a detailed account of opportunities and predictions across a selected set of vertical sectors. In my opinion, this gives the content of the book more research depth and greater brainpower. Collectively, these experts have had several decades of experience both in working with and in researching Indian firms. The contributors for this book come from a variety of outstanding organizations, including the University of Michigan, New York University, Purdue University, the University of Texas at Austin, the University of North Carolina, the Indian Institute of Management, Deloitte Consulting, and Brickwork India.
- Third, the organization of the book as modular chapters allows readers to selectively focus on the industries in which they are most interested. Each of these chapters, which cover different sectors of the Indian economy, begins with a brief review of what has happened in that sector in India in the last 20 years. This is followed by a discussion of current opportunities and challenges. Finally, the authors discuss what needs to be done in the sector in the upcoming years. Contributors to this book have all tried their very best to provide a balanced perspective of the challenges and opportunities India has faced, and continues to face, in these areas.

This book consists of 11 chapters. The first chapter on "Sea Change" highlights factors that have led to the rapid economic development in India over the last two decades. These changes are both significant and radical, and they have provided much momentum to the Indian business economy. Chapters 2–7 provide accounts of the vertical sectors of outsourcing, software, manufacturing, land and aviation logistics, and healthcare. Each of these chapters starts with a description of the history of the sector along with characteristics that are unique to India, then goes on to describe the current and future trends in that sector in India. Chapter 8 provides specific advice and caveats for firms that are seeking to leverage Indian product and service markets for cost reduction or for growth in revenue or market share. Chapters 9 and 10 then offer concluding discussions on the challenges faced by India as it tries to attain the status of a world economic superpower, along with projections regarding what multinationals can expect from India in the upcoming decades. In Chapter 11, I provide a brief analysis of the impact of the recent global financial crisis. Before each chapter, written by other authors (Chapters 2 to 8), I have provided a brief summary of the content, linking the chapter to the overall perspective of the Indian economy, so that readers wanting to skip a chapter can quickly get an overview of the issues and challenges in that sector, maintaining continuity as they move on.

Although this book covers a number of crucial sectors, other important sectors such as retail, finance, insurance, power, real estate, and agriculture are not addressed in detail, in some cases because the sectors are still regulated (some partially). Hopefully, the brief discussions that I provide in Chapter 10 on some of these sectors will be insightful to the reader. Despite this limitation, I hope that this humble attempt on my part (with the collaboration of the contributors) to provide an informed perspective will be of value to any individual or organization interested in better understanding and benefiting from the Indian economic growth story.

Cutting edge research of this nature cannot take place in an academic environment without active support from the business school. I am thankful to Dean Steve Jones, Senior Associate Deans Doug Shackelford and Jim Dean for their continued interest and support of this project. I wish to thank the Kenan Institute of Private Enterprises for supporting part of my research related to this project. The Center for International Business Education and Research (CIBER) at the Kenan-Flagler Business School funded several MBA students for their trip to India in 2004 when the global immersion course on Doing Business in India was first started. This enabled to jump start the course in the first year. I wish to thank Sherry Wallace, Candice Ward, Patricia Collins, Allison Reid, Emily Wilkins, and Erin Benavides for co-ordinating all logistics related issues during our visits to India which allowed me to channel my efforts towards research of these firms while we were in India. The multiple repetition of this popular course over the last four years enabled extensive research of business in India which eventually has led to this book. A selective group of over 125 business students who came with me to India over the last four years, I believe influenced this project in a big way. Their excitement, passion, and interest in understanding the nuances of doing business in India led to several interesting research questions to me which I have tried to address in this book.

The depth and perspective of research presented in this book could not have been achieved without the full support of all the contributing authors of the different chapters — Vivek Kulkarni, M.S. Krishnan, Narayan Ramasubbu, Ramnath Subramanian, Ananth Iyer, Peter Koudal, Haritha Saranga, Sridhar Seshadri, Pankaj Chandra, Nimit Jain, John Kasarda, Rambabu Venkalayapati, Ravi Anupindi, Mainik Sarkar, Sridhar Balasubramanian, and Prabhudev Konana. Many of them are world renowned experts in their areas and collectively have more than a 100 years of experience researching, managing, and educating Indian firms. I would like to thank each one of them for taking time out from their extremely busy schedules to write their respective chapters and further agreeing to a uniform format for all the chapters. Once all the chapters were submitted, it was important to create a book that flowed reasonably well. I wish to thank Vidya Mani, one of my doctoral students, who provided research support during this project as well as helped in creating a uniform organization of the different chapters. I also wish to thank Lynn Hand for her professional editorial help in creating a uniform writing style across the different chapters of this book. The World Scientific Editor, Ms. Sandhya, was also very helpful in co-ordinating the various stages of this project and helping me with various queries in a timely fashion. In the final stages of the book, I got very useful comments from several colleagues of mine. I wish to thank Saravanan Kesavan, Ann Maruchek, Adam Merserau, Sriram Narayanan, Brian Tomlin, and Harvey Wagner for their thoughtful comments and suggestions that helped me in improving the presentation of the contents of this book.

Last, but not the least, a project of this magnitude could not have been accomplished without the support of my family. My special thanks to my wife Shanti for all the additional parenting efforts and patience that was needed from her end during the hundreds of hours of research and writing that I spent on this book. Also thanks to Aishwarya and Anand, our two kids, who despite their young age, showed a great deal of maturity in understanding and working around the time requirements this project posed on me. Without their help and support, this book would still have been a dream.

I sincerely believe that this book provides a deep and balanced perspective of the Indian economic story and hope that this in turn will answer many of the questions of the present day managers as they attempt to leverage and include India as a powerful player in the global economy of the 21st century.

Jayashankar M. Swaminathan
Chapel Hill, NC

CONTENTS

CHAPTER 1

SEA CHANGE IN THE INDIAN ECONOMY

Jayashankar M. Swaminathan[†]

As the clear blue waves from the Arabian Sea splashed on the walls of Fort Aguarda, which had been turned into a nice five-star hotel, the bollywood music from the beach boy's transistor brought me to the realization that I was indeed in India. This was the summer of 2004, and I was in Goa with 25 MBA students from the Kenan-Flagler Business School at the University of North Carolina–Chapel Hill. Our time in Goa was a short break for us in-between our hectic 10 days in Delhi, Mumbai, and Bangalore studying top firms in India and the challenges and opportunities of doing business there. This was our first year in India. This trip has subsequently become an annual pilgrimage for me, to learn more about the Indian economy and to impart that knowledge to a group of future global managers.

Interestingly, during our visit to India in 2004 there were several times when I temporarily forgot that I was in India because of the surrounding environment that would often resemble and sometimes exceed that in the developed world — while we were visiting the Network Operating Center at Reliance in Mumbai (now Reliance Infocomm) and the Failure Detection Center at Power Grid Corporation in Delhi; while observing the manufacturing excellence at Hero Honda in Gurgaon and Intimate Apparel in Bangalore (MAS Holdings); and also while visiting the software development facility at Infosys in Bangalore and call center operations at Wipro BPO in Delhi (formerly Wipro Spectramind). This experience was not only limited to corporate environments but extended to day-to-day activities, while shopping at the extravagant malls in Delhi and Mumbai, observing the in-flight service and baggage handling of JetAirways, and (during another visit earlier

---

[†] Senior Associate Dean of Academic Affairs and Kay and Van Weatherspoon Distinguished Professor of Operations, Technology and Innovation Management, Kenan-Flagler Business School, University of North Carolina-Chapel Hill.

Fig. 1.1.   Map of India.

that year) leading a classroom discussion at the Indian School of Business in Hyderabad. In each of these situations my expectations were far exceeded.

During the next four years several more trips back to India provided me the opportunity to closely interact with outstanding individuals from firms such as the Reliance Group of Industries, Ranbaxy, Aditya Birla Group, TVS Motors, ICICI Bank, GMR, HCL, Maruti, Mahindras, Godrej, Shoppers Stop, Kingfisher Airlines, Brickworks, and Evalueserve, among others. I have sensed a great deal of passion and energy and the drive to excel during my conversations not only with corporate executives but also with engineers, investment bankers, bureaucrats, and even the country's politicians.

A sea change is taking place in India today. Just like the sea, from a distance the Indian economy appears to be calm and smooth. However, there are rapid and turbulent changes happening at the very core of the Indian business economy whose power and energy are not perceived till one experiences and studies it carefully.

1.1. Earning and Spending More than Parents

First and foremost, the economy has been growing at an amazing rate: more than 7% annually on average over the last decade. According to the World Bank, India is on track to record a growth rate of approximately 9% in 2007 (Table 1.1).[4] This makes India the second fastest-growing economy in the world after China. Although the projections are that the Indian economy is slowing to an extent and will be growing at only 7.5% by 2012, this is still a very fast growth pace. Optimistic estimates, such as those by Goldman Sachs, predict that India's GDP will reach USD1 trillion by 2011, USD2 trillion by 2020, USD6 trillion by 2032, USD10 trillion by 2038, and USD27 trillion by 2050. That would make India the third-largest economy in the world after the United States and China. In this projection, India's GDP will overtake Italy's by the year 2016, France's by 2019, the

Table 1.1.   Snapshot of Indian economy.

Annual data	2007[a]	Historical averages (%)	2003–2007
Population (m)	1110	Population growth	1.4
GDP (USD billion; market exchange rate)	1147	Real GDP growth	8.9
GDP (USD billion; purchasing power parity)	3083	Real domestic demand growth	9.3
GDP per head (USD; market exchange rate)	1033	Inflation	4.9
GDP per head (USD; purchasing power parity)	2777	Current account balance (% of GDP)	−0.4
Exchange rate (average): USD	41.3[b]	FDI inflows (% of GDP)	1.3

[a] Economist Intelligence Unit estimates.
[b] Actual.
Source: www.economist.com/.

United Kingdom's by 2022, Germany's by 2023, and Japan's by 2032. India's current GDP based on market exchange rates is already at USD1.14 trillion.[6]

India's economic growth over the last 20 years has been triggered by the knowledge-based service sector, particularly services related to information technology and business process outsourcing (BPO). As a result, the Indian economy, which in 1990 had a GDP split of 15%, 43%, and 30% among the manufacturing, service, and agriculture sectors, respectively, had changed to 15%, 52%, and 22% by 2003.[9] Over the last four years, the manufacturing sector has also grown quite well in some fiscal quarters, outpacing the growth in services, so that the latest split among these sectors is roughly 16%, 54%, and 17%, respectively.[4]

Much of this growth in the Indian economy has benefited the burgeoning economic middle class, which now comprises over 200 million people. It is important to remember that the middle class in India does not earn the same amount as the middle class in the developed world. A household income of roughly USD5000 qualifies one to be in the middle class in India, while the same status requires closer to USD45,000 in developed countries. Still, the overall purchasing power of the Indian consumer market is quite large. Today's young Indian middle class earns much more than the previous generation (their parents), and due to Indian culture many of these young workers continue to live with their parents even after getting a job, giving them more disposable income on hand. This is one reason that India has been witnessing a consumer spending boom (Fig. 1.2). In 2003, the Indian retail market was estimated at USD250 billion, which put it in the top 10 countries in the world. This market is projected to reach USD400 billion by the year 2010, which would place India in the world's top five retail markets. This growth has had a tremendous impact on many sectors. One such sector is mobile phones: India adds 5.5 million new subscribers every month, according to iSupply. In 2006, the number of subscribers in India reached 149.5 million, and that number is projected to grow to 484 million by 2011. In the

Fig. 1.2.   Affluent Indians are driving consumer spending.

same year, 69.3 million new handsets were sold to Indian consumers, making India the second biggest market after China.[7] To put this in perspective, this is roughly equivalent to every fifth adult or child living in the United States buying a new cell phone every year.

1.2. Collaboration in Infrastructure Development

Whenever the Indian economy is discussed in any forum, very soon the focus turns to the fact that India lacks standards for the infrastructure of basic amenities such as power, water, and transportation. For decades, the Indian government and politicians have talked about improving these, but very little was seen in terms of actual action. Today, there is a sense of urgency among business and political leaders about the improvement of India's infrastructure. My conversation with Mr. Chandrababu Naidu,[a] former Chief Minister of Andhra Pradesh, clearly indicated that the government, as much as the private sector, realizes that infrastructure improvement is one of the keys to economic development in India. Such a focus has led to some outstanding achievements on this front in the last few years.

The Golden Quadrilateral project,[b] valued at USD12 billion, connects India through more than 3000 miles of expressways running from Delhi (in the north) to Kolkata (in the east) to Chennai and Bangalore (in the south) to Mumbai (in the west) and back to Delhi. This initiative was started by the Bhartiya Janata Party during its tenure and was continued by the Congress and Alliance parties after they took office in 2005, and it is now almost complete. On a recent visit to India, I was astonished by the speed and relative ease with which one could travel from Chennai to Bangalore by road, which 25 years ago could only have occurred in a dream. The Delhi Metrorail, which was started in 2002 with just 8.5 km[c] of track, has been a tremendous success over the last five years. Phase I of the project, with 65 km of track, was completed on time in 2005, and Phase II of the project, which is currently underway, is expected to have 121 km of its route completed by 2010. On a busy day, the Delhi Metrorail has the capacity to carry 650,000 passengers, and it is

---

[a] Mr. Naidu, who is the leader of the Telugu Desam Party, is often credited with making Hyderabad, a city in southern India, one of the most sought-after locations for multinational operations. He is considered a revolutionary leader who believes that change at all levels in the government is needed to take India to the next level of development. He is also credited with bringing several high-tech firms such as Microsoft and world-class institutions such as the Indian School of Business to the city of Hyderabad.

[b] The Golden Quadrilateral project and other transportation logistics issues are discussed in greater detail in Chapter 5 of this volume.

[c] 1 km = 0.62 miles.

Fig. 1.3.   Rajiv Gandhi International Airport in Hyderabad.

expected to expand to a capacity of 2.6 million passengers by 2010. Following up on Delhi's success, several other major cities in India are planning to build metro-rails as well. Last year, I had the opportunity to visit the greenfield international airport being built at Hyderabad (Fig. 1.3). The airport was expected to have an initial capacity to handle 12 million passengers per year, subsequently expanding to about 40 million passengers per year. This international airport, with several state-of-the-art features, was completed on time in March 2008, something unique worldwide as far as infrastructure projects are concerned. It is a public–private partnership between the GMR group, the Malaysian Airport Holdings Berhard, the state government of Andhra Pradesh, and the Airport Authority of India. This public–private collaborative model is being replicated at other airport projects across the country.[d]

1.3. Going Beyond Software and Information Technology

There have been a number of books that highlight India as a prime offshore destination[1,2] — a place where firms can outsource most of their difficult or routine tasks, such as software maintenance and technical helpdesk services. Bangalore is considered the Silicon Valley of India, where most of the multinationals in the high-tech industry as well as some of the largest Indian software firms such as Infosys, Wipro, Tata Consultancy, and Hindustan Computers Limited (HCL) are located. Clearly, this is an area in which Indian firms have gained a lot of ground over the last 15 years. For example, a recent advertisement by the Government of India indicated that 50% of the Fortune 500 firms have outsourced their information technology operations to India.

Although for a novice, India is mostly about outsourcing technology-related activities, there are other significant things happening today in other industries as

---

[d] See Chapter 6 of this volume for an in-depth look at historical, current, and future trends in India's aviation industry and aviation logistics.

well. The big successes in the software and BPO sectors at the international level have imbued business leaders and managers in other industries with the confidence that they too can excel on the world stage. Some firms such as Reliance Industries are already world leaders. Reliance is the world's largest producer of polyester fiber and yarn, one of the top 10 producers of chemical components such as paraxylene, polypropylene, and purified terepthalic acid. Several other Indian manufacturing firms, in their aspiration to become worldwide leaders in their industries, are taking the acquisition route. In March 2008, Tata Motors signed a deal to acquire the Jaguar and Land Rover brands from Ford Motors. In 2007, Tata Steel acquired Corrus, making it the fifth-largest steel producer in the world, while Aditya Birla Group's Hindalco acquired Novelis, which made it the world's largest aluminum rolling company. The previous year, Mittal Steels acquired Arcelor to become the biggest worldwide producer of steel. Ranbaxy, India's largest pharmaceutical company, acquired Ethimed in Belgium, Terapia in Romania, and the unbranded generic business of Allen SpA of Glaxo Smith Kline in Italy. Recently, Bharti Airtel and Reliance Communications, India's two largest wireless provider have shown interest in acquiring a stake in MTN wireless in South Africa. More recently, Sterlite Industries announced that it plans to acquire the copper mining assets of Arasco in the United States for USD2.8 billion. It is no surprise that when the Boston Consulting Group (BCG) published the recent list of top 100 emerging multinationals from the rapidly developing economies of Argentina, Brazil, Chile, China, Egypt, Hungary, India, Indonesia, Malaysia, Mexico, Poland, Russia, Thailand, and Turkey, India — with 20 companies on the list — was second only to China. These firms are creating exciting new innovations for the world.

One of these innovations is the Nano car, introduced by the Tata Motors earlier this year. The four-door Nano is a little over 10-feet long and nearly 5-feet wide. It is powered by a 623cc two-cylinder engine at the back of the car. With 33 horsepower, the Nano is capable of traveling up to 65 miles an hour. Its four small wheels are at the absolute corners of the car to improve handling, and it has a small trunk, just big enough for a duffel bag. The Nano will go on sale in India later this year for USD2500, with an initial annual production run of 250,000. When plans for this car were unveiled a few years ago, almost no one in the industry could believe that it could be manufactured at this price. Tata says that it will offer the Nano in other emerging markets in Latin America, Southeast Asia and Africa within four years.[5] This is just the tip of the iceberg as far as Indian manufacturing is concerned. Many of the firms on the Boston Consulting Group list will go on to challenge existing multinational firms, but there are many other outstanding firms in India that are not yet on that list, and they are equally hungry to join the world stage in their industries. In the upcoming years, we are likely to witness a change in which India will come to be known for something much more than just being a great location for offshoring tech services.

1.4. Young, Educated, and Motivated Workforce

India is the second-largest country in the world in terms of population and is expected to overtake China sometime in the first half of this century. It is interesting that more than half of the population is under 25 years of age. In comparison, that same percentage is about 40% for China, 30% for the United States, and 25% for Germany. It is true that many in the Indian population are very poor by international standards, but roughly one-third of India's population is in the lower middle class or above. This translates into 350 million people that are eager for success, about 175 million of whom are less than 25-years old. These young men and women have witnessed the growth of multibillion dollar companies such as Infosys and Reliance, both of which were started with personal finances and loans by motivated, bright, and hard-working individuals from the middle class who sought the right opportunities at the right time. They have also heard great success stories about their uncles, aunts, and distant relatives who emigrated from India and now are a part of a vibrant and successful Indian community in different parts of the world, including the Middle East, Malaysia, Singapore, the Caribbean, Kenya, the United Kingdom, the United States, Europe, and Australia. Most of the people who have left India since the 1960s have been the highly educated (from the upper middle class) or highly skilled (from the middle and lower middle classes). The current lower and middle classes believe that they can replicate the success of their relatives and friends who are working in other countries. This "can do" attitude is extremely powerful, especially since India's strength lies to a great extent in its human resources. If a large proportion of the people are energized by a strong positive attitude, then they will be instrumental in changing the whole society — as was witnessed in countries such as the United States in previous centuries.

1.5. Politics and Development Get Decoupled

For several decades after India gained its independence in 1947, political parties in India's democracy were notorious for stalling or scrapping development projects started by the parties of their predecessors (particularly when they were from the opposition). This led to serious problems with development, since one step forward would be followed by two and sometimes three steps backward. Democracy became a curse for India's development plans. However, starting in the early 1990s and even more so recently, I have seen a shift in the way that political parties react to development projects. It would be foolish to claim that political leaders completely support and advance the development projects initiated by their rivals. However, it would not be an understatement to say that there are many cases in which the politicians are supportive of development projects in general. While highlighting the deficiencies in the previous government's execution, these leaders have tried to move the projects forward during their own time in power. This has led to a democracy in which two steps forward are followed by only one step backward. The net effect is that development projects in India are going forward at a slow, yet, positive pace. Once this becomes one step forward followed by another step in the same direction, these projects will start having a major impact on the everyday lives of the Indian people.

1.6. Capital Infusion

Clearly, there is a lot of positive energy and optimism flowing in the Indian economy today. While the world stock indices receded in anticipation of a U.S. recession in 2008, the Sensex (the Bombay stock exchange index, which comprises 30 large Indian firms) set yet another milestone, reaching the 21,000 mark in early January. Since then, it has receded somewhat and is currently at 16,000. To put this in perspective, the Sensex was at about 4000 in 2003. Thus, in the last five years, the Indian stock market has increased fourfold. Given the growing economic momentum, major multinationals such as GE and IBM are expanding their India operations significantly, making this an integral part of their global operations strategy. In 2006, GE announced that by the year 2010 it expects to have USD8 billion in assets in India and would set a target of USD8 billion in revenue from India.[8] The same year IBM announced that it planned to invest USD6 billion by 2010. GE's India Innovation Center is today among the largest design and development centers for the company's global industrial business, while IBM has over 53,000 employees in India, making India its biggest operation (in terms of employees) outside the United States. GE and IBM are not only making asset investments but also aggressively pursuing R&D activities in India, tapping into the large talent pool. Such investments have infused much-needed capital into development. The foreign direct investment (FDI) in India in 2005–2006 was USD5.5 billion, which increased to USD15 billion in 2006–2007. For the 2007–2008 fiscal year, the FDI is anticipated to be roughly USD30 billion, and it is likely to grow in the years to come.[11] But it is clear to see that more is needed, when one compares the level of the FDI in China to that in India: in the past year, China had an FDI of about USD80 billion. However, the ball is now rolling. Considering that in the latest round only USD6 billion of investment has been in the manufacturing sector, which is typically the major component of such investment, future investments in India (barring some unusual situations) should only rise dramatically. For someone like me, who was born in India and is quite familiar with the Indian firms and the Indian economy, the above changes seem to be neither usual nor superficial. They are part of a brewing wave of powerful currents that are leading to this sea change.

1.7. Overview of the Book

In the next seven chapters, various experts provide a comprehensive set of views on important vertical sectors in India, including technology, BPO, manufacturing, logistics, healthcare, and aviation, as well as highlighting how individuals and multinational firms can leverage this growth in India. The contributors include distinguished researchers from top business schools around the world and senior executives from industry and consulting firms, as well as policy makers. Collectively, these experts have had several decades of experience working with and researching Indian firms. They are from outstanding organizations including the University of Michigan, New York University, Purdue University, the University of Texas at Austin, the University of North Carolina, the Indian Institute of Management, Deloitte Consulting, and Brickwork, India.

Each of the following chapters describes the history of a sector along with sector characteristics that are unique to India, followed by a description of current and future trends in that area. Before the chapters, I have provided a brief summary of the content from the perspective of the Indian economy, so that readers can quickly get the gist of the discussion on each sector before going on. The book begins with service-sector industries, such as information technology and BPO, which have been subject to a minimal amount of bureaucratic regulations, then moves on to the manufacturing and logistics sectors, which historically have been tightly controlled by the government but recently have been significantly deregulated. The book subsequently focuses on the rural healthcare sector which has been largely neglected thus far. The final three chapters are intended to help readers gain a better understanding of common pitfalls that multinationals need to avoid, roadblocks to India's achievement of economic superpower status, and potential opportunities in India in the upcoming decade.

India's rise in the global economy over the last couple of decades can be primarily attributed to firms such as Infosys, Wipro, and Tata Consulting Services (TCS) in the ITES (Information technology-enabled services) sector. As it was one of the earliest sectors to be deregulated, and required minimal amount of infrastructural support, it has witnessed phenomenal growth. It is estimated that of the USD100 billion in offshored IT activities worldwide, USD60 billion worth of services will be provided by Indian firms by 2010. In the next two chapters of this book, leading researchers in these sectors explain the story behind

India's success in the IT-enabled services sector. In Chapter 2, Mr. Vivek Kulkarni, the former Secretary of Information Technology in Karnataka and current CEO of Brickwork India,[c] provides first-hand details of the way that Bangalore, once a paradise town for retirees, turned into the Silicon Valley of India. He also provides an analysis of the alternative business models used by firms in these sectors — both low-cost providers and value-added solutions partners — and the challenges they face. In Chapter 3, Dr. M.S. Krishnan, a chaired professor at the Ross School of Business, University of Michigan, and a well-recognized name in the area of software management and information technology, along with his co-authors Dr. Narayan Ramsubbu and Dr. Ramanath Subramanian, provide a detailed account of the historical development of India's information technology and software industry. Based on their experiences in the software sector in India during the early stages of its development in the 1980s and on their research in that sector in both the United States and India over the last 15 years, the authors provide an overview of the developments in this area in India while highlighting the potential pitfalls. In these two chapters, the authors explain subtle differences in the evolution of the information technology (IT) and BPO sectors. While multinationals have tried to participate in this growth, their success has been rather mixed. GE, for example, has been highly successful with its strategy in the BPO sector (as explained in Chapter 2), but firms such as Dell and IBM have had mixed results. On the other hand, in the IT sector IBM seems to have solved the puzzle and is now the leading provider of IT solutions to firms in the growing Indian economy (as explained in Chapter 3). The authors of these chapters also discuss the future of these industries and their potential for multinational players.

While much is known in the Western world about India's strength in terms of IT services, less is known about the strength of Indian manufacturing. In sectors such as automotive components, electronics, and textiles, India is emerging as a leading player. Given that manufacturing has been regulated for a long time (during License Raj) and depends to a great extent on infrastructure, growth in the manufacturing sector has been slow to take off. However, the manufacturing sector in India has registered a higher rate of growth than the service sector for several quarters in the last year. In fact, many leading brands such as Nike, Nokia, Hugo Boss, Samsung, and GM, among others, manufacture products in India. In Chapter 4, Dr. Ananth Iyer, a chaired professor at the Krannert School of Business at Purdue University and a leading scholar in the area of global manufacturing operations, along with his co-authors Mr. Peter Koudal, Dr. Haritha Saranga, and Dr. Sridhar Seshadri, provide a framework for understanding the growth and development in the Indian manufacturing sector (Fig. 1.4). The authors discuss the impact of the formerly tight regulations in this sector on current and

---

[c] A leading knowledge process outsourcing firm, www.b2kcorp.com.

Fig. 1.4.   Apparel manufacturing plant in Bangalore.

future economic prospects. While the manufacturing sector has in the past decade picked up its pace, India still lags behind countries such as China and Mexico when it comes to its role in the global manufacturing supply chains. In an earlier piece,[10] I highlighted logistics (defined as the physical movement of items) as one of the major impediments to supply chain management in India. For example, in 2006 India had 3700 miles of major expressways, while China had 25,000 miles of major expressways and the United States 47,000 miles.[3] India had only 17 major airports, in comparison to 56 in China and 189 in the United States. Similarly, while only 400 million tons of goods went through the ports in India, the same year China shipped 2.9 billion tons through its ports, and the United States 1.4 billion tons. These differences are, in large part, a result of the amount of money that the respective governments have been investing in infrastructure. While China spent roughly 8.5% of its GDP on infrastructure in 2005; the corresponding figure for India was less than 4%.

Recently, the Indian government has recognized the need to improve the logistics infrastructure in the country, and as a result, this is a booming sector today. In Chapter 5, Dr. Pankaj Chandra, Director of the Indian Institute of Management at Bangalore and a sought-after expert on logistics in India, along with his co-author Mr. Nimit Jain, describe the current state of India's ground logistics and highlight the challenges of operating a logistics network in India. In addition to discussing the deficiencies in the logistics network and the current plans of the government to modernize the road network in the country, these authors provide a handful of excellent examples of innovative logistics systems

(a)   (b)

Fig. 1.5. Dabbahwallahs of Mumbai and their tiffin boxes.

in India that have been able to overcome the obstacles posed by India's poor network of roads. For example, the authors discuss the nuances of the Dabbahwallahs (Tiffin Men) of Mumbai (Fig. 1.5). The Dabbahwallahs pick up and deliver 200,000 lunch boxes in a standard container every day and return the same to the place of pickup. The firm has an annual turnover of about USD12 million and employs around 5000 people for pickup and delivery. However, there are less than 10 boxes which have errors in delivery or pickup in a month. According to one estimate, their delivery accuracy is comparable to that of Fedex without usage of computer-based information technology. In Chapter 6, Dr. John Kasarda, a chaired professor at Kenan-Flagler Business School, University of North Carolina–Chapel Hill, who is world-renowned for his work on the "aerotropolis" concept (cities and economic development coupled with airports), along with his co-author Mr. Rambabu Vankayalapati, shed light on the development of the aviation sector in India. They focus on the rapid changes that are occurring in this sector as the Indian economy continues to gain momentum and discuss the upcoming economic revolution in India in terms of the modern aerotropolis, which promises to provide unique advantages to the Indian cities of Delhi, Nagpur, and Hyderabad. Such developments are preparing India to assume a powerful economic position in the next century.

Despite these positive signs, however, several sectors still require major changes before the Indian economy can truthfully claim to be a leading economic superpower. Dr. Ravi Anupindi, a chaired associate professor at the Ross School of Business, University of Michigan, along with his co-authors Dr. Madhuchanda Aundhe and Dr. Mainak Sarkar, highlight some of the formidable hurdles that India is facing in the area of rural healthcare. Although health tourism is on the rise, the daunting task of taking care of the rural poor is also beginning to attract attention. These authors explore new developments in telemedicine in India that can help provide low-cost, high-quality healthcare to people living in the more remote areas of the country. They cite the example of Aravind Eye Care System, which consists of five eye hospitals owned and operated by Aravind as well as two Aravind-managed hospitals. Together, these facilities provide healthcare for over 1.7 million patients and perform over 250,000 surgeries annually. The authors highlight the importance of technology-based innovations that may indeed become an important catalyst in bringing basic health amenities to India's rural poor.

The challenges faced by the Indian economy are many. In Chapter 8, Dr. Sridhar Balasubramanian, a chaired associate professor at the Kenan-Flagler Business School, University of North Carolina at Chapel Hill, along with his co-author Dr. Prabhudev Konana, discuss what precautions and approaches a multinational should take to successfully leverage the opportunities that the Indian economy presents. While the success stories have been many, there have also been many failures, and those firms hoping to take advantage of India's growing product and service markets need to be aware of the pitfalls to be avoided, in both the planning and the implementation stages.

Following this, in Chapter 9, I highlight some of the critical hurdles the Indian economy will need to overcome to claim its spot as a true economic superpower. The biggest challenge, in my opinion, is that of creating mechanisms of inclusive growth. While the middle and upper middle classes in urban areas have flourished over the last 15–20 years, the rural and lower economic classes have been left behind. It is crucial for the Indian government to find mechanisms to include all of India's citizens in the tremendous opportunities for present and future economic growth. This will enable India to continue on its promising route towards an open economy backed by a democratic form of governance. In Chapter 10, I provide an overview of the opportunities that lie ahead in terms of growth and investments in India, as well as thoughts on the reasons that the sea change that we are witnessing will continue and create a storm of outstanding future economic opportunity for the Indian economy and the rest of the world. Finally, in Chapter 11, I provide a brief analysis of the impact of the recent global financial crisis. Sail on!

References

1. Ferris T (2007). *The 4-Hour Workweek*. New York: Crown Publishers.
2. Friedman TL (2005). *The World is Flat, A Brief History of the Twenty-first Century*. New York: Farrar, Stauss and Giroux.
3. Hamm S (2007). The trouble with India (19 March 2007). *Business Week*.
4. http://web.worldbank.org/.
5. http://wheels.blogs.nytimes.com/2008/01/10/tata-nano-the-worlds-cheapest-car/.

6. http://www.economist.com/.

7. http://www.emsnow.com/newsarchives/archivedetails.cfm?ID=18558.

8. http://www.ge.com/.

9. Sinha J. Checking India's Vital signs (2005). *McKinsey Quarterly 2005.*

10. Swaminathan JM (2006). Managing supply chain operations in India: pitfalls and opportunities. In *Supply Chain Management in Emerging Economies*, Lee, H and C-Y Lee (eds.), pp. 137–154, Springer. New York, USA.

11. "To cap it all". (17 April 2007). *The Economist.*

OUTSOURCING

Jayashankar M. Swaminathan

"I've been Bangalored" is a phrase often used in the United States by people whose jobs have been offshored to low-cost destinations. It is estimated that by the year 2010 close to USD25 billion in revenue will be generated by India's offshore industry, which provides business process/knowledge process outsourcing (BPO/KPO) services. The year-to-year growth rate in this industry has been close to 40%. This has generated immense interest not only among multinational corporations, who are offshoring processes to India, but also among graduating students from all over the world. Each year, our MBA students are positively surprised and sometimes jolted when we visit firms such as Wipro (BPO), Brickwork (KPO), or Evalueserve (KPO). When visiting Evalueserve,[2] one of the largest KPO firms in India, last year with our MBA student group, we were welcomed onto their campus by Andrea and Sigrid. Andrea has a master's degree in Economics from Germany, while Sigrid has a master's in Journalism and Communication. They both had decided to work for Evalueserve to gain experience in the offshoring sector, global operations, and working in India. There is a growing number of students who, like Andrea and Sigrid, want to gain experience in working for Indian firms. And why not? Firms such as Evalueserve or Brickwork[1] engage in a number of high-end, value-added activities related to market research, business research analytics, investment research, intellectual property services, and marketing and sales services that can lead to a fulfilling career. This is a win-win situation for both sides, since these firms, which are beginning to set up operations in Europe and Latin America, need employees who can speak languages other than English. As a result, Evalueserve today has 50 international employees in its ranks, up 150% from the same time last year.

The outsourcing activities that started with call centers for technical help are much deeper in both scale and scope today. How did India become such a giant in IT and BPO services? How did Bangalore — the city of retirees — become a globally renowned city?

Fig. E1.1. Call centers.

There is a trend from call center-based outsourcing to knowledge-based outsourcing activities.

In the next chapter, entitled "Offshore to Win, Not Shrink," Mr. Vivek Kulkarni, former Secretary of Information Technology in the state of Karnataka (of which Bangalore is the capital) and the founder and current CEO of Brickwork, Inc., a leading provider of BPO and KPO services, gives an account of the key historical developments that have made Bangalore the services offshoring hub of the world. Mr. Kulkarni also provides an account of lessons learned from offshore winners such as GE and IBM, while highlighting the reasons that other initiatives have failed. He notes the key factors related to failures, including picking the wrong process or activity to offshore; not understanding cultural and communication nuances; not choosing top executives correctly; underestimating the turnover in employees; choosing the wrong partner; and not paying enough attention to security and quality-related issues. He then goes on to discuss alternative offshoring models — the use of captives, third-party vendors, or the build, operate, and transfer model — and their trade offs. Next he provides a framework to enable firms to choose a country, specific city and location, and finally a vendor in India. He discusses current challenges facing offshoring (BPO/KPO) businesses, based on his experience with Brickwork, and he also highlights issues related to operational excellence as well as the crucial need to manage the workforce. Mr. Kulkarni concludes with a description of the growing domestic market and new sectors for business and knowledge process offshoring. It is very clear that call centers are just the tip of the iceberg, as far as BPO is concerned.

References

1. http://www.b2kcorp.com/.
2. http://www.evalueserve.com/.

CHAPTER 2

OFFSHORE TO WIN AND NOT SHRINK!

Vivek Kulkarni[†]

The terms "outsourcing" and "offshoring" have become the bane of the general population of developed countries. And understandably so! After all, they result in jobs being exported to foreign lands. Yet, multinational companies continue to use these two processes to enhance productivity and cut costs. As Thomas Friedman[2] says in his masterpiece, *The World is Flat*, "Outsource to win and not shrink" is the right mantra. Companies should use offshoring to win new customers and new markets and not to cut back the workforce at home.

According to a recent research paper, *Offshoring: Beyond Labor Cost Reduction*, by the Boston Consulting Group, the Indian outsourcing services industry as a whole helps its clients save USD1.5 billion annually. General Electric (GE) alone saves more than USD350 million annually by offshoring about 900 different processes to India. The U.S. banking and financial services sector's costs are 7%–10% lower than that of its European counterparts. For every USD1 invested in India, the value derived by the U.S. economy is between USD12–14. American finance companies have saved USD6 billion in the last four years by offshoring to India. Offshoring has resulted in quality and productivity gains of 15%–20% and customer satisfaction of almost 85%.

Many of the Fortune 500 firms have already taken advantage of this offshoring opportunity, but small and medium enterprises (SMEs) have yet to plunge into outsourcing. How can the small and medium companies win? How can they retain their competitive advantage against large companies that have

---

[†] Former IT Secretary to the government of Karnataka, Bangalore and presently founder CEO of Brickwork India.

already outsourced to India? What lessons can they learn from the successes and failures of large corporations?

Historical Development

2.1. Bangalore — The Birthplace of Modern Offshoring?

Bangalore is the place where it all began. It is a beautiful city in the state of Karnataka in south India. The city is a beautiful sight, full of lakes, gardens, and natural greenery. At over 3000 feet above the sea level, the city has a climate like that of San Diego and is a pleasure to live in. No wonder Bangalore was the choice for most people wanting to relax after retirement. It was called *Pensioners Paradise*.

Over the last decade, outsourcing has changed Bangalore for better and for worse. The number of people employed in IT and BPO outsourcing has been more than those so employed in the entire country of China. Banneraghatta Road, where Accenture and IBM have made their headquarters, boasts over 50,000 jobs in less than a kilometer. The growing number of apartment buildings and the exponential increase in the number of vehicles has made the city a very crowded place now, and the quality of life for ordinary citizens has deteriorated.

In spite of infrastructure bottlenecks that the coalition governments have failed to solve, the city continues to attract foreign companies interested in outsourcing. The secret, of course, is the very versatile talent that is available here. The city produces annually over 30,000 engineering graduates, and several thousand MBAs, doctors, chartered accountants, and more. IBM, with 59,000 employees in India, has made Bangalore its main base of Indian operations. Goldman Sachs, JPMorgan, and Fidelity find their best financial talent here. General Electric, General Motors, Honeywell, and other firms have started over 106 R&D centers here. Astra Zeneca chose Bangalore as the location for their security level-4 biotechnology laboratories. The U.S. National Institutes of Health conducts stem cell research collaboration in the city. Countless multinationals and universities have established joint education programs with India's premier university, the India Institute of Science (IISc). Of late, the city has become the Mecca of medical tourism.

The success of Bangalore has been reproduced in multiple cities across India. Hyderabad, Chennai, Pune, Mumbai, and Gurgaon are leading the pack. The Indian IT revolution has also been expanding to many smaller, formerly sleepy towns like Belgaum, Hubli, Goa, Mangalore, Mysore, Coimbatore, Vishakapatnam, Jaipur, Raipur, and Bhubaneswar.

2.1.1. *The Move Toward Outsourcing*

As the IT and Biotechnology Secretary of the Government of Karnataka, Bangalore, I was fortunate to be a witness to the outsourcing saga since its genesis. Each week during my tenure, I saw at least one new foreign IT company opening an office in Bangalore. After the September 11 terrorist attacks, we expected this pace to slow down. However, although business was very slow for 2–3 months, gradually it picked up as firms continued to express their vote of confidence in Indian offshoring. Later, a number of BPO firms set up bases in Bangalore as well as in other cities in India. This growth meant the creation of thousands of professional jobs. Some estimates put the number of IT professionals currently in Bangalore at 150,000. The consistent growth in the four years beginning from 2000 now ranks Bangalore as the world's biggest IT hub. Presently, Bangalore is home to over 1500 application development firms, 150 systems software firms, and 120 telecom software firms, as well as 100 chip design firms. A UN report recognizes Bangalore as the fourth most advanced tech hub in the world. How did Bangalore develop such a vibrant eco-system?

2.1.2. *Texas Instruments and the First Offshore Development Center*

The year 1984 was a significant one for India, because it was in this year that the IT revolution began in India with the arrival of Texas Instruments' (TI) first offshore development center (ODC) on Indian shores. They came up with a blueprint of an IT outsourcing plan, which proposed that TI would hire Indian engineers to write software code, which would then be electronically transmitted to TI offices in the United States. For this purpose, TI asked the Indian government for a 64 Kbps telecom line, a request that caught India off guard. The proposal was studied in detail by panels of experts, government ministries, and committees. Bureaucrats wondered if national secrets would be compromised, as these could also be electronically transmitted to other countries. A total paradigm shift was required in the thought processes that were the foundation of India's foreign and trade policies. After about three years of deliberation on the pros and cons, the government finally agreed in 1987 to give TI the telecom line. TI now has grown and has filed hundreds of patents from its Bangalore campus.

2.1.3. *IBM Did Not Pull the Plug!*

In the 1990s, telecom connectivity continued to be a major issue. At this time, last mile meant actually digging in the ground to connect the company's network center to the telecom exchange via copper wires. Dealing with the state monopoly — the Department of Telecommunication (DOT) — was not easy. People would wait for years to get a simple landline connection. A few fortunate ones could get them out of turn, thanks to quotas meant for the ruling elite (members of the Indian Parliament). In 1991, IBM finally got tired of waiting for the last mile connectivity for its software operations and threatened to move out of India. In the same year, the Indian government was under severe foreign exchange pressure: the rupee was losing ground and the country's foreign exchange reserves had bottomed out. IBM's withdrawal would have sent a bad signal to the market and led to a considerable outflow of foreign investment. The problem was ingeniously resolved by creating one of the most successful government organizations: the Bangalore-based Software Technology Parks of India (STPI).

STPI solved the last mile problem by collecting signals via wireless radio waves. It eliminated the use of DOT copper lines by setting up a satellite dish on the top of the IBM building in Bangalore and another one at Electronic City to transmit signals from the IBM office to Electronic City via radio waves. Electronic City then beamed the signals via satellite to installations in Europe, and they traveled on to the United States via submarine cables. IBM stayed on!

STPI continued providing service to many more firms. At its last count, the number of IT firms served in Bangalore had surpassed 1200, all of which sport dish antennas on the top of their buildings facing STPI's central satellite dish in Electronic City. Thanks to the STPI's innovative work, telecom liberalization has continued at a feverish pace, putting Bangalore on the world map.

2.1.4. *Y2K Helps India Consolidate*

Although offshoring began with TI in 1984, the single most important driver of the offshoring phenomenon has turned out to be the technological problems related to the year 2000 (or Y2K). Many large firms all over the world were rightly worried about the impact of the date change on their computer systems, as critical portions of their software had to be rewritten. To address this issue, they hired many Indian firms, which in turn hired many Indian programmers to complete the task in time. The same year the world discovered the *Indian Geek Squad*, the tech talent.

2.1.4.1. *The Internet Bubble*

In the same year the Internet bubble burst. Companies like Global Crossing that had built undue capacity in telecom were riding high. Time Warner saw more value in America Online. Rupert Murdoch came to Bangalore to hand over a check of over USD70 million to an entrepreneur to start the Internet company *Indya.com*, which soon went bust.

2.1.4.2. *9/11 Incident*

The terrorist attacks of September 11, 2001, raised concerns all over the world. Many companies canceled their investment plans in India in an effort to reevaluate the risks in a new world in which terrorists signaled their dominance. Even the *Bangalore IT.com* exhibition and tradeshow event that I was managing as the IT secretary saw unprecedented cancellations. With our new slogan airing on the BBC, *"There's more to the future,"* we were able to persuade a large number of exhibitors to reconsider and join in the event that concluded on November 1 of the same year. Although companies slowed down a bit for about six months, after that business was back to normal. Offshoring continued and even boomed: the value of Indian software and services exports is now expected to jump nearly 30% to reach USD40 billion during the fiscal year ending March 2008.

Current and Future Trends

2.2. What can you Offshore?

In India, offshoring began in the late 1980s with small IT application development projects. Traditional IT services include hardware/software maintenance, network administration, and helpdesk services. The IT maintenance will continue to require low-cost labor and will keep up the offshore growth in this sector for quite some time. Application development and maintenance has been one of the mainstays of the Indian IT revolution, currently accounting for about 30% of the business in this area. In systems integration and consulting, only a small portion of the market has been captured by large Indian players such as TCS, Infosys, and Wipro. The remainder of the market resides with multinationals such as IBM and Accenture.

Indian companies used to write small software modules without much idea of how they fitted into the larger system. Many critics described Indian programmers as "software coolies" doing repetitive simple coding. Although the industry started in this manner, it has quickly matured and grown into high-tech areas. The quality of software writing has gone up substantially, and numerous firms have been set up in the areas of system software, telecom software, chip design, analytics, and R&D using very talented Indian manpower.

Offshoring Facts

- In the IT-BPO offshoring industry, Indian employees constitute 28% of the global workforce, followed by China with 11%, Russia 9%, the

Philippines 8%, and Turkey 7%. The city of Bangalore alone has as many IT employees as, if not more than, the entire country of China.

- The Indian market share of the worldwide offshore BPO industry is 46%, while its share in the offshore IT industry is 65%.
- Though these market shares are huge, they represent just 10% of the potential market of USD300 billion dollars that is waiting to be tapped.
- There is a tremendous scope for future growth of business process and IT offshoring. NASSCOM–McKinsey (2005)[3] estimates that India will capture 35%–40% of the still-untapped market over the next five years.
- Within the sector of business process and IT outsourcing, application development and maintenance (ADM) and R&D services have been growing very rapidly. These services currently have a share of 30%–35% and, as other services take their place, are unlikely to grow dramatically in the future.
- As of 2007, the Indian IT-BPO sector (including the domestic and export segments) is growing at an estimated rate of 28%. The turnover of the offshore IT industry grew from USD8.5 billion in 2001 to USD18.4 billion in 2005, which represents an annual compound growth of 21%. During the same period, the BPO industry grew from USD2.3 billion to USD11.4 billion, which translates into a growth of 49% per year.
- The total turnover for the IT-BPO sector in India is expected to exceed USD47.8 billion, nearly a 10-fold increase over the figure of USD4.8 billion reported in the fiscal year 1998.
- As a proportion of national GDP, the aggregate revenue of the Indian technology sector has grown from 1.2% in 1998 to an estimated 5.4% in 2007.
- The Centre for Monitoring Indian Economy (CMIE) says that the BPO and IT outsourcing industries accounted for almost 95% of foreign exchange inflows related to services industries between 2000 and 2004.
- In 1991, the country was plunged into a foreign exchange crisis that compelled the RBI to pledge gold to foreign banks in London; today, thanks to outsourcing, the country has over USD300 billion of foreign reserves.

Quality Software

Software quality depends on user satisfaction. While this is hard to measure, the software development process has to capture users' requirements correctly and produce error-free software. Some firms that have quality processes in-house choose to be audited by standard-setting agencies such as Carnegie Mellon University's Software Engineering Institute, which audits a company's processes and assigns them a Capability Maturity Model (CMM) level. More than 75% of software firms that have the highest CMM levels are from India. Half of these firms are located in Bangalore.

2.2.1. BPO/KPO and Technology Services

In addition to the regular IT services, the new wave of BPO and knowledge process outsourcing (KPO) has been all-pervasive. In the age of the Internet, a company's location is of little consideration. With fast communications and an improving Internet infrastructure, companies can now send knowledge work anywhere — India, China, or the Philippines. The Indian outsourcing industry has evolved from services such as call-center support or check processing to KPO services in which cognitive skills, analysis, and judgment are the tools. A recent outsourcing deal between the British Telecom and the Mumbai-based tech firm Mahindra highlights India's expansion from the world's "back-office" source of data processors and call-center workers to a provider of refined and knowledge-based skills. Currently, about 65% of India's 180,000 outsourcing services workforce is involved in transaction-intensive services.

In the BPO sector, banking and insurance represent 50% of the potential offshore market. Service providers have exploited less than 10% of the total opportunity. In the healthcare sector, India can be a dominant center for global outsourcing. The other most popular areas of business processes that have been offshored are call centers, customer service functions, telemarketing, data entry, content building, medical billing, and insurance claims processing. The more knowledge-oriented sectors are now classified as KPO, including high-end analytics, equity research, financial modeling, valuation, healthcare consulting, market research, business plan drafting, high-end architecture drawings, and more.

Presently, almost half of the IT offshoring services are delivered by a couple of large Tier I players. Tier II players make up another 20% of the IT services market. The captive offshore units of players such as Microsoft, IBM, and Oracle account for 10%–15% of IT services. In terms of BPO, the captive units play a very important role, accounting for 50% of the industry. There are very few emerging players, and companies seem to be using their own captive centers as the answer. Established IT players are also in BPO, but their penetration has been quite nominal (4%–5%). The Tier I companies are maintaining margins of about 25%, which are growing rapidly. Small-scale companies do not have this kind of margin; rather, they are attracted via additional billing rates.

Table 2.1:   Offshore IT and BPO revenues (USD billion).

	2006	2010	CAGR* (%)
India's offshore IT revenues			
R&D services	3.6	6.6	16
Consulting services	0.3	0.7	28
System integration	1.5	4.8	34
Application development and maintenance (ADM)	7.7	13.7	16
Traditional IT	1.6	9.0	55
	2006	2010	CAGR (%)
India's BPO revenues			
Horizontals	1.2	4.5	38
Others	0.8	2.5	33
Pharmaceuticals	0.3	0.9	35
Telecom	0.5	1.7	34
Manufacturing	0.7	2	32
Travel and hospitality	0.3	1.3	45
Banking	2.2	7.6	37
Insurance	1.1	4.8	43

* Compounded Annual Growth Rate.
Note: Based on Brickwork India research estimates.

2.2.2. *IT Infrastructure Management*

Many companies nowadays prefer remote infrastructure management of IT, either through working with third-party vendors in India or by setting up their own. The typical arrangement consists of a round-the-clock network operations center with the monitoring of servers, desktops, ports, and other network elements. Some firms have opted for remote support of their users' desktops worldwide. Once again, the first mover GE supports over 30,000 users in its company via remote IT management based in Bangalore.

2.2.3. *Integrated Offshoring*

Integrated offshoring gives firms a tremendous advantage, in that they are able to control many of the risks related to infrastructure and processes and thus are able to have better control over the overall offshoring process. In terms of planning offshoring strategy, it is useful for companies to plan in an integrated way, such that all the possibilities for offshoring IT, BPO, and infrastructure are considered. In the case of IT, the processes are already defined: the infrastructure must be conducive to such processes as remote desktop management and helpdesk service for the companies. However, in terms of BPOs, the processes could be different. The firms that have adopted integrated offshoring have obtained operating profits in the order of 11% in comparison to companies that have implemented only one or two of the individual offshoring strategies.

2.2.4. Back-Office

Rapid development of IT has led to a class of firms that specialize in back-office work, call centers, financial and accounting services, medical billing, insurance claims processing, and so on. A large number of captives have set up their own centers and are reducing costs while increasing productivity. Dell has set up its technical support center in Bangalore and other cities in India. HSBC's Indian centers support their credit-card operations as well as many other firm-internal processes. GE has professionals in India who write management discussion analysis for the company's annual report. Ernst & Young prepares IRS tax returns for many U.S. clients from their Bangalore center, and a European multinational likewise uses its India center to handle the finance and accounting for their worldwide entities.

2.2.4.1. Medical Billing and Insurance Claims Processing

While insurance claims processing is hugely popular, very few firms do medical billing. In fact, billing requires a thorough understanding of the policies of various healthcare payers, and firms are obliged to hire smarter agents to cope efficiently with the complexities of these policies. Many hospitals in the United States have in-house billing departments that are unable to cope with mounting claims, repeated correspondence with healthcare payers, and complicated patient paperwork. Both the hospitals and the billing firms find themselves unable to recruit and retain quality billers, and they face acute attrition. For these institutions, highly qualified graduates at an offshore Indian center would be able to reduce typing errors, advise on coding, and repeatedly follow up with the payers to enhance revenues for the providers. U.S. hospitals and group practices could save about 40% in billing costs by offshoring, and even more as revenue improves.

2.2.5. Investment Research

Goldman Sachs, Fidelity, JPMorgan, and many other investment firms have their presence in Bangalore and carry out processes connected with investment research. Information providers like Reuters are also competing for local talent. A few third-party vendors also offer investment research. The key to success in all these ventures is the ability to recruit high-quality employees in finance. A large number of the finance professionals in India have mastered the U.S. GAAP (generally accepted accounting principles). This has been possible due to the work of large multinationals that outsource finance and accounting processes, as well as to the drive by NASDAQ to list Indian companies.

2.2.6. Analytics

Quite a number of firms in Bangalore are involved in analytics. However, many of their projects are code-named, as these firms do not want to disclose their competitive advantage. Numerous credit-card players use Indian talent to do pattern matching to provide early warnings of fraud. Some use advanced CRM analytics to leverage a better understanding of customer satisfaction. Advanced analysis aids in market research projects and clinical trials for pharmaceuticals firms. India provides advanced manpower resources in Cognos, Hyperion, Informatica, and SAS. The Indian Statistical Institute, the country's premier institute in statistics and econometrics, has campuses in both Kolkata and Bangalore from which expertise can be sourced. The IISc, Bangalore, with a large number of departments, boasts an excellent faculty as well as talented students in analytics.

2.2.7. Destination R&D

Bangalore has over 106 R&D centers that are involved in extremely innovative research and save millions of dollars for their respective companies. This multidisciplinary research cuts across fields, with engineers and scientists in chemistry, biology, computer science, and mechanical engineering working together to build complex models. Major R&D centers in Bangalore include the General Motors Engineering Center and centers for Delphi and Honeywell. Both the GE's Bangalore R&D center and the John F. Welch Technology Center, described in detail in the next section, illustrates the multiple facets of R&D in India.

2.2.8. *Knowledge Centers*

Many multinationals have established knowledge centers in India. These centers employ highly qualified professionals that support analysts and consultants in the United States. The knowledge center analysts do web and market research and competitor and industry analysis. They also summarize articles, prepare concept papers and PowerPoint presentations, and produce Excel sheets and financial models. When a brand manager wants to introduce a new product, the knowledge center can provide with various options for positioning the product as well as information about how to avoid violating competitors' patents.

Knowledge center professionals are relatively difficult to recruit. Some centers employ engineers, doctorates, and intellectual property attorneys. While India has plenty of talent, recruiting qualified analysts has become a significant challenge and requires an in-depth understanding of the Indian educational system, described elsewhere in this chapter.

In summary, outsourcing to India includes not just simple application processing, but many complex knowledge-oriented sectors. The bulk of outsourcing in BPO, not surprisingly, predominantly involves mundane, repetitive tasks, however.

2.3. India Strategy

This section highlights how firms can articulate their India offshoring strategy. We first discuss several innovative winners that have profited from offshoring, followed by the stories of a few losers that made strategic and tactical mistakes. Based on these lessons, some possible offshoring models emerge. Along the way, this section gives specific tips on how to choose a specific country, location, and vendor for offshoring.

2.3.1. *Offshore Winners*

Since it is mostly large companies that have taken advantage of offshoring opportunities, most winners are, naturally, large organizations. Offshoring, however, offers benefits for small- and medium-sized companies as well.

2.3.1.1. *General Electric*

General Electric, one of the most innovative companies in the world, is a guide to what can be outsourced. In the early 1990s, GE's former chief executive

Jack Welch stated that "70–70–70" would be his company's rule for technology offshoring: 70% of the GE work would be done by outside suppliers, 70% of this outside work overseas, and 70% of this overseas work in India. Welch's vision was to rebuild the company using Indian resources. GE now has over 20,000 employees in India, 70% of whom support GE's global operations. The company's activities in India can be grouped into six categories: (i) local market sales and services; (ii) sourced software in Global Development Centers and Global Engineering Centers; (iii) GE-owned technology and software operations; (iv) back-room services such as call centers and legal and accounting processes; (v) exporting of components and products made by GE; and (vi) sourcing of components from key suppliers for export to GE's global manufacturing locations.

GE began by offshoring traditional software services to a couple of Indian vendors, with whom it could drive hard bargains due to its large-volume deals. The "big three" IT firms in India have all had work from GE. While GE concentrated on knowledge services in Bangalore, the company began with routine transactions processing in Delhi. GE's shared services center in Delhi offered back-office solutions, call centers, and legal and accounting services to their constituent companies all over the world. GE grew this entity to over 20,000 people. Finally, the company was able to monetize its offshoring operations by selling the services center entity to private equity investors.

GE's knowledge service initiative in Bangalore has been spectacular. GE has set up the John F. Welch Technology Center on over 50 acres of land in Whitefield Bangalore, and it has become GE's biggest research center outside the United States, with 1700 Indian engineers, designers, and scientists carrying out advanced R&D. It now employs over 2000 Ph.Ds, and GE is looking to expand this number to 3000. Among the current employees, 60% are from India and the remainder from other countries. This gives an international and cosmopolitan feel to the campus.

As the Finance Secretary of the state, I had to persuade a powerful lobby that opposed the allocation of land for this facility. GE persevered through a roller coaster of land allotment, cancellation, and court cases and finally was permitted to begin construction. In spite of revenue pressures and concerns about Karnataka's high budget deficit, I realized the importance of this vital initiative. Considering the prestige it would bring, I agreed to a number of special incentives for this research center. The state government spent substantial sums to provide a redundant electric network for the company, which ensured that GE would have two secure power sources from the utility. GE also set up its own power plant as a back-up in case the state power failed. The existence of a multiple-level uninterrupted power supply system protects GE's labs, servers, and work stations.

GE has also set up several associated laboratories to support their goods and services. The center has patent lawyers and Ph.Ds in IT, materials science, chemistry, biotechnology, nanotechnology, data analytics, and more. A group of 18 professionals from the India team has enabled GE to increase production in its Spain plant by over 25% with no extra capital expenditure by studying the lean manufacturing processes, simulating them in their Bangalore lab, and coming up with the optimum process. Thanks to their efforts, GE has been able to save at least USD150 million while achieving this increase in production.

GE's Knowledge Center in Bangalore shares the same campus. The center employs over 100 professionals in finance, intellectual property, the manufacturing domain, and marketing. The company, thus, has essentially established a consulting unit in its own backyard. If GE had hired an agency such as McKinsey, it would have had to spend millions of dollars to obtain similar results.

As successful as it has been, GE is not just one isolated example. The following section describes how offshoring has saved other companies millions of dollars and made firms in the developed world more efficient and productive.

2.3.2. *Profit from Outsourcing*

Foreign companies in sectors as diverse as banking, IT, aviation, retail, and engineering can win through offshoring. Here are some typical examples of firms that have achieved success through outsourcing partnerships with India.

- IBM employs over 59,000 people in its different offshoring centers. In a recent address to a group of Wall Street analysts at the Bangalore Palace grounds, CEO Sam Palmisano announced IBM's plans for a three-fold investment increase in India over the next few years. Almost 30% of the world's offshore talent is in India — no wonder then that IBM has more employees in India than in any other country except the United States.
- Although Sony was content with the services provided by Cap Gemini, a leading provider of consulting technology and outsourcing services, it decided to switch to India's Wipro in 2002. Cap Gemini could not compete with Wipro's low-priced offshore resources. In signing a USD5 million contract, under which Wipro would write IT applications for Sony's TV and computer assembly plants in the United States, Sony expected to save 30% in costs. Wipro won because it could not only offer low-cost labor but also help Sony build expertise and achieve economies of scale.
- Companies such as Citibank and American Express have achieved savings in millions of dollars through offshoring. Often, firms worry about their data security, particularly in financial transactions. A leading U.S. bank discovered a large number of instances of fraud in the course of domestic business in the United States. When the same operations were handled in India by a different set of graduates working in a different culture — employees having

greater diligence and showing more attention to detail — the company was able to save millions of dollars through avoiding fraud.

- Delta Air Lines outsourced some of its worldwide reservation services to India-based Wipro Spectra mind. This third-party vendor manages Delta's reservations from its Mumbai call center, a move that saves Delta over USD30 million a year.

- In the telecommunications industry, BellSouth Corporation outsources IT work to Accenture in India. The company plans to move one-third to one-half of its IT application work offshore, saving USD275 million over five years.

- In the software industry, Microsoft announced a USD100 million investment to improve its Indian product development and R&D center. Microsoft began its operations in Hyderabad, but as IT Secretary, I began wooing Microsoft to come to Bangalore. Following a meeting in Delhi with Bill Gates and the Karnataka Chief Minister, Mr. Gates expressed interest in our drive to make Karnataka a zero-piracy state, and he visited Bangalore soon thereafter. We signed a memorandum to create *BangaloreOne,* an e-governance initiative, as well as an intellectual property protection memorandum. Microsoft subsequently opened a technical support center in Bangalore that serves their premium customers in the United States, as well as a scalability lab and an R&D center, for which Bangalore offers the best technical resources in the world.

- Oracle announced plans to double its software development workforce in India to 10,000 people. This company now owns at least five facilities in India, three of them in Bangalore. Oracle's Bangalore facility writes most of the firm's advanced software, as well as conducting sales and operations. Indian engineers support their U.S. counterparts in business development, prepare research on prospects, do presentations, and talk to customers to understand their requirements.

- In the retail industry, Home Depot sent some of its IT application development offshore to India-based Wipro. Starting with the development of a comprehensive security system, the partnership has spanned a wide range of projects — from the globalization of store applications to the development of point-of-sale and merchandise systems.

- The investment bank Goldman Sachs has relocated part of its IT, equity research, and administrative operations to its Indian center in Bangalore, employing about 500 IT and administrative staff. In the private equity sector, General Atlantic announced a USD100 million investment in India's sixth-largest software services exporter, Patni Computer Systems. This provides a tangible evidence of the American private equity market's belief in the outsourcing industry.

- Fluor is currently offshoring architectural design work. The company employs more than 1200 engineers and draftsmen in the Philippines, Poland, and India to turn draft plans of giant, multibillion-dollar industrial projects into detailed blueprints. Some of these construction projects, including a petrochemical plant in Saudi Arabia, require nearly 50,000 separate construction plans. To develop these plans, Fluor has offshore engineers to collaborate with their U.S. and British engineers via Web portals in real time.
- Bechtel Group, a large engineering-construction firm, employs 400 engineers in New Delhi, India. The average starting salary of a Bechtel engineer in India is USD4000 per year, compared to USD70,000 in the United States. With such salary differentials, it is obvious why Bechtel and other engineering firms (including Fluor) are outsourcing much of their architectural and design work.

The brain chips for many brand-name cell phones are designed in Bangalore. If one rents a car from Avis online, the data management is done in Bangalore. Tracing lost luggage on Delta or British Airways is done from Bangalore. The back-room accounting and computer maintenance for scores of global firms are done from Bangalore, Mumbai, Chennai, and other major Indian cities. The range of firms and sectors benefiting from offshoring to India is growing and will continue to expand in the future.

2.3.3. *Learn from Failures*

While winners inspire, the stories of losers provide valuable lessons for firms looking to take advantage of the offshoring phenomenon. Since companies usually cover up failures, it is hard to find case studies of firms that have not succeeded in their offshoring efforts. Nevertheless, this section offers a few examples of companies that failed in outsourcing, for reasons as diverse as the lack of work-process planning, the overlooking of regulatory problems, inadequate HR practices, the misunderstanding of local culture, or inadequate support from top management.

2.3.3.1. *Data Centers May Not Be a Good Idea*

Offshoring the operations of a data center may not be the best idea, since the cost savings are not huge — for offshoring to India, the savings are only 5%–6%. Companies thus may be better off locating their data centers in their own countries. The data center cost components include costs related to hardware, software, the network, and the facility. The firm's offshoring savings might only come from the labor cost, however, which is a very small component of the overall data center cost. One prominent U.S. investment bank had a bitter experience with their data center in Bangalore. The bank's honest admission that no one was employed in their data center created peculiar regulatory issues, and as a result, the bank had to grapple with customs and other regulatory authorities. If offshore data centers must be set up, the choice of location and the structure of the organization must be carefully considered to avoid future pitfalls.

2.3.3.2. *Get the Local Culture Right*

The corporate governance models employed by offshoring companies vary. Some companies trust in their Indian management and primarily hire local staff. Other companies have tried to bring in Western culture in very substantial doses — and failed miserably. One large technical support operation that came to India from the United States decided to set up its offshore operations in an extremely expensive location for real estate. Once set up, the company indulged in lavish practices, and the senior management organized a large number of night parties for all the staff. The management felt that this would motivate the staff to stay with the company as well as improve their productivity. However, in the end these parties created a sense of a different culture within the organization. Employees felt that attending such parties and engaging in witty conversation were more important than the firm's actual operations. This company, which had expanded to almost 600 employees, eventually could no longer sustain its operations in Bangalore, and the firm's operations were shifted to the Philippines.

2.3.3.3. *Choose the CEO Carefully*

A large Korean conglomerate set up its software development center in India. Departing from their usual model of retaining a local Korean to head the center, they hired an Indian CEO for this role. However, although the center spent a considerable sum of money, it could not scale up, nor was it profitable. This was a case of poor recruitment of the Indian CEO. Choosing an Indian CEO has to be done very carefully, by means of a number of interviews with the local team, face-to-face meetings with the candidate, and if possible having the candidate visit the company's headquarters to observe his/her vision, communication skills, and understanding of the corporate culture.

2.3.3.4. *Communicate Right*

Apple began its offshoring with a bang, recruiting a former executive from Dell who had scaled up its technical support operations to a 2000-employee center in just two years. Apple bought the servers and networking and other equipment, recruited senior staff and then suddenly closed. Their public communication was confusing and unclear: it was felt that Apple had left India in order to offer better service to Americans by hiring local U.S. agents in their call centers. While the decision to leave is understandable, Apple's communication could have been better. The hiring of as few as 30 people would not have been a huge drain on a billion-dollar company like Apple, and they would have been able to make a slower and more honorable exit. With its products now being big money spinners, Apple may not presently need to achieve cost savings, but eventually it might. Furthermore, India and China are expected to represent 45% of the world GDP within the next few decades, and it will be important for multinationals in these countries to manage the local sentiments well.

Dell likewise withdrew certain divisions of its offshoring agents, shifting operations to the United States. This resulted in a lot of publicity for the company in the United States, where the sentiments against offshoring ran high. The company, however, communicated well with its Indian staff and the local community and averted any major conflicts with local sentiments. Dell continues to expand its operations in India.

2.3.3.5. *Manage Attrition Well*

A French company that is big in smart cards failed in Bangalore. They hired some of the best talent and started their operations in the most advanced IT park. But just when the going seemed great, the company decided to close the operations. The managers never connected with their local staff and made an ugly exit. The company suddenly closed its doors, packed the belongings of their employees, and said it had moved to Dubai. The employees were shocked and protested. An indication of underlying problems, however, was that this company had been experiencing an unusually high attrition of 45%, while the industry average in Bangalore was just 12%. It was, and it still is, an employee's market in Bangalore. Each worker gets three or four job offers and has a lot of choices. If the company had informed its workers as little as three months in advance, many would have happily found other jobs, while others might have been willing to travel with the company to Dubai. Even though multinationals may pay high salaries, it is important for them to keep in close communication with their Indian employees. Managing the human resources function can be the single biggest challenge in offshoring operations.

2.3.3.6. *Pay Attention to the Security of Information*

A number of captives and third-parties have faced the issue of the leakage of sensitive financial and health information of their customers in developed countries. These cases have been reported both in the press and on television. While leakage cannot be entirely prevented, it is critical for firms to work with the local authorities to identify the culprits and take appropriate corrective action. Most employees are honest and can help to prevent or stop such leaks by informing the management, if the right culture exists. In fact, keeping employee morale high is the best way to prevent such occurrences. Also, the standard agreement on the nondisclosure of confidential information has to be drafted properly, with the relevant local laws in mind.

2.3.3.7. *Choose Third-Party Vendors Carefully*

India has a history of too many companies rushing in to make money in whatever sector is hot. This can lead to the proliferation of third-party vendors that are of doubtful quality. There have been cases in which the results of a firm's clinical trials were reported without actual delivery or testing. When medical transcription was the talk of the town, hundreds of companies came in and the rates per line fell to ridiculous levels. When call centers became popular, many companies sprang up virtually overnight, without proper quality-control processes in place. Many Indian politicians back such ventures, investing considerable sums of "black money." While the infrastructure of these firms may be good, the underlying management can be a serious problem. Choosing the right third-party vendor in India can be a daunting exercise and must be done with due care.

2.3.3.8. *Choose the Right Hospital*

India is fast becoming a center for medical tourism, which is a burgeoning business. European and U.S. patients come to India for surgery that is very cost-effective relative to their home country: heart bypass surgery, for example, can cost just USD4000 in India, compared to USD40,000 in the United States. However, hospitals must be chosen with caution. In India, the entire hospital sector is unregulated, and while many hospitals have an excellent infrastructure, the quality of care can differ widely. Many lack standardized protocols of treatment and depend on the judgment of the physicians. Serious errors can occur: a German patient visiting a city hospital of dental surgery was injected with a brine solution instead of local anesthesia. The patient developed severe complications and had to return to Germany to complete her treatment. Furthermore, choosing provider network partners in India can be a daunting task for health insurance firms in developed countries. While life insurers are doing quite well, health insurance companies have thus far been unable to enter the Indian market.

2.4. Offshoring Models

Based on the successes and failures of the companies described above, I have highlighted a few possible models for offshoring, along with other issues that are critical in setting up an offshore development center.

There are three basic offshoring models that companies can adopt: setting up a captive unit; hiring a third-party vendor; or using the build-operate-transfer (BOT) model. Hybrids of two or more of these may also be used. There are pros and cons to each model, which I briefly describe below.

2.4.1. *Captives*

This has been by far the most popular model, one that particularly suits large multinationals. These firms set up their own branch office in India, appoint an expatriate manager to oversee the operations, recruit and employ local talent, and keep their processes in-house. This model is beneficial when the company believes that its processes are the key to its competitive advantage and cannot be shared.

Many U.S. firms appoint managers of Indian origin who are educated in the United States and who may even have had experience in the captive's U.S. headquarters. However, most non-U.S. firms appoint managers from their home countries, due to the lack of supply of managers of Indian origin. Expatriate managers often set up extremely expensive facilities, as they lack local knowledge and find many items relatively inexpensive compared to the prices they are used to back home.

Captives display several short-term gains, primarily their ability to scale up quickly. They recruit at a pace much faster than is possible at home, train these new agents, and migrate processes from their country to India much faster than they had envisioned. Dell, for instance, came into Bangalore with a business plan to scale up to 900 agents within three years. They were able to scale up to 1800 in less than 18 months, recruiting more than 600 employees in a month. Their present workforce is over 5000 in Bangalore alone. Most captives lease their facilities from private real estate players. Leasing, however, does not lessen the challenges of understanding the value proposition based on real estate location, and this is where local managers can help to enhance a firm's return on investment.

There are a number of long-term risks associated with captives. First, the cost structure of captives gets bloated faster than that of a comparative third-party vendor. Other risks include ineffective recruitment that leads to heavy losses; a large headcount, which turns management and training into a mammoth task; lax monitoring, which can lead to quality issues; and communication issues arising out of a lack of appreciation of the Indian work culture.

Most captive managers end up negotiating relatively high costs for their facilities, transportation services, and employee salaries. Quite often, this occurs when the facilities are set up by expatriates, who find Indian salaries and costs far lower than those they are used to. Eventually, this shows up in a bloated cost structure. We find the same phenomenon in a few third-party vendors, recklessly funded by foreign venture funds.

2.4.1.1. *Faulty Recruitment*

Many captives are carried away by the rapid pace of recruitment, but in that process, many things can go wrong. In one such case, the senior vice president of HR in a multinational captive forgot his cell phone near the CEO's table. The CEO picked it up and decided to return it later. When the cell phone rang, the CEO answered the call and was dismayed to find that the caller was asking where the money was to be delivered. After further conversation, the CEO realized that his HR manager was receiving money from external recruitment consultants. The vice president was, of course, fired. This episode illustrates how careful captives must be in their recruitment. If they are not, they will pay the price in terms of increased costs and poor quality of recruits.

India has many companies that give false experience certificates. A multinational might feel that it has hired the most experienced candidates, when in reality it has hired workers who simply have not got jobs elsewhere. Candidates have learned to fudge experience letters and salary certificates in other ways also: they scan the real salary slip, insert a new, higher rate, and then make a good print-out. Technology has made such frauds much easier. For this reason, administering a test to candidates and holding an internal panel interview with them would be a better way to judge their credentials. It is also important to check with previous employers before hiring. Since some recruitment consultants themselves sometimes engage in questionable practices, it is better to use other methods to hire quality personnel.

2.4.1.2. *Managers or School Monitors?*

Most captives recruit fast and promote even faster. Their employees, including team leaders and managers, are often young. These managers may not have dealt with labor issues before, and the outsourcing industry may not yet have gone through the full business cycle of ups and downs. Captives' employees are paid some of the highest salaries and work in the best environments. After a few years, associations and groups may arise within the organization. For instance, a call center group may threaten the captive management, saying that they will stop taking calls unless their salaries are increased. Such labor troubles could arise in the future, and if they do, the captives' young managers might not be able to cope with them.

2.4.1.3. *Quality Issues*

BPO operations require daily monitoring. There is never a time when firms can be assured that everything is under control and that all processes will continue on smoothly. If not monitored properly, employees may find ingenious ways to beat the incentive schemes, at the expense of captives' end customers. For example, unless carefully monitored, agents may report incorrect performance metrics. This problem, however, is not unique to captives. There have been instances of third-party vendors with lax monitoring systems that have committed fatal mistakes in their operations. Third-party operations audits must also be encouraged.

2.4.1.4. *Indian Work Culture*

Unless the Indian work culture is understood well, it can lead to long-term failures. Indians respect their elders and expect a fair degree of hierarchy. Women have traditionally been homemakers, but they now are entering the workforce in considerable numbers. Indian families believe in simple living and consequently save substantially.

The entry of captives has ushered in several changes in the work style. On the positive side, the captives operate with a friendly, informal management style. Indians are learning professional management styles, are beginning to use first names while talking to their managers, and are getting used to teamwork. Indians' work ethic, sensitivity to deadlines, and oral and written communication skills have improved substantially, thanks to expatriate managers.

There are some negatives, though. Most captives recruit young workers who are paid much more than their parents ever dreamed of earning. These young people have a lot of money and are getting used to an American life style. They attend more parties and spend more. Some have taken up smoking or drug abuse, and a few centers are seeing problems with this in their facilities. Unless monitored properly, these issues can result in lower work quality. Large captives with deep pockets can even be the targets of lawsuits that could emanate from drug abuse in their facilities.

2.4.2. *Third-Party Vendors*

The second offshoring model is the use of third-party vendors. These companies can deliver just like the captives, and they remain the only solution for small- and medium-sized American firms that would like to take advantage of the economies of offshoring. Even the larger firms would do well to selectively use these vendors as a risk-mitigating measure.

The Indian centers of global third-party vendors are subject to the same risks as captives. However, as the third-party vendors are local, they have certain advantages. Their primary advantage is their ability to understand local issues, recruit effectively, and operate under a low-cost structure. But challenges abound. A large number of third-party vendors lack investments in infrastructure and quality processes, and they may also lack an articulate management that understands the U.S. work culture. A few third-party vendors with large facilities have been set up by nonprofessionals primarily with the backing of black money. The key to selecting the right third-party vendor is to evaluate the ability of the management to set up, operate, and run high-quality U.S. processes as well as having an in-depth understanding of the Indian scenario. The engagement model should be supportive and provide up-front help in investments. The vendor may not be able to obtain the necessary investments from commercial banks, as they have little experience lending to companies involved in outsourcing. Having established a relationship with the vendor, the large multinational can then cultivate it as their eventual captive, reaping rich rewards.

2.4.3. *Build, Operate, and Transfer*

Many large corporations have recently negotiated BOT deals that transfer all the set-up risks to a third-party vendor initially, with a plan to take over the center three to five years later. This model combines the benefits of the first two models. It allows big players to institute certain security processes to preserve their intellectual property and gives the centers the option to transfer core processes back to the parent and continue with the third-party vendor in most other processes. As with the two previous models, there are examples of both success and failure among firms employing BOT.

2.5. Where to Offshore?

Having got the model right, the next question is where to offshore. Companies could offshore to India, China, Eastern Europe, or a number of other countries. Assuming a firm chooses India, it must choose a city and specific location. The following paragraphs describe how to practice effective offshoring in regard to the choice of country and city, specific location, facility, infrastructure, telecommunications, transport, airports, and other issues. Most of these factors play a separate role, and they are not presented in any particular order of importance. Being the most critical issue, talent management is discussed separately.

2.5.1. *Choosing a Country*

Client companies would be well advised to study the geopolitical stability and infrastructure capabilities — among other factors — in the outsourcing service provider's country. Corporations should moreover consider a risk-mitigation approach in which they spread operational risks across multiple locations.

India is the undisputed leader in both IT and BPO offshoring, offering a menu of possibilities in application software, system software, chip design, R&D, back-office processes, knowledge processing, and more. Canada comes second to India in terms of both IT and BPO offshoring. Being near to the United States and having similar political conditions, outsourcing in Canada is actually "near-shoring," but it is relatively expensive. Ireland has been the traditional center, with excellent software talent, but it is also relatively more expensive. The Philippines offers excellent manpower for customer services and call centers. China is more focused on Japan and presently offers services primarily in embedded software. Russia has excellent engineering manpower, but its political system has not been developing well. South Africa has specialized in actuarial services that are particularly useful for the insurance industry. This country has strong linkages to regulators in the United Kinngdom and provides a pool of excellent talent in this industry. Sri Lanka has many accountants. Eastern Europe is an important location for companies that follow the Eastern European Data Protection Act. Poland, the Czech Republic, Hungary, and Romania are also fast emerging as sources for European back-office processing, as they offer skills in

IT and BPO services global exports

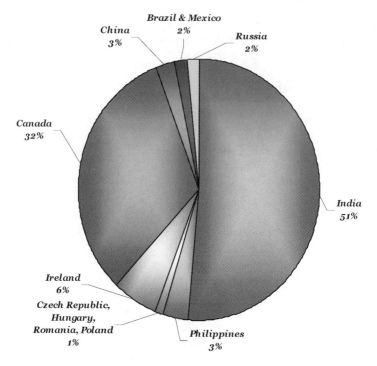

Fig. 2.1. Outsourcing-related market shares of various countries (Total market size — USD45 billion).

Table 2.2: Total outsourcing market IT and BPO.

India story	IT(%)	BPO(%)
Market share	65	46
Projected growth (CAGR)	21	49

German and French. Mexico offers Spanish-language capability and custom software development. The pie chart below shows the outsourcing-related market shares of these countries (Fig. 2.1, Table 2.2).

India continues to lead in offshoring, especially in traditional IT processes such as application development (which has two-thirds of the market share).

In regard to call centers and helpdesks, India leads with a large talent that can speak English and communicate well with customers. Even in high-end engineering, business research, and analytics, India accounts for half of the global market. Finance, accounting and human resources are other areas in which India has a 50% share. Only in the R&D of certain already established industries have countries such as China and Russia come in. The market for this kind of R&D, which mostly involves the testing of engineering products, is divided among India, China, and Russia.

In choosing a country, firms must take into account physical security, including the level of risk for their employees. In this respect, India scores high and comes close to what Ireland can offer. There are a number of ways to mitigate potential losses caused by political instability, power cuts, and *bandhs* (a local phenomenon lasting 1–2 days in which a section of society protests on a particular issue by blocking roads and forcing shops to close, leading people to stay indoors). With in-house Internet capability, collaborative software, and adequate planning, operations can still be kept running despite these events.

India's labor cost, taken as an average across different categories of employees in an offshore enterprise, is one of the lowest — about 15% of the comparable U.S. labor cost. Of course, the labor cost for higher-end workers, financial researchers, CPAs, R&D personnel, and IT project managers will reflect a different (and more expensive) relative picture. Other countries with low labor cost are the Philippines, China, and Malaysia (in one bracket) and Mexico, Brazil, and Poland (in another bracket). Labor cost in the Czech Republic and Russia is 50% of the U.S. cost, while Canada offers only a 15% savings. Ireland, the United Kingdom, and Japan are all more expensive than the United States, and Germany is 1.5 times more expensive.

2.5.1.1. *Choosing a City in India*

The Indian government offers offshoring companies many incentives and concessions, some of which have been in place for a long time. Although these concessions continue, the 2006–2007 budget has been somewhat unfavorable to the IT sector, with hikes in taxes. At the same time, stable state governments (such as that of Andhra Pradesh) have created special bodies — trade bodies, investment bodies, and single-window agencies — that help create good value propositions for investors. Karnataka, which was in the forefront earlier, has slipped due to inadequate attention by the coalition governments.

In terms of relative advantages of location, the southern and the western areas of the country generally have stable state governments with well-defined functional processes, greater transparency, and more progressive ways of doing business. Foreign companies will prefer to locate where contracts are enforced with greater diligence.

Currently, about 50% of BPO and IT offshoring is concentrated in four major metropolitan cities: Delhi, Mumbai, Chennai, and Hyderabad. Another 40% is concentrated in a single city, Bangalore. There are many Tier II cities in southern and western India, as well as emerging locations such as Belgaum, Mysore, Hubli, Mangalore, Goa, Cochin, Vishakapatnam, Bhubaneswar, Jaipur, Raipur, and Kolkata. These could be cost-effective locations for companies willing to undertake the risk of operating in an unfamiliar city that is otherwise well known.

In the BPO and IT offshoring business, Bangalore continues to be the pioneer in the country. The other cities of note are Hyderabad, Chennai, Pune, and Navi Mumbai. Besides Bangalore, other cities in Karnataka hold out attractive possibilities, with lots of available talent and other advantages. Belgaum is an excellent location, with engineering colleges, proximity to Goa, and air connectivity. Mangalore is another location with unique talent. This district has numerous banks and innovative institutions, and it has a literacy rate of 95% (compared to the overall Indian rate of 64%). Mysore is just 150 km from Bangalore and is well connected; it also may become an important outsourcing destination. Bhubaneswar is an emerging location in the state of Orissa.

2.5.1.2. *Choosing a Specific Location in a City*

The real estate market in certain Indian cities is heating up to the extent that prices have become exorbitant for both commercial and residential real estate. Planning an offshore center in India, therefore, requires careful consideration of not only the city in which to operate but also the specific location for the firm's facilities within the chosen city.

India offers plenty of real estate projects, with lots of players in the market. Real estate firms must be assessed and evaluated carefully with reference to their credibility, financial strength, management quality, and other pertinent characteristics. Some companies offering real estate for sale or lease do not have clear titles and documents for their properties. This can later lead to unexpected and serious problems. In one major outsourcing project in India, for example, a center set up by a U.S. multinational with over 5000 employees is currently the subject of litigation. The builder who offered the space in one of the central areas of Bangalore is involved in a dispute with the landowner, who believes that the contract has not been honored. There is also the suspicion that several floors of the building violate building codes. This may lead to further litigation and even the demolition of the higher floors. This highlights the importance of choosing builders carefully and examining all related documents. While foreign lawyers can do this, many of them do not understand local realities; thus, it is important to engage a local firm that can undertake due diligence with respect to both builders and real estate agents.

2.5.1.3. *India Needs More Cities*

The infrastructure required for offshoring is minimal compared to the infrastructure required for a manufacturing facility. For example, there is no need for roads that can handle huge container trucks. The roads required for commuters in cars are on a lower scale, but nevertheless many cities in India are not able to provide satisfactory infrastructure. Unless both the central and state governments act immediately, infrastructure bottlenecks will become severe constraints on the future growth of outsourcing in India.[a]

NASSCOM–McKinsey (2005)[3] estimates that at least 10 more large cities will have to grow up in India to support the IT-BPO industry. Office space creation in many cities in India has been growing very rapidly. In Bangalore alone, over 12 million square feet of office space is being built every year. In a survey done by a global real estate consultancy firm, the city was ranked third among global cities for the amount of office space absorbed in 2006. In Hyderabad, Chennai, Navi Mumbai, and the Delhi-Gurgaon area, 8–10 million square feet of new office space is added annually to each city. These additional facilities, and their associated personnel, have clogged the roads, and traffic has become unbearable in most cities. India needs to create many more satellite cities and townships around the existing cities to provide improved infrastructure and decongest the existing cities.

2.6. How to Choose a Vendor

Once a company has decided on an outsourcing model and location, the choice of vendor or Indian partner is the next critical decision. It is important that client companies balance several factors before segmenting away their services overseas. Understanding and defining acceptable risk levels is one of the first challenges. Clients need to consider both operational risks such as natural disasters and technology failures and performance risks such as pricing traps and

---

[a] For a more in-depth discussion of the infrastructural issues in the logistics sector, see Chapter 5 of this volume.

nondelivery on service-level agreements. The Boston Consulting Group points out that all of these risks can be managed by the right delivery model, vendor selection, service-level agreements, and price negotiations. Caution is necessary, because Indian vendors might misrepresent facts, over-promise, or under-deliver, as well as failing to properly handle sensitive client information. The most important qualities to look for in a vendor are its management quality and its security infrastructure. Firms must undertake due diligence of vendors before awarding a specific contract, and this due diligence should include an intellectual audit component.

2.6.1. *Intellectual Property Audit*

Several U.S. firms have had unhappy experiences in dealing with Indian firms regarding the protection of their intellectual property (IP). While this was commonplace 10 years ago, Indian IT and biotech firms today are much more sensitive to IP rights. In recent years, India has also begun to provide tighter regulations and more specific laws on data protection. Many offshoring firms invest substantially in IT infrastructure, firewalls, and virtual private networks to maintain the confidentiality of their client data and information. Employees are required to sign non-disclosure agreements, and employees who violate them are subject to prosecution. Employees, likewise, have been arrested and tried for IP infringements. In one case, a group of engineers in Bangalore formed a small company and developed a software product. A large multinational then acquired this company, and the engineers worked for this multinational for a while. The engineers later set up a new company and used the same software code, violating the multinational's IP. Based on the company's complaint, the engineers were arrested and brought before the court for violation of IP. This sent a clear message that authorities were very concerned with the IP rights of offshoring companies.

In another instance, an employee of a knowledge-processing firm had complete information about the entire range of market research reports prepared by one of the world's best-known companies. The cost of all these reports would run into millions of dollars. The employee left the KPO, started his own unit with a similar web site and company name, and offered all the reports for less than USD20,000. The police became involved and ensured that the employee voluntarily destroyed all the files that he had.

Even though IP protection *per se* seems reasonable, the problem lies in the details. It is important, therefore, for firms to keep in touch with the local police if they need to take action against IP infringements. Otherwise, the IP laws may go unenforced. Firms may also hire trusted companies to do an IP audit before signing any business deals.

2.7. Grow with India

India presents tremendous opportunities for future growth. Companies can take advantage of the growth in the Indian domestic market as well as entering newer areas of outsourcing that can be big money spinners. Even SME can grow and become more competitive with help from India.

2.7.1. *The Indian Domestic Goldmine*

Multinational firms that come to India for offshoring are discovering the domestic goldmine. The very foreign firms that came to India to save money by outsourcing may eventually make money by participating in the growth of the domestic market in India. With the rapid automation of Indian banks, the domestic IT market is growing rapidly. Thousands of ATMs have been set up and retail branches connected. There is tremendous growth potential for companies in the manufacturing and service sectors, which are making their processes more IT-based. The IT sector has been growing at a rate of 35% (CAGR); for hardware services, the growth is 45%, while for software it is 38%. The current turnover of the domestic IT industry is more than USD7.5 billion annually.

PC installation is growing rapidly in the country, with an installed base of 4–5 million computers. The addressable market is as big as 30–40 million units, and it is likely to expand with the introduction of low-cost PCs. Companies such as HP have set up labs that are trying to develop an inexpensive computer that would be unique for the market.

In the private sector, the adoption of IT will increase if channel partners are properly trained. Most computer sales take place through over 35,000 channel partners in India. Many of these are small organizations, and if the people in these organizations are trained properly, the smaller cities will be better able to adopt IT. In small cities, the companies providing software and helpdesk services are extremely primitive in nature, using pirated software and not providing complete service to the satisfaction of the customer. Large companies can gain substantial market share in these cities if they are able to identify these smaller companies, train them, and make them their channel partners.

The market size for e-governance has recently crossed half-a-billion dollars. Many state governments have published e-governance programs. The state of Karnataka has put in real-time treasury computerization that makes information available in real time on the amount spent by 34,000 officers spread over a few hundred kilometers. The state's railways have a well-designed and complex reservation system, and the entire railway reservation system was streamlined with the advent of computerization in 1995. Of the 11 million passengers who travel daily upon 8520 trains, about 550,000 have reserved accommodations.

Such projects provide plenty of opportunities for foreign technology players to participate in Indian domestic market growth.

The domestic market has been attractive in non-IT sectors, too. More and more multinationals are setting up manufacturing operations in India, attracted by India's burgeoning domestic market and its relatively low-cost, highly skilled workforce. At least 270 million square feet of residential space and 60 million square feet of commercial space are added every year across the country; in addition to this is another 45 million square feet of new space added for the retail and hospitality sectors. Retail is a fast-growing sector, and as it is 96% unorganized, it offers a wealth of opportunities for foreign companies to do business. In the hospitality and food business, the case of Nammura Hotel in Bangalore is exemplary. It has grown from humble beginnings to become a large company with a modern kitchen that supplies 25,000 lunches to IT workers in Accenture and IBM.[b]

2.8. New Areas of Outsourcing

Many industries in which offshoring has yet to take a hold, could bring about substantial benefits for foreign companies. I foresee tremendous growth in these sectors, assuming that business will grow as usual and that protectionist tendencies do not intensify from the present levels. I highlight below some of these areas of potential growth through outsourcing.

2.8.1. *Education*

The U.S. universities have the benefit of an excellent infrastructure and enjoy both a good name and good reputation in the higher education market. Yet, they could gain from outsourcing their activities as well as setting up new campuses in India. Some of the activities that could be outsourced include content development for e-learning portals; the design and publishing of brochures; the management of the admission process; and also R&D. The University of Michigan Business School has set up an R&D center in Bangalore. Senior professors routinely visit this center, select faculty and Ph.D students, assign projects, train groups of students over several weeks, and continuously monitor progress in R&D from Michigan. The results of this endeavor are high-quality academic

---

[b] For another example from the lunch-delivery industry, see the case study of the Dabbawallahs of Mumbai in Chapter 5 of this volume.

publications and useful research for companies that frequently consult with the school. As far as India is concerned, the U.S. universities have tremendous possibilities for expansion in business programs, arts and science graduate courses, commerce, accounting, new IT technologies, and healthcare and medicine (including nursing, paramedical work, specialized technical skills, and radiology). The millions of secondary-school graduates in India constitute a strong and as yet untapped potential market base for such programs.

The U.S. universities are showing a growing interest in Indian education. Columbia Business School, for example, started a student exchange program in early 2008 with the Indian Institute of Management at Ahmedabad. The institutions teamed up to write case materials to teach American students about doing business in India. The Americanization of Indian education takes a variety of approaches. Champlain College, based in Burlington, Vermont, runs a satellite campus in Mumbai that offers degrees in one of the three career-oriented subjects that college administrators have found to be attractive to Indians: business, hospitality industry management, and software engineering. California State University, Long Beach, has agreed to help start American-style four-year degree programs at the state-run Lucknow University in northern India. Cornell University is seeking to expand research collaborations, particularly in agriculture and public health. Rice University envisions faculty and student exchanges, particularly in technology. Carnegie Mellon offers a degree in partnership with a small private Indian institution, and the state does not regulate fees. American universities are just beginning to experiment in India, and the law is still vague about how foreign educational institutions can operate.

2.8.2. *Government*

Enormous possibilities for offshoring exist in the realm of government. Different state governments in the United States and in Germany have set up promotional offices in India. These days, government activities are very critical, and the government must be supportive of industry so that companies can enter new areas and generate more domestic jobs. The U.S. and German government offices provide help to enable companies to win to India. Furthermore, the governments themselves can outsource some of their activities and thereby save money, getting more services for each taxpayer dollar. Typical outsourced activities include generating content, running government portals, making drawings available for municipal bodies, converting paper drawings into electronic form using CAD/CAM and other tools, and setting up 24/7 network centers to provide help to citizens. Governments can even look at the possibility of outsourcing part of their citizens' work during off-hours. A great deal of scope exists, particularly in the area of e-governance projects: governments in the United States and Germany can use the Indian expertise to help implement these projects in an expanding market.

2.8.3. *Wholesale Market*

While Indian banks have always provided loans to the manufacturing sector, they have not developed the skills necessary for lending to the services sector. As a result, certain communities that are able to lend to each other internally dominate the wholesale trade in India. Wholesale trade is family-dominated: for example, the Marwari, Gujarati, and Shetty communities have familial links that have helped them in cornering business. Most of this sector is still unorganized; there-fore, there remains a lot of scope for wholesale companies to come to India and set up major operations.

2.8.4. *Transportation*

The transportation sector in India is a weak and fragmented one. State-run buses are not up to the mark: they are old and not maintained properly. Except in one or two states, transportation represents a severe bottleneck. People traveling on the rooftops of buses are a common sight. Foreign transportation companies can come to India and set up domestic and offshore operations that make use of vehi-cle monitoring via GPS, maintain the inventory of transport stock, and update ERP systems and other software. Multinational transportation companies can use advanced R&D in India, drawing on sophisticated operational research models for running fleets. Huge opportunities exist for both local and offshoring activi-ties. The infrastructure for shipping is generally lacking, but it is currently being built up and improved in a number of areas. A large player could develop a minor port into a specialized one for its industry — whether for cargo bulk handling or container handling.

2.8.5. *Petroleum and Coal*

Fossil fuels are a big emerging sector in India, which has perhaps the world's second largest reserve of coal. Many states offer low-cost power possibilities for industries like mining and aluminum. It is possible to enter these states with a multiyear contract on a power purchase and then set up power-dependent indus-tries, such as aluminum extraction.

2.8.6. *Machinery and Construction Industry*

The electrical machinery industry as well as the general machinery industry hold out wide possibilities. India is in the process of building many steel mills, aluminum plants, bridges, and highways. The development of the Golden Quadrilateral highways along with their diagonals is a major event in the world transportation industry that is generating tremendous opportunities for the machinery, construction, and electrical sectors in India.[c] Construction is a booming sector in many cities, bringing in a number of players in both the construction and engineering services industries. Consultants can set up offices in India and play a critical role in the country's development, especially in the construction industry. Hospital construction is one area that presents many possibilities for companies interested in outsourcing to India.

2.8.7. *Engineering Design with Specialized Software*

Engineering design is another important area of offshoring. Many architects are now sourcing their CAD/CAM requirements from India. Foreign firms (e.g., Bechtel) have set up enterprises in India employing thousands of engineers. These engineering operations currently are highly fragmented, and it would be both possible and desirable for consulting companies to set up one-stop centers offering services in architecture, structural engineering, drawings production, electrical fitting, air conditioning, plumbing, sanitation, and civil construction.

2.8.8. *Chemical and Pharmaceutical Industries*

The manufacture of chemicals and pharmaceutical formulations and products is of equal importance. Some states in India have set up centers in which the effluents are treated by the state. The state government comes in as an intermediary to take care of the effluent, and then regulators inspect the facilities of the government rather than those of the private company. This significantly reduces the risk for manufacturers and can be a major attraction for companies setting themselves up in the chemicals sector.

---

[c] See the discussion of the Golden Quadrilateral project in Chapter 5.2 in this volume.

2.8.9. KPO Projects

An illustration of high-end KPO work is the Pipal Research of Chicago, which
was founded five years ago and now employs about 100 analysts. Until recently,
the bulk of its assignments came from equity research, fixed-income asset
research, and asset pricing-related work. A year ago, it created a branch called
PipalAnswers that functions like a "quasi spot-market for knowledge." The new
division offers speedy research on tightly focused client requirements such as
snapshot insights of rival companies' ad spends and public relations.

Large U.S. companies have offshored 30% of their services to India, but the
remaining 70% of the services represent outsourcing possibilities that have yet to
be studied. Industrial companies may have started with the outsourcing of
accounting, legal, commercial, and other administrative processes, but analysts
see others in line — environmental health and safety-related functions, for
instance. A big multinational with 100,000 employees may employ between 500
and 800 people to handle just environmental health and safety-related work, gath-
ering statistics that need to be sent to regulators for analysis and other back-office
functions. Similar opportunities for outsourcing exist in areas such as quality control and quality assurance, production planning, and cost analysis. Although these
higher-value services might be more difficult to outsource, as Indian companies
learn how to deal with such clients and understand their requirements and styles
of functioning, they will also upgrade their capabilities.

The future development of the offshoring industry is primarily dependent on
demand — how aware foreign companies are of outsourcing, how willing they
are to make use of it, and whether they have the organizational preparedness to
engage in outsourcing in a major way. The supply-side factors include India's
intelligent talent pool, and a friendly environment that keeps business policies
transparent and readily understood. More than the supply factors, the demand factors (internal preparedness, willingness, risk-taking, and understanding new possibilities in offshoring) will determine how the industry will evolve. The vast
majority of the U.S. companies have not even thought of outsourcing. Others are
aware but have not yet taken steps to study the possibilities and visit foreign
countries to gain firsthand knowledge of how outsourcing can work.

2.9. Can SMEs Win?

While large companies are reaping the benefits of offshoring, SMEs are still
unaware of outsourcing's untapped potential. They are subject to cost pressures
and are losing customers as well as employees. In fact, it is the SME sector that
can benefit most from outsourcing. Outsourcing is no longer just for Fortune 500

companies. Small- and medium-sized firms, as well as busy professionals, can offshore their work to increase their productivity and free up time for more important commitments. However, they may have to depend on Indian players to assist them in this, as setting up their own center in India would not be cost-effective. It is time for the world to take advantage of this revolution. Timothy Ferris,[1] in his best seller, *The 4-Hour Workweek*, shows how to do this.

About 95% of the Fortune 1000 companies have already articulated their offshoring strategy, while only a quarter of the next 1000 companies have been able to do this. Most of the Fortune 1000 companies are already global and have experience in managing a global workforce, a task that requires sophistication in terms of understanding different cultures and managing different personnel. Thus, many smaller companies prefer to work with providers who will be able to address their specific needs. They are also looking for deeper levels of partnership that can bring in a revamping of their own processes.

As firms become more mature, their emphasis changes from cost to innovation and productivity. Offshoring companies come to India with a basic emphasis on cost, quality, and risk. As they get comfortable with the Indian players, the perception of risk goes down. Their degree of urgency on the cost and quality fronts also decreases a little bit, but their concern with innovation and productivity grow in emphasis.

Companies, especially small- and medium-sized ones, could begin offshoring on a small pilot basis and then undertake larger projects. They could visit the offshore destination and learn from others. These companies could also, in the course of a visit, investigate India's emerging market and try to sell their products in a limited way. Companies have to understand that internal preparedness is the most important part of any success in offshoring. This primarily means understanding the process, the activities that would be outsourced, the method of monitoring, and the relationship with the offshore partner. Often foreign companies do not trust their Indian counterparts, for valid and cultural reasons, and this can lead to finger-pointing and one-upmanship. The net result is an overall deterioration in offshore delivery and productivity. It is, therefore, important to have a leadership that is culturally sensitive, balances risk-taking with the trust factor, and is willing to experiment, travel, and bring the offshoring culture into the organization.

2.10. Conclusions

The world economy is more integrated now than at any time in the past 100 years. Just after the World War II, Europe was in shambles, but America provided the growth engine for the world. When America was painfully adjusting to the oil price shock in the 1970s, Europe came to its rescue. Asia, led by Japan, lent a helping hand in the 1980s when America had not yet come out of its second oil shock. In the 1990s, it was the turn of the Southeast Asian countries to lift the world economy. China rescued Japan from its decade-long recession and now leads the world in economic growth. India has emerged and is expected to provide the right growth impetus now.

Earlier, when one economy was in recession, some other economy provided a growth stimulus. Now, the world economies are more integrated, and this liberalization has made it easier for firms to sell in other countries. The advent of technology has made it easy to get work done anywhere in the world, as long as it can be transported electronically. Companies located in developing countries can have access to latest technology now more than ever before. This process of globalization has forced companies to adapt, exploring new ways of cost-cutting as well as new markets and customers.

India and China had historically accounted for 45% of the world GDP in the ancient world. Only in the last 300 years has the story been quite different. It is critical for companies based in developed countries — particularly America and Europe — to have a presence in these developing countries, both to outsource (and thus save money) and to sell and enter the market. Most of the Fortune 500 companies have already blazed the path to success. It is now up to the SME to take the lead and offer tougher competition to the bigger players. Outsourcing is no longer just for Fortune 500 companies alone: small- and medium-sized firms, as well as busy professionals, can offshore their work to increase their productivity and free up time for other more important activities. It is time for the world to take advantage of this revolution.

References

1. Ferris, T (2007). *The 4-Hour Workweek*. New York: Crown Publishers.
2. Friedman, T (2005). *The World is Flat*. New York: Farrar, Strauss and Giroux.
3. NASSCOM–McKinsey (2005). Extending India's leadership of the global IT and BPO industries. In *"NASSCOM–McKinsey Report 2005*. New Delhi: NASSCOM.

INFORMATION TECHNOLOGY

Jayashankar M. Swaminathan

Nine out of 10 times when I introduce myself to the person sitting next to me on the plane in the United States, they are surprised to find that I am not a software programmer. They are quite relieved when I mention to them that, indeed, my undergraduate degree happens to be in computer science and engineering. It has become an expectation among many people in the United States that any Indian (or Indian-looking) person would be a trained IT or software specialist. Even for someone like me who grew up in India, it is hard to believe that this change could have happened over the last 25 years.

I recall the excitement my fellow students and I had in the early 1980s when our high school received a personal computer, which had been donated by the British government as part of a special type of federal program for the whole school (1500 students). Most of the excitement associated with the computer room was centered around the air conditioning, since that was the only room in the whole school that was temperature-controlled. Also, there was only one person in the school — the computer teacher — who knew how to switch it on. It was not surprising that in the years that we had access to this machine, hardly anyone was taught anything about it. When I entered the IIT in Delhi to major in computer science, the situation was better but nowhere close to what one would expect to have in terms of computing resources at one of the country's premier institutions. We had great professors who were excellent teachers of computer science, but when it came time to do the programming assignments, I still remember the mad rush to the centrally air conditioned main computer center to get access to a terminal. There were about 40 terminals for a class of 250 students. Given that the IIT had by far the best resources in the country, one can only imagine what was available in terms of computing resources at other institutions. However, when I did my internship at the Center of Development of Telematics (CDOT),[1] a pioneering organization set up with the help of the government for

Fig. E2.1. Infosys campus in Bangalore.

the development of the nation's telecommunications backbone, I saw glimpses of what could be achieved if Indian software engineers were provided adequate computing resources.

Last month, on a visit to Infosys,[3] one of the major software firms in India, I learned that they have grown from 60,000 to more than 90,000 employees in one year. As we walked through the spectacular 93-acre lush green campus in Bangalore, which houses close to 20,000 employees and features 40 buildings with outstanding facilities for work and leisure, I did not need a lot of brainpower to conclude that India had become a "lead factory" for software development and maintenance.

How did India transform itself into this leading destination for software- and technology-related activities? What are the current areas of focus for firms in this sector? Where is this industry headed? What has been the role of multinationals in this development? How is this growth going to play out in the next decade?

In the next chapter, entitled "The Evolution of the Indian Software Industry: The Emerging Model of Mobilizing Global Talent," Prof. M.S. Krishnan, Professor and Chair of the Management of Information Systems area at the Ross School of Business, University of Michigan, along with Prof. Narayan Ramsubbu, Assistant Professor, University of Illinois at Urbana Champaign and Prof. Ramanath Subramanian, Assistant Professor, Singapore Management University, give a detailed account of the evolution of the software industry in India. They start with the 1970s, when Indian engineers were primarily assigned low-end testing work by multinationals such as Burroughs Limited. In the 1980s, more software engineers were deployed overseas in various projects, while at the same time the Indian government recognized software as a major initiative and opened up various degree programs and universities with this as their focus. The decade of the 1990s saw immense growth in the software sector, and smaller firms started appearing on the horizon. At the same time, some of the Indian firms started moving from the testing domain toward more value-added activities related to application software, and in addition they invested heavily in quality-based initiatives. This was also the period that saw the rapid rise of Indian software giants such as Infosys, Wipro,[6] Tata Consulting,[5] HCL,[2] and Satyam,[4] among others. Since the beginning of the 21st century, large multinationals have been investing significantly in India, making it a software hub in their global operations. These companies include Microsoft, Oracle, Google, IBM, Texas Instruments, and HP. The authors highlight that the major issue for the software sector in India is that the growth has primarily come from project-based outsourcing services, and that there currently is a dearth of product-based innovations. They project that, going forward, the growth of this industry will mainly come from multinational players operating in India, from small- to medium-size Indian software enterprises, and from solution-driven integrated services provided by the large domestic players. The authors conclude with a brief discussion of the kinds of innovations that may be necessary to tap the full potential of this sector in the upcoming decades.

References

1. http://www.cdot.com/home.htm.
2. http://www.hcltech.com/.
3. http://www.infosys.com.
4. http://www.satyam.com/.
5. http://www.tcs.com/homepage/Pages/default.aspx.
6. http://www.wipro.com/.

CHAPTER 3

EVOLUTION OF THE INDIAN SOFTWARE INDUSTRY: THE EMERGING MODEL OF MOBILIZING GLOBAL TALENT

M.S. Krishnan,* Narayan Ramasubbu**
and Ramanath Subramanian[†]

This chapter focuses on the growth and transformation of the Indian software industry over the last three decades. While there is a common misconception that the year 2000 (Y2K) problem was the primary driver bringing Indian software talent to the forefront of the global market, this transformation had, in fact, begun much earlier. The Y2K problem was simply one of the catalysts in this journey. The fact is that this industry had begun to mature even before the rise of the Internet.

While the liberal policies of the Indian government did help the growth in this sector, at times the software industry grew in spite of some of the government's contrary policies. The growth in the initial stages (as early as 30 years back) was under a bout of essentially unfriendly policies and incentives. However, the rate of growth was evident to leaders in government think-tanks, such as the then Department of Electronics in the mid-1980s. Both the Indian government and the large software firms discovered the enormous potential for this industry in the global IT market, and this led to friendlier policies and greater investment in human talent and education in the late 1980s and early 1990s. The emergence of the Internet and the digitization of business processes in the corporate world led to a tremendous rise in the demand for IT services. Indian IT firms, with access to low-cost and high-quality software talent in large numbers from Indian universities, began to thrive. This transformation is not just about the size of the

---

*Professor and Chair of the Business Information Technology, Ross School of Business, University of Michigan.
** Assistant Professor at the Singapore Management University.
[†] Assistant Professor at the College of Business, University of Illinois at Urbana-Champaign.

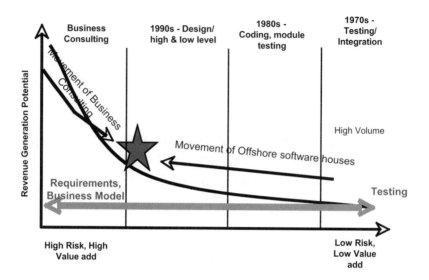

Fig. 3.1.   Software industry trends.

industry. The nature of services rendered by the Indian software firms and the role of the captive Indian software centers of multinational firms has morphed from mundane low-cost services such as testing to integrated product development, research, and broader ownership. The evolution of the Indian software industry is illustrated in Fig. 3.1. In this chapter, we track this journey and the transformation of the Indian software industry and conclude with the emerging role of the Indian software talent in the global context.

Historical Development

3.1. 1970s — The Age of Support Services

As early as 1974, the large U.S. computer hardware manufacturer Burroughs sought programmers from TCS to help meet their programming needs. Although the late 1970s was a time when the Indian government was severely restricting monopolistic trade, especially by large multinationals such as Coke and IBM, multinational firms started sensing the opportunity to leverage low-cost resources in India for software support services. For example, based on the quality of work delivered by Tata engineers, Tata and Burroughs set up a joint venture named Tata Burroughs specifically to meet the global needs of Burroughs' customer installations.

In this early stage, the nature of support services provided by programmers from India-based firms involved low value-added auxiliary needs in the software product life cycle. Early on, firms most commonly used programmers to perform tasks secondary to research and development, such as the provision of testing services for software programs developed abroad. The economics and quality of testing services offered by Indian firms encouraged their global customers such as IBM, ICL, and Burroughs to expand into other services, such as porting of large applications from one hardware platform to another. The competition among large mainframe vendors was accompanied by large banks and insurance companies porting their existing application software into new hardware platforms. This was followed by software programmers travelling to various customer sites of these mainframe firms. The demand for these services always exceeded the supply base of major Indian firms such as TCS. Although the testing and porting of applications offered modest revenues, these services provided an enormous opportunity for Indian programmers to gain knowledge and experience in working on the latest hardware platforms. Even at this early stage, the contribution of Indian software firms was not limited to application software space (i.e., commercial applications for large organizations). A small segment of the Indian software firms also served in the systems software domain. Indian software firms were collaborating with global hardware firms in database and network software utilities.

3.2. 1980s — The Decade of Local Awareness

The success of joint ventures and independent business units set up by the Tatas and other Indian groups increased the social and economic awareness about the software industry. Given the strength of foreign currency against the Indian rupee (INR) in the 1980s[a] and the opportunity for Indians to work abroad at the client sites of large multinational firms, the industry started attracting top talent from India's highly reputed engineering and management institutions. Multinational banks such as Citicorp and ANZ Grindlays also spotted this opportunity to leverage global resources. These financial sector units started setting up their own captive units in India to provide software services for their international operations in countries such as New Zealand, Australia, the United Kingdom, and the United States.

The target set by the Indian government for annual software export was often met within a year. The Department of Electronics, under the central government, gradually but continually adopted policies to grow the education infrastructure by legitimizing existing courses and introducing new degrees in computer science as well as in applied computer technology. The three-year Master's in Computer Applications (MCA) degree approved by the government was an innovative

---

[a] In 1980, 1USD = 7.89 INR.

program that combined within the course requirements the technical content of computer science programs with basics in business applications, economics, and accounting. This program also required a six-month internship in a commercial setting. Such programs prepared a talent pool that could be readily deployed in commercial software projects. Education in software also attracted the interest of the private sector. Software training houses such as NIIT and Aptech[b] began professional training centers in all major cities. The software certificate in tools and technologies from these institutes emerged as a respectable pathway for both science and arts undergraduates to land a rewarding career in the conspicuous and prestigious software industry. The global demand reaching India and the increasing supply base of Indian software programmers soon started feeding one another.

The second half of the 1980s also witnessed a new level of confidence in the Indian software talent on the part of the multinational electronics and telecommunications equipment manufacturers. First, the Indian government had set up innovative organizations such as C-DOT (Center for Development of Telematics) and C-DAC (Center for Development of Advanced Computing) to develop indigenous technologies in telecommunications and supercomputing. The progress of work in such organizations instilled further confidence both in the minds of software professionals and in the market as a whole. Multinational firms such as Motorola and Texas Instruments (TI) launched India-based development centers to meet their global software needs. These software services were mostly part of their R&D and new product development efforts. In the absence of the required bandwidth and reliability in the regular telecommunication channels, these multinationals started setting up private satellites to beam software directly from their centers in India to global new product development and design sites. By the late 1980s, Indian software talent was recognized globally for domains beyond traditional application software.

The role of Indian software professionals in firms such as Motorola and TI was much greater than mere programming or testing. Software teams in India were actively involved in the design and architectural decisions of new products. The nature of services offered by Indian software firms in the applications domain also began to shift toward broader ownership of responsibilities. Software teams from India were able to deliver mission-critical and real-time applications in finance, insurance, and other domains. These software teams also took exclusive responsibility for delivering the entire system, as opposed to merely managing a piece of the project such as testing or coding of specific modules. While captive units of multinationals were leveraging Indian talent espousing a more integrated approach by including teams from India as part of their design groups, most

---

[b] Aptech — Apple Technologies.

Indian commercial software firms were still predominantly delivering software services through cost-plus or time and materials contracts. These software firms had yet to take significant risks in project execution. The source of competitive value delivered by the Indian software firms to their clients was still primarily comparative in nature. That is, these clients were leveraging lower software labor costs in India.

3.3. 1990s — Global Awareness and Confidence

While the Indian software industry was growing rapidly in exports, the overall Indian economy was struggling with low single-digit growth. The decade of the 1990s marked the beginning of a number of economic liberalization policies in which the government recognized, among other things, the potential for further growth in the software sector. In 1991, the government adopted policies that reduced import duties on hardware. Furthermore, the adoption of more enhanced policies in 1993 granted income tax exemptions to firms for software exports. The growth in the software industry and lucrative offers to work on projects with foreign clients further captured the attention of the Indian society, and this led to higher enrollments in existing technical degree programs and the introduction of new degrees. The country soon witnessed a profusion of talent, mainly in engineering and the sciences, which annually amounted to more than 100,000 young "trainable" graduates.[8] However, the lack of a local market for software services limited graduates' job prospects within Indian projects. The belated growth in the overall Indian economy also limited the number of attractive opportunities for engineering graduates in the areas of civil, mechanical, and chemical engineering. Their grounding in technical knowledge and quantitative skills made it easier for these graduates to jump ship and join the software exports movement. This further added to the supply base.

Global awareness of Indian software talent further expanded. Multinationals such as GE discovered the enormous potential in leveraging Indian resources for their various business units. As stated by their former CEO Jack Welch, "GE went to India for cost advantage but found quality and capability in addition to cost".[3] This era also witnessed the emergence of hundreds of small software firms focusing on niche technologies such as local language editors, database engines, and other utilities, based on the work from Indian research institutes and universities. These firms enabled the development of pockets of local expertise by creating dedicated centers of software excellence around the country. Gradually, the software divisions of firms such as Citibank and Hewlett Packard established more prominent and larger software development centers in India.

In the United States and global economy front, this era witnessed the rise of the Internet in the corporate world. E-commerce and e-business were emerging. Meanwhile, large firms had to shift their IT systems from mainframe-based to client server computing, leading to an increase in demand for system redesign. As smaller firms were built around the growing demand for software-related services, a strong resource base began to emerge. Opportunities grew immensely on the external front, and foreign firms began utilizing Indian talent to satisfy their global software and design needs. This was manifested in the origin of "body placement" services and firms such as TCS that acted as conduits for exporting human talent. While uncertainty due to the limited local market and so-called "brain drain" was a concern, the accompanying upsurge in educated local talent and the attractiveness of computer-related education helped prepare the country for the impending growth of the software industry due to exports. The Indian government recognized the demand for talent and adopted policies encouraging industry growth, primarily through software export.

In the previous decades, Indian outsourcing firms generated revenues primarily by performing services that were relatively expensive to perform onshore (i.e., within the geographical confines of Western countries such as the United States). Barring a few exceptions, these initiatives rarely involved innovation and consisted of highly "programmable" tasks (services that could be clearly and unambiguously specified) that were moved offshore to countries like India for financial reasons. The firms generated significant revenue by the placement of skilled personnel in onshore initiatives that were facing a shortage of programming and testing talent. However, one limiting factor was that the rapid outburst of small, medium, and large firms that participated in the market resulted in a high variance in the quality of work. Firms that had made the necessary talent investment began seeking means to differentiate themselves from the pack. Toward the mid- and late 1990s, capable firms began refining their processes and pursuing certifications that would be recognized on an international scale, for instance in vendor-selection processes. Some examples were the ISO certifications and Capability Maturity Model (CMM)[c] certifications that had gained wide popularity. A by-product of these certification initiatives was that project life cycle management and project management expertise also began to flourish locally. A select few firms such as Infosys, TCS, and Wipro took on more active roles in this learning process and demonstrated exceptional levels of quality, which have continued to this day.

With an abundance of programming talent budding locally, and with the increasing certified expertise in project management and co-ordination skills

---

[c] CMM refers to a widely accepted set of processes of software development associated with the Software Engineering Institute at Carnegie Mellon University.

emerging from the performance of relatively limited programming services to offshore client firms, select firms began growing up the value chain. Established companies began shifting to an offshoring-based business model in which they would set up co-ordination mechanisms to own the entire life cycle of software and perform end-to-end solutions development on a small scale. Firms traditionally good at software maintenance, programming, and testing services began demonstrating design skills and providing affordable alternatives to onshore development. These firms also established facilities onshore to facilitate customer contact. Undertaking the full spectrum of activities from design to customer delivery was the logical next step in the evolution of this business model.

Toward the end of the millennium, the Y2K problem served as a catalyst for further growth, due to the need for software maintenance expertise and programming expertise in the mainframe environment. Indian companies had retained the maintenance expertise of legacy systems, and the software porting skills that had accumulated locally were also important in taking on opportunities created by the concerns of the United States and other Western countries about the potentially dangerous implications of Y2K computer software glitches.[4]

Due to the abundant supply of programming skills, firms were mildly successful in software product design, but the limited local market for such products and various shortcomings of international marketing and business expertise resulted in a sizable number of failures. Firms learned expensive lessons and had to bear the significant costs of these failures. This inertia in product design prowess and the enticement of continuing business from offshore agreements resulted in a majority of firms limiting their R&D efforts and focusing on profitable long-term agreements for tasks that were not necessarily technically challenging. A great number of firms were still engaged in time and materials contractual agreements in which they were compensated periodically for the technically non-challenging services performed.

Product design expertise and the complementary entrepreneurial skills that would encourage significant local R&D investments were lacking on a larger scale. As a consequence, innovations in products and processes were limited, though they were growing at a slow and steady rate. The growth in consumers' purchasing power and the escalation of salaries in this environment, with its competition for differentiating talent, resulted in the bridging of the salary gap between developed countries and firms involved in software development in India. Such an environment meant that to sustain the momentum gained over the decade, firms had to engage in innovative solutions and product development efforts. While there had been progress in niche high-tech product development on a marginal scale, considerable inroads were yet to be made.

3.4. New Millennium 2000⁺ — Global Firms Bet on India

As they entered the new millennium, large global firms experienced the comfort that either the turning of the calendar on December 31, 1999, was not as big a problem as envisaged or they had taken adequate measures to correct the date formats. But this event emerged as a big bonus for the Indian software industry. During the late 1990s, the CIOs of these multinational companies had approached Indian software firms as a low-cost resource base to test the Y2K compliance issue. This was a perfect strategy from the global firms' perspective, since Y2K compliance was something they had to do in addition to their routine operations, and thus to seek outside help for this standalone test function was well accepted. For the Indian software firms, this created an enormous opportunity to get exposure to the large live applications used by multinational banks, insurance companies, and firms in other industries. For many large multinational firms, the Y2K challenge led to the discovery of Indian software firms: they found that it was not any more difficult to engage Indian software vendors directly for their software applications outsourcing needs. Hence, in a way, we witnessed the same cycle as in the late 1970s and early 1980s, but on a much larger scale. Global firms used Indian software firms for testing during Y2K and became aware of their capability and quality, and they subsequently expanded their engagement with the Indian firms. The traditional application development and maintenance business then flourished further as a major contribution to the total Indian software export, which had surpassed USD30 billion by 2002.

In the meantime, this surge in global confidence in Indian software capability also led to other software research and development initiatives in India. As noted earlier, while some multinational companies like Texas Instruments had had a research footprint in India since the 1980s, the start of the new millennium saw a rapid growth in knowledge-intensive R&D investments in the software sector. Several new product development groups that worked independently and in collaboration with development centers outside India were beginning to be formed as part of these new initiatives. A snapshot of some well-known R&D activities is provided in Table 3.1.[d]

In addition to the larger and rapid investments by multinational companies in software R&D activities in India, domestic software firms also began to strike significantly larger deals with Fortune 500 firms. For example, TCS and Infosys closed a USD2.2 billion deal with ABN AMRO,[2] and TCS and the Netherlands-based Nielsen, Inc., signed a contract worth USD1.2 billion for the

---

[d] The URL at http://www.expresscomputeronline.com/20030609/focus1.shtml is one of the sources of information in this table.

Table 3.1.   Research and product development initiatives.

Companies	Highlights	Product components developed
Sun Microsystems' India Engineering Center	Established in mid-1999 with 20 people, it has scaled up to more than 500 people today.	Portal server, Web server, identity server, and meta-directory.
Texas Instruments' R&D Center	Established in 1984. The Center, started with just 20 people, now has 900 people working on VLSI and embedded software, which goes along with a chip or into the chip.	Fully developed at least 20 products, including the Ankur Digital Signal Processor; Sangam, a bridge router for the DSL; and Zeno, which runs multimedia applications.
SAP Labs	The largest single-location R&D lab for SAP outside Walldorf, Germany (3600 employees across Bangalore and Gurgaon).	Largest location for supplier relationship management (SRM) development. Contributes to more than 2/5th of the SAP ERP and CRM development. Prime contributor to other SAP products and solutions such as XApps and Duet.
I2 Technologies' R&D Center	Established in 1988 with 20 people, it has scaled up to 1000 people today.	Fully developed a strategic sourcing solution for i2, besides delivering nearly eight manufacturer-industry template and retail solutions from India.
Philips Innovation Campus	20% of the total software resources of Philips	Develops most of the software required for

(*Continued*)

Table 3.1. (*Continued*)

Companies	Highlights	Product components developed
	worldwide. Established in 1996 with 10 people, it has scaled up to over 950 people today. It is the largest software center for Philips outside Holland.	Philips product divisions such as consumer electronics, medical systems, and business systems. Almost every Philips product containing software has a contribution from the Bangalore campus.
IBM Research Center	One of the eight IBM research labs worldwide. Established in 1998, it expanded recently to Delhi and Bangalore.	Pure and applied research in the areas of Blue Gene, speech recognition, distributed and high performance computing, and services innovation.
HP Labs	Established in 2002 with just two people, it has scaled up to over 40 specialists today.	Focuses on opportunities and challenges faced by customers in emerging economies, especially the development of diverse languages and scripts.
Oracle India	Oracle's Bangalore center was established in 1994, and the center in Hyderabad in 1999. Oracle's largest development center outside the United States has 3700 employees.	Does work on Oracle's database products, applications, business intelligence products, and application development tools, in addition to other activities.

outsourcing of IT operations and maintenance. Moreover, domestic outsourcing deals involving home-grown software companies are also exploding in value. The USD80 million HDFC-WIPRO deal is a case in point.[9]

The explosive growth of the Indian software companies in the new millennium has been attributed to several factors. First, there is a worldwide movement among firms across the industrial sectors to search for low-cost outsourcing partners. Second, there has been an intense, collaborative effort by a joint forum headed by the National Association of Software Companies (NASSCOM) to promote the Indian software industry and its capabilities both to Fortune 500 clientele as well as to the central government. Third, Indian software firms have invested heavily in their process capabilities and have revamped their ability to handle complex and large scale projects.[1] Combined with the low-cost advantage, this improved capability to handle complex projects has made the Indian software service firms a force to be reckoned with and a viable alternative to established IT consulting firms such as EDS and Accenture. Apart from the rapid growth, we are witnessing a phase of continued capability improvement in the Indian software services sectors.

Current and Future Trends

3.5. Climbing the Slippery Rope: Migration to Products and Value-added Services

While the Indian software services industry has seen tremendous improvement in revenue growth as well as in its capability to execute large-scale and complex projects over the decades, the Indian software product market cannot boast of such a record. Despite the availability of a world-class employee pool and favorable economic conditions, software product entrepreneurship has thus far been lacking in the Indian software industry. This is attributable to several causes, ranging from the work culture to the economics of software product development.

First, while there exists a burgeoning services industry with low barriers to entry, it is difficult to make a case for long-term product development investments. Furthermore, product development activities require a different mix of skills among the work force. While a large engineering skills set is widely available in the Indian labor market, the marketing and management work force may not exist in a corresponding ratio to make large-scale product development effort sustainable in the long run. Also, for successful product development, collaborations with a broad range of consultants and implementation partners is necessary. Lacking the solid reputation of an incumbent, new entrants in the market will find it a challenge to leverage network effects in order to partner with reputable consultants.

Despite these drawbacks, there are recent success stories in the Indian software product market. For instance, Iflex has pioneered the Flexcube range of products, which has become the leading solution for the financial services industry. Iflex has indigenously developed a wide range of products for the financial services industry and has established a customer base of more than 775 customers in 130 countries. Iflex is now part of the Oracle group of companies. Similarly, Ramco systems has created a flexible approach to software development and has developed several packaged solutions (ERP, Supply Chain) for the SMB segment as well as a robust software development platform called VirtualWorks for custom software development.[6] Similarly, IRobot opened a design center in Mysore, their first R&D division outside the United States, to extend their capabilities by working in concert with their U.S.-based R&D team and their manufacturing divisions in Hong Kong/China. Their goal was to be a product development and design center involved in the design of both current and future products. Such moves suggest measured growth in R&D initiatives, but proliferation across the economy is still far from being realized.

A major stumbling block for product-oriented business models within large Indian software firms is the prevailing internal logic.[7] Most large Indian software firms have thrived on the growth in demand for low-cost offshore services for the development and maintenance of software applications. Their business model exhibits an annual growth rate of above 40% in revenues and 30% in gross margins, and their capital market valuations are based on these growth rates. The incentives for managers are primarily based on meeting quarterly targets in revenues and gross margins. It is a known model for them to hire engineers in large numbers, train them in months, and place them in global client projects at offshore locations initially and then on-site as required. The product-based business model is a shift that pushes these Indian software firms beyond their comfort zone. It requires a significant investment upfront and a new approach to risk management, and it demands a radical shift in marketing, customer engagement, pricing, and operations. Hence, it is no surprise that despite over USD40 billion of annual software exports from India, successful software products entirely designed and developed by the large Indian software firms are few.

However, the emerging global competition for talent will require large Indian software firms to revisit their business models. The growth in their current business models is nearly linear in the number of employees. This means that for Indian firms such as TCS and Infosys to maintain their current growth for five years, they would have to employ the population of an entire city.[7] Thus, the search is imminent for business models that either are software product-oriented or move toward value-added services such as customized business solutions for each client, business consulting, and/or business process management for large clients. The trend in decisions by Indian IT firms to merge their IT services and BPO units is a step in the right direction.[5] Nevertheless, this shift to a consulting and IT solutions-based business model directly confronts existing players in this market. Figure 3.1 illustrates the industry in transition. While Indian firms move to enhance their presence onshore by recruiting onshore talent, seeking marketing expertise, and improving their ability to stay in touch with customers, established consulting firms such as IBM and Accenture with considerable expertise in these areas are seeking complementary cost-effective capabilities by leveraging offshore talent in India.

The transition to the high risk (and high value-added) realm has been a difficult one for firms in India. As noted earlier, while the local technical talent is strong, the educational infrastructure for the development of complementary skill sets, such as the management of technology, marketing, new product development, and technology entrepreneurship, has been lacking. The limited supply pool in these areas is one reason that local firms have found it difficult to build the capabilities to provide complete end-to-end IT solutions for firms. Although companies such as Infosys and TCS, which have significant financial resources, are seeking talent outside the country to bridge this gap (for instance, by recruiting overseas talent for positions involving customer contact), other firms without the wherewithal might find it difficult to develop these complementary skill sets necessary for long-term survival and success.

3.6. The New Face of Indian Software Industry

The popular face of the Indian software industry in the last decade has been the celebrated success of the offshore business model leveraged by Infosys, TCS, Wipro, and other similar firms. They have created enormous wealth for their shareholders and have surpassed all expectations in software exports through application design and testing services. But we believe that this face of the Indian software industry is changing in both the "who" and the "what." This change is multifold. First, the emerging face of the Indian software industry will be more about multinational firms leveraging Indian talent for their software needs. As seen in Table 3.1, almost every major player in the high-tech industry is expanding its software-based R&D centers in India. This trend is likely to continue as these firms leverage their talent base in India to develop unique solutions for their customers worldwide. For example, Honeywell's center in Bangalore is developing several unique embedded software-based products and services for their global market.[7]

Second, the recent emergence of an ecosystem of over 5000 small and medium-sized software firms in India will play a significant role through their partnership in the provision of unique value-added solutions to both multinational and Indian firms. The spirit of software entrepreneurship in India has taken a new turn in the last few years. This change is from a plethora of attempts to start yet another offshore-based firm to the seeding of niche software solutions via a unique approach to the co-creation of value with customers. This ecosystem is about the emerging new Silicon Valley in Bangalore and beyond. For example, Robosoft, a small software firm based in the Tier 2 city of Udupi, won the Product Award in 2004 for enabling Bluetooth headsets for Apple iPods. Robosoft has also developed unique software-based solutions for Hewlett Packard and Philips. Matrixview,[e] a Chennai-based software firm with operations in Singapore and the United States, has developed a compression algorithm called SWISH that beats the best standards of JPEG and GZIP (the compression technology used by Google) by a significant margin (www.matrixview.com). Robosoft and Matrixview are not alone. The flow of venture capital in U.S. dollars to India in the last two years validates this. We expect to see the role of this ecosystem of small- and medium-sized software firms in India become more visible and pronounced by 2015. We envision more multinational firms mobilizing Indian talent through partnerships with firms such as Robosoft and Matrixview to co-create unique value for their global customers. This is also a part of the emerging model of business innovation.[7]

Third, we expect the portfolio of services in the business models of large Indian software houses to change as well. This change will be in the form of a shift away from project-based application development and testing services. We expect the major Indian software houses to take on larger solutions-based engagements that will include ownership of IT infrastructure and global business process management for large multinational clients. This change will not be a choice. It will emerge as a requirement for success in the emerging competition for Indian talent. We also expect the local demand for such IT services in India to grow significantly, as the Indian economy continues to leap forward at 9%–10% annually. We anticipate that global consulting firms such as IBM and Accenture will compete and collaborate with Indian software firms such as Infosys, TCS, Wipro, and Satyam for both global and local markets. We also anticipate that the mix of employees in these firms will emerge from across the globe in an inter-mixing of cultures and values, posing new challenges for the management of human resources and organization values.

3.7. Challenges for the Future

Several different pathways need to converge for Indian firms to maintain their current momentum through the next decade. The gradual loss in strength of the

---

[e] Professor M.S. Krishnan serves on the advisory board of Matrixview.

U.S. dollar has diminished the profitability of offshore initiatives and reduced the comparative cost advantages of Indian firms. Compounding this concern has been the escalating salaries of the Indian workforce. The proliferation of high-paying multinational firms and abundance of alternatives have increased local costs and affected the returns on investments in software and technology for Indian firms, and the increase in salaries has led to speculations that the "charm of India" in software is over. We disagree. We believe that the opportunities for mobilizing talent in India remain open — but only to firms that are willing to innovate in their search for talent and their talent development. While costs are likely to increase, one source of consistent advantage has been the strong supply of analytical minds in the Tier I and Tier II cities of India. This resource base also includes readily available, English-speaking professionals. We expect that the direct involvement of large software firms and innovative public/private collaborations with the local governments will unearth this talent. In terms of complementary skills in management and the management of new product development, only a handful of Indian universities and institutions (for example, the Indian Institutes of Technology, the National Institutes of Technology, and the Indian Institutes of Management, to name a few) have been successful in consistently developing this expertise. A more concerted effort by the government to grow such institutions through effective educational policies is essential to meet the demand for skilled talent.

As noted earlier, today's large Indian outsourcing firms such as TCS, Infosys, Wipro, and Satyam have no choice but to expand their resource base outside India to build the complementary skills of business domain expertise and a deeper understanding of their customers for the co-creation of unique values. With the support of appropriate policies, as was the case in the early 1990s, we envision the Indian software industry emerging as a dominant player in the ecosystem of resources and partners, mobilizing talent in both Indian and global firms to create value for their global customers. Successful firms will innovate the next round of ways to leverage the growing Indian software talent.

References

1. Ethiraj, SK, P Kale, MS Krishnan and J Singh (2005). Where do capabilities come from and how do they matter? A study in the software, *Strategic Management Journal*, 26(1), 25–45.
2. Financial Times (2005). http://www.ft.com/cms/s/0/79ac61de-1b4d-11da-a117-00000 e2511c8.html) [Retrieved 17 November 2005].
3. Friedman, T (2005). The World is Flat 3.0: A Brief History of the Twenty-First Century. New York: Farrar, Straus and Giroux.

4. Keogh, JE (1998). Working to solve the year 2000 problem. In *COBOL Programmer's Notebook*, JE Keogh (ed.), Ch. 12, pp. 307–329. Upper Saddle River, NJ: Prentice-Hall PTR.

5. Narayanan, S and JM Swaminathan (2007). Information technology offshoring to India: pitfalls, opportunities and trends. In *New Models of Firm's Restructuring after Globalization*, Prasnikar, J and A Cirman (eds.), pp. 327–345.

6. Prahalad, CK and MS Krishnan (2002). The dynamic synchronization of strategy and information technology. *MIT Sloan Management Review*, Summer, 43, 24–33.

7. Prahalad, CK and MS Krishnan (2008). *The New Age of Innovation*. The New Age & Innovation: *Driving Co-created Value Through Global Neworks*. New York: McGrath Hill Publications.

8. Ramamritham, K (2001). A Detailed Report on R&D at Indian Computer Science Establishments. um-cs-1995-085, University of Massachusetts.

9. The Financial Express (2007). http://www.financialexpress.com/news/TCS-Nielsen-Co-in-10yr-1-2-bn-pact/229725/.

Connecting Wave

MANUFACTURING

Jayashankar M. Swaminathan

A couple of years ago, as I was watching the "swoosh" of the Nike logo being printed on T-shirts at the Intimate Active Wear factory in Bangalore,[a] I realized that India had finally joined the global manufacturing network. In fact, textiles make up 14% of India's total industrial production, constituting 4% of its GDP and 17% of its total export earnings. Since liberalization, the Indian textiles industry has grown significantly, from USD27 billion in 2005 to USD49 billion in 2007. India currently exports textile products and handicrafts to more than 100 countries. Continuing the centuries-old tradition, Europe remains India's major export market, with a 22% market share in textiles and 43% in apparel, while the United States is the largest single buyer of Indian textiles (19% share) and apparel (32.6%). Recently, India overtook the United States to become the world's second-largest cotton-producing country after China, according to a study by the International Service for the Acquisition of Agri-biotech Applications. It is no surprise that the textile industry is the largest foreign exchange earning sector in the country. The industry employs over 35 million people, and with its continuing growth momentum, its role in the Indian economy is bound to increase. The Indian sourcing market is estimated to grow at an average annual rate of 12%, from an expected market size of USD22–25 billion in 2008 to USD35–37 billion by 2011.[1] All of the above factors have led some key international fashion brands, such as Hugo Boss, Diesel, and Liz Claiborne, to increase their sourcing from India.

But why has it taken so long for India to join the global manufacturing networks? Is it because people in India did not like "Made in India" products, and as a result the foreign confidence in Indian manufacturing was minimal?

---

[a] Intimate Clothing is part of MAS Holdings, a leading supplier in the apparel sector, for major multinational brands.

I remember my younger days when I heard people all around me comment that if a product did not work well, then it must be domestic. There was a joke that even the glue made in India would not stick properly. Or is India's delayed entry a result of the extremely tight regulations during the "License Raj" that strangulated the Indian manufacturing industry? According to Mr. Gurcharan Das, between 1960 and 1989 the Tatas made 119 proposals for new business or expansion and each one of them "ended in the wastebaskets of the bureaucrats".[2]

Today, there are many top-class Indian manufacturing firms that have some of the brightest talent, best processes and technology, and, of course, world-class products. The Indian operations of some multinationals are being recognized for being among the best in their global supply chains. In a recent conversation with executives from Nokia, for example, I learned that their Chennai plant is generating the highest number of kaizen improvements among all the plants in its global supply chain network. Toyota is planning to invest USD340 million for a second plant in India outside of Bangalore, and in doing so it joins Renault, General Motors, Hyundai, and Suzuki in making India an important part of its global production network for small- and less-expensive cars.[3] While speaking to us last year at the Supply Chain Thought Leaders Roundtable in Japan, Prof. Fujimoto, a leading expert in the area of product design and development, applauded Indian manufacturing firms in the motorcycle business for their quality improvements. In fact, there are many exceptional companies that are very large and successful in their respective sectors. However, most of the products that are sold in India come from small- to medium-sized industries. So is it the

Fig. E3.1.   Small and medium scale manufacturing is widely prevalent.

scale of operations that has caused the Indian manufacturing sector to lag behind the curve?

In the next chapter, entitled "Indian Manufacturing — Strategic and Operational Decisions and Business Performance," Prof. Ananth Iyer, Susan Bulkeley Butler Chair in Operations Management at Krannert School of Management, Purdue University, along with Mr. Peter Koudal, Director of Global Manufacturing at Deloitte Research, Prof. Haritha Saranga at the Indian Institute of Management at Bangalore, and Prof. Sridhar Seshadri, Toyota Professor of Manufacturing at the Stern School of Business, New York University, present a detailed research perspective on the development of the manufacturing sector in India. They begin with a historical description of the economic restrictions of a policy environment that strongly regulated monopolies; controlled capacity expansion decisions and technology imports; and favored the small-scale sector, investments in public sector enterprises, and the substitution of critical imported materials. The authors go on to discuss how these restrictions affected firms' operational choices in terms of scale and operating focus; product and process technologies; and planning, control, and execution systems. Different industries evolved in different ways in response to the types of restrictions imposed on them. As a result, the industries in the manufacturing sector have each generated unique manufacturing capabilities and achieved varying levels of performance. For instance, in the auto components industry, firms have quickly adapted to the deregulated environment and are competitive on a global standard and are constantly innovating. The authors present the example of Rane Brake Linings (RBL) to highlight the improvements and global competitiveness in this sector. Finally, they draw on both research and industry analysis to suggest the possible future evolution of industries in the manufacturing sector, providing a brief description of the necessary steps for the significant growth and development of manufacturing firms operating in India in the years to come.

References

1. CII-Ernst and Young Textile and Apparel Report, November 5, 2007. http://www.ey.com/Global/assets.nsf/India/Report_Summary_CII_Textile_Event/$file/Report
2. Das, G (2002). *India Unbound: From Independence to the Global Information Age.* UK: Profile Books Ltd.
3. Reed, J (2008). "Toyota to invest $340m in Bangalore plant". *Financial Times* (13 April 2008). http://www.ft.com/cms/.

CHAPTER 4

INDIAN MANUFACTURING: STRATEGIC AND OPERATIONAL DECISIONS AND BUSINESS PERFORMANCE

Ananth Iyer,* Peter Koudal,[†]
Haritha Saranga[‡] and Sridhar Seshadri[§]

Over the last decade, developing countries have increased their share of global manufacturing value-added from a mere 15.73% in 1990 to 23.58% in 2002,[44] and their share in world export from 24.3% in 1990 to 32.1% in 2003.[43] The average annual flow of FDI into developing countries has more than quadrupled, from USD16.9 billion in the 1989–1991 period to USD70 billion in 2001–2003, growing more than twice as fast as the rate of investment into developed countries.[43] These trends suggest that developing countries will play a significant role in the future of global manufacturing.

Several studies suggest a possible increase in manufacturing activity in India in the upcoming years, following the ascent of China's manufacturing industry. The next wave of offshoring is going to take place in skill-intensive industries, and India has an advantage in this segment.[29] Various demographic studies have revealed that while the aging population in the developed world is driving manufacturing jobs to the developing countries, among the low-cost manufacturing destinations (including countries such as China, Brazil, and Russia), India is

* Susan Bulkeley Butler Chair in Operations Management, Krannert School of Management, Purdue University, West Lafayette, Indiana IN. USA. E-mail aiyer@mgmt.purdue.edu.
† Director of Global Manufacturing, Deloitte Research, New York, NY, USA. E-mail pkoudal@deloitte.com.
‡ Production and Operations Management, Indian Institute of Management, Bangalore, Bannerghatta Road, Bangalore 560076, India. E-mail harithas@Iimb.ernet.in.
§ McCombs School of Business, The University of Texas at Austin, Texas. E-mail Sridhar.Seshadri@mccombs.utexas.edu.

expected to have the largest percentage of young working-age population in the years leading up to 2050.[46]

The Indian manufacturing sector has witnessed significant growth in productivity since the economic reforms of 1991. Empirical studies have shown that there has been approximately a 15% increase in aggregate productivity growth in FDI-liberalized industries and a 20% increase in tariff-liberalized industries during the period 1987–1995.[41] Further, there has been a significant increase in the average productivity of the Indian auto-component industry (about 40%) and the Indian pharmaceutical industry (about 15%) during the decade after the liberalization took place.[5,15] The overall share of Indian exports in the world trade of goods and services has increased from 0.5% in 1990 to 0.8% in 2003.[43] However, there is a great amount of heterogeneity across the Indian manufacturing sector. While some industries are highly evolved, others have lagged far behind.

In this chapter, we first focus on the historical restrictions placed on Indian manufacturing and provide a summary of the operational choices made by firms in a policy environment that strongly regulated manufacturing and industry. We discuss how regulations related to monopolies, capacity expansion, and technology imports affected firm-level decisions. In response to different regulations, each industry developed its own unique manufacturing capabilities and performance; we classify firms in the manufacturing sector into different categories based on their objectives and practices. We hence provide our thoughts on the future trends in the manufacturing sector, concluding with a short summary of the changes in one of these firms, Rane Brake Linings (RBL), to highlight its improvements and its global competitiveness.

Historical Development

4.1. Policy Restrictions and Firm Decisions

Most industries in the Indian manufacturing sector were subject to strict licensing requirements and capacity controls during the 1960s and 1970s.[3] In particular, the restrictions that seem to have had significant impact on operational choices are the following:

1. Public sector dominance: In 18 industries, significant market share was reserved for the public sector, including manufacturing industries such as iron and steel, heavy plant and machinery, telecommunications equipment,

and petrochemicals. But there were exceptions in each industry (for example, Tata Steel in the steel sector).

2. Small-scale advantage: Some industries were reserved for the small-scale sector, including mechanical engineering, chemical products, and auto ancillaries. Production of certain items (e.g., garments, shoes, and toys) was also restricted to the small-scale sector.

3. Capacity restrictions: Most sectors were subject to capacity restrictions and industrial licensing. The restrictions meant that a license from the government was necessary to expand capacity.

4. Monopoly control: The Monopolies and Restrictive Trade Practices Act of 1969 (MRTP) allowed the government to monitor the investments of large industrial houses by inviting objections and holding public hearings before granting a license for production.

5. Foreign investment control: The Foreign Exchange Regulation Act of 1973 (FERA), among other restrictions, limited foreign equity share to not more than 40%, unless the company was engaged in "core" activities, was using sophisticated technologies, or met certain export commitments.

6. Import duties: High import tariffs on capital goods and technology were levied to encourage firms to develop in-house R&D and complementary technologies and to discourage the importing of capital goods.

7. Process patents: Process patenting laws permitted firms to develop alternate production approaches to existing patented products. This was particularly significant in the pharmaceutical industry.

8. FDI: Restrictions on FDI limited the participation of global corporations in Indian markets. It also affected access to technology and the scale of existing companies.

4.1.1. *Scale of Operations*

One of the major effects of these restrictions was on firms' scale of operations. In the case of Indian manufacturing industries, policy restrictions regarding capacity, together with government favoritism towards smaller firms, discouraged the majority of smaller firms from growing, as they would have had to cope with a much more difficult licensing policy, higher labor costs, and substantially higher excise duties once they exceeded a certain size limit.

As a result, manufacturers of products such as chemicals and auto components, which were reserved for the small-scale sector, were operating at capacities below the minimum efficiency scale because they risked losing their preferential status if they expanded their output.[11] Also, smaller firms performed

82   *A. Iyer et al.*

better in industries in which vertical integration was discouraged by policy makers and in which there were few or no economies of scale in management.[11,a] As a result, SMEs[b] constituted roughly 73% of the Indian manufacturing enterprises in 2002, according to a World Bank survey.[c] Small-scale production was negatively correlated with per capita income levels across other developing countries and also within these countries through time.[42]

The decision to stay small could additionally have been influenced by several market factors. The domestic orientation of the Indian government, unlike the other emerging economies (e.g., those of East Asian countries) might have influenced firms to focus only on meeting local demand. Infrastructural problems such as poor transportation networks and warehousing facilities could also have influenced firms to stay small, spread out, and produce locally to meet small, diffused pockets of demand. The higher volatility in developing markets might have discouraged the use of advanced mass-production techniques and encouraged firms to remain small and rely more heavily on labor, to stay flexible (Tybout, 2000).

Smaller firms, being more labor-intensive and less automated, are more flexible in their ability to respond to demand volatility and may not have allocational inefficiencies, unlike the larger firms that try to adapt capital-intensive imported technologies. In order to stay in the small-scale category, many companies split their businesses into multiple entities but ran them as a single value chain. In this way, they were able to achieve efficiencies and at the same time enjoy the benefits available to small-scale units. In many cases, these businesses operated as clusters and achieved efficiencies in that manner.

Licenses allocated in the 1960s and 1970s were extremely specific with regard to what could be manufactured. In many ways, the effect of licensing was similar to that of capacity restrictions. Firms that were trying to differentiate products were affected most by licensing requirements, as both technology upgrades and entry into new product ranges required licenses from government. The early deregulation of the 1980s introduced "broad-banding" of production licenses. This change allowed firms to use their existing licensed capacity (previously tied to a narrow product specification) to manufacture a broader range of related products. Though licensing requirements were formally retained, they were granted more easily. Firms such as Reliance in the textile industry took

---

[a] Gang (1992) found that if an industry sales structure, regulatory environment, or technology is such that there are significant economies of scale in management, then small firm presence is reduced, where the economies of scale in management are measured in terms of worker-to-employee (managerial staff) ratio. Thus, economies of scale in management are present if the worker-to-employee ratio in large firms is greater than that in small firms.
[b] A firm is defined as an SME if it has fewer than 150 employees.
[c] http://lnweb18.worldbank.org/sar/sa.nsf/Attachments/wbcii/$File/FACSReport.pdf.

advantage of broad-banding to increase scale and backward-integrate most of the raw materials and intermediates for the manufacturing of polyester fiber yarn.

The capacity allocations at the level of individual firms and plants more or less determined the market share of each firm. The MRTP Act of 1969 imposed additional capacity restrictions on large business houses. Production as a share of the total manufacturing sector in the textile industry, which employs more workers than any other manufacturing sector in India, fell from 79% in 1951 to under 30% in the early 1990s, primarily, as a result of curbs on capacity expansion and new equipment, as well as differential excise duties.[d] The fertilizer industry too faced these restrictions, but they were compensated by a subsidy that was based on cost, and transportation costs were borne by the government.

As laws pertaining to market share changed, firms tended to adjust within the limits imposed by the MRTP, FERA, capacity-constraint, and industrial-licensing policies. Lacking the ability to grow organically, firms chose to grow through acquisitions in unrelated areas. For example, the large family businesses such as Birla, Tata, and Reliance entered diverse sectors ranging from agriculture, automobiles, oil, and steel, to aviation, entertainment, hospitality, IT, retailing, and telecommunications. Did the restrictions on size lead to loss of efficiency?

4.1.2. *Efficiency of Operations*

If indeed scale inefficiencies were present due to these restrictions, one would have expected to see firms operating in the increasing returns-to-scale region prior to liberalization, and thus being in a position to exploit scale economies after the partial reforms of the early 1980s and the new industrial policy of 1991. However, the actual outcomes depended on the nature of the industry and the market growth as well.

From 1976 to 1985, large firms belonging to six major manufacturing industries, namely automobiles, electrical machinery, non-electrical machinery, basic chemicals, pharmaceuticals, and paper, on average were operating close to constant returns to scale.[6] After liberalization, the firms in these industries grew to take advantage of scale economies. Firms in other key manufacturing industries, such as chemical and chemical products, machinery and equipment, leather and leather products, metal products and parts, and electrical and related parts also experienced technological progress and exploited scale economies subsequent to the lifting of restrictions in 1991.[32] In industries such as television manufacturing, small-scale manufacturers took advantage of the benefits offered by the government and grew rapidly, resulting in an efficient and rapid growth of the Indian

---

[d] http://reference.allrefer.com/country-guide-study/india/india108.html.

television industry during the period 1973–1987.[13] A number of studies have indicated that regulations impeded smaller firms' efforts to attain an optimal level of efficiency, but the industries that have been liberalized to a great extent seem to have recoiled faster.[22, 24]

In fact, examples from low-growth industries such as fertilizer show that more efficient firms took advantage of liberalization and grew to capture market share. Other firms from diverse industries for which this was the case include Bombay Dyeing (textiles and garments), Coramandel Fertilizer, Larsen & Toubro (heavy engineering and construction), NTPC (thermal plant construction and operation), ONGC (oil and natural gas), Reliance (various industries, including textiles, petrochemicals, and telecommunications), and Saint Gobain (float glass).

Another factor that might have influenced firms' choices and efficiency is their ownership. During the 1988–1992 period, escalating competition in product markets propelled the state-owned enterprises (SOEs) to realize greater levels of technical efficiency.[34] However, these SOEs did not perform as well as their private sector counterparts,[35] and the magnitude of the private vs. SOE performance differential increased with increasing competitive intensity in the industrial and commercial machinery, chemicals, food, and metals industries. This can be attributed to the fact that even after many regulations were lifted by the 1991 reforms, SOEs still needed government approval for the capital investments required for capacity expansions and technical upgrades, which in turn were necessary to improve scale and technical efficiencies.

In summary, firms in medium- and high-technology sectors, those in which there was rapid growth or scope for rapid growth in demand due to greater competition, and those that were liberalized early seem to have benefited the most from the improvements in scale and technical efficiency that followed liberalization. It is worth noting that these factors might not be independent.

4.1.3. *Product Differentiation vs. Cost Focus*

Prior to liberalization, when facing constraints to growth, firms had the choice of focusing on cost or differentiating through products or services. The former choice might have been more attractive for companies serving markets that were regulated or for which technology could not be imported. Firms in this category would have to focus on cost reduction. Thus, when the import restrictions were lifted, firms that were cost-efficient would have been expected to pursue their existing trajectories even more, in an effort to capture market share through a low-price strategy.

In contrast, firms that could differentiate themselves based on product changes could, after liberalization, try to upgrade to more sophisticated technologies and strengthen their position within their niche. This assumes that firms with differentiated products would be more likely to import technology and capital goods, provided there was enough demand to recoup their investments. When Indian market liberalization was implemented, domestic prices would be expected to fall with the influx of cheap imports, thus pushing firms to become more efficient or to exit. In either case, it would be hard to separate out the portion of the effect due to the operating focus of firms.

Evidence shows that firms manufacturing less-differentiated products, such as chemical products, electrical machinery, and transport equipment, increased their capacities and grew by increasing their factor inputs rather than improving technical efficiency during the reform period.[17]Anecdotal evidence from firms such as Orpat, Samay, and Aurobindo Pharmaceuticals Ltd. indicates that they took advantage of liberalization to leverage their efficient operations to grow and capture market share, supporting the prediction regarding firms with low-cost as their focus.

The evidence related to firms pursuing a strategy of differentiation is limited. For such firms, we would expect to see an increase in technical efficiency, that is, an improvement in productivity due to the substitution of capital equipment and technology for labor. Consider the auto-component industry in India. For decades the industry had stagnated with obsolete models and technologies, but following the trade liberalization, the entry of global auto majors into the Indian market and high demand forecasts by consultants encouraged some auto-component makers to increase their scale during the late 1990s. The global slump in demand during 1997–1998 subsequently had a negative impact on their capacity utilization and the automotive firms became more cautious in their capital investments.[38] A benchmark study by Deloitte Research finds that depreciation rates still are below growth rates for the majority of Indian manufacturers studied and that the industry continues to suffer from capacity constraints and a lack of capital investment. It appears that Indian manufacturers have fallen behind in adopting technology and investing in R&D relative to global manufacturing industries overall. This lack of investment may be due in part to the high cost of capital and the lack of internationalization of finance. It might also be due to the pursuit of a differentiation strategy in a relatively small market. However, the main point is that there remain opportunities for significant improvement.

Reliance Industries Ltd. (RIL) provides a good example of a corporation that followed both cost-efficiency and differentiated strategies based on the industry in which it was operating. Being one of the few Indian companies that was successful in vertically integrating most of its operations, RIL followed a differentiated strategy in the fabric business by offering an entire range of high-quality products manufactured with world-class technology, while opting for a cost-efficiency strategy through scale economies in the manufacturing of raw materials like polyester filament yarn, polyester staple fiber, and fiber intermediates such as PTA and MEG. Post-liberalization, RIL not only expanded its capacities in its existing businesses but further backward-integrated by entering into the manufacturing of raw materials and intermediates for its own use and sales.

Thus, the empirical evidence gathered so far suggests that the behavior of manufacturing firms pre-liberalization was, in general, consistent with what was expected, but with exceptions due to government policies for small-scale and state-owned enterprises. However, the evidence on Indian manufacturing industries is *not* similar to the case of emerging economies in general: unlike firms in other developing nations, Indian companies do seem to have realized major gains from better exploitation of scale economies, particularly in sectors such as electronics, fertilizer, telecommunications, textiles, transport equipment, and non-electrical industries. There is evidence that firms facing growth in demand (or being able to grow demand through price) in more competitive industries and also those in medium- or high-technology industries have improved their efficiency. Only the relaxation of all restrictions will allow us to make this statement with confidence, however.

4.1.4. *Technology Adoption*

High tariffs and restrictions on the importing of technology and capital goods are intended to induce firms in developing countries to develop in-house technological capabilities, in addition to generating government tax revenue and improving the balance of trade. Many classifications of technological capabilities and their modes of transfer exist in the literature, in the context of both developed and developing countries. A number of researchers have identified factors that influence the ability of developing countries to improve their technological capabilities through technology transfers.[21,31,45] It is expected that firms that invest in a certain amount of in-house R&D in order to complement imported technologies will be better able to assimilate and adapt the new technologies to the local environment. To achieve import substitution of raw materials and intermediate goods, as well as to develop the local capability to repair imported machinery and modify product and process technologies, firms must invest in local R&D and employ a certain number of R&D personnel in-house. These activities fall under basic capabilities.[25] This in turn enables firms to carry out minor modifications and create incremental innovations, which are adaptive and duplicative in nature and are considered intermediate capabilities. In the long run, these basic and intermediate technological capabilities are expected to give rise to advanced, research-based capabilities that are innovative and risky (such as new molecular development in the pharmaceutical sector) but can result in breakthrough products and technologies.

With the intention to gradually develop these technological capabilities and achieve technological self-reliance, India followed an "import and adapt technology" (IAT) strategy after its independence in 1947. Under this strategy, partial restrictions were placed on the importing of new technologies in order to encourage firms to adapt the imported technologies and to develop complementary technologies in-house. The overwhelming emphasis on import substitution in all branches of industry fostered considerable technological effort, primarily directed toward the adaptation of processes to the use of local materials.[7] Thus, it seems that the Indian government was successful in creating basic technological capabilities through an amalgamation of IAT and other import substitution strategies.

Did the IAT strategy stimulate local R&D? Studies by Katrak[18-20] using data from a variety of Indian industries during the pre-liberalization, liberalization, and post-liberalization periods suggest that although the importing of technology appears to have stimulated in-house R&D, the magnitude of this effect was limited and weaker for more complex technologies. Although R&D expenditures increased with enterprise size, larger firms appear to have invested in proportionately less R&D. However, the use of industry-level data might have affected the results. Katrak also found that the technological effort was higher in firms whose technology imports included those intended to strengthen their in-house technological capabilities, but lower in the enterprises that negotiated an exclusive right of sale in the home market. Further, the probability of importing technology was only weakly affected by the initial in-house capabilities, though the probability of impact was greater among larger and older enterprises.

These mixed results suggest that the technological activities of Indian firms were considerably influenced by the technological complexity of the industry and size of the firm during the pre-liberalized era. These findings are in line with Alam's arguments that the nature of the market and industrial structure had a significant impact on the development of the technical capabilities of Indian firms.[2]

Also, the effect of the IAT strategy appears to have been moderated by the adaptability of technologies to the local market. Complex technologies developed elsewhere might not have stimulated in-house R&D, because they either were not easily adaptable, did not have a sufficient market, or could not be improved to preserve advantage. The restrictions on the importing of ready-made technologies essential for the mastery of more complex technologies would have further contributed to this inertia. Results of a study by Basant and Fikkert show that the returns from technology purchases were high and significant for both scientific firms[e] (166%) and non-scientific firms (95%), while the returns from in-house R&D were high and significant only for non-scientific

---

[e] The "scientific" subgroup of firms consists of firms in chemicals, drugs, and electronic industries, while the "non-scientific" firms are in all other industrial categories (Basant and Fikkert, 1996).

firms (64%) (returns were a mere 1% for scientific firms). Katrak also observed a considerable underutilization of local technology compared to imported technology. This may be because firms preferred to import reputable foreign technology in lieu of experimenting with relatively less well-established local technology, which was most often developed in Indian government laboratories isolated from production.

In addition, industrial structure, firm size, public-private ownership, and the pool of purchasable foreign technology influence the relative levels of firms' own R&D and technology purchases in Indian manufacturing industries.[9] Empirical evidence shows that purchased foreign technology and in-house innovation activity complemented each other in Indian manufacturing industries from 1960 to 1970. Thus, the industrial structure, pool of purchasable foreign technology, and complementary nature of in-house R&D point towards the importance of the *adaptability* of technology, but firm size and public-private ownership appear to play an important role in developing and sustaining the technological advantage. This is illustrated by the large private industrial conglomerates such as the RIL, the Birla Group, and the Tata Group, which invested heavily in technology imports as well as in-house R&D in industries including auto components, steel, and textiles and contributed significantly to the technological growth of these industries in India.

In his study of Indian technology exports and technological development, Lall argues that while India's highly protectionist strategy created various inefficiencies, it also led to the creation of a substantial technological capability that enabled India to become the leading exporter of industrial technology in the Third World, in terms of the range, diversity, and complexity of technologies it exports.[25,26] He attributes this technological development to firm-level technological efforts such as the tailoring (*adaptation*) of capital goods to local customer needs, transmission of technology to subcontractors, product diversification, and new product development in response to internal competition and cost-reducing process improvements. Public-sector units such as BHEL, IRCON, HMT, and RITES are a few examples of firms with significant exports of technology and turnkey projects. Kumar and Saqib qualify Lall's finding, suggesting that Indian firms exhibited greater R&D and technological capabilities in sectors such as electrical equipment, non-electrical machinery, and machine tools in order to exploit the greater opportunities for product adaptation present in these sectors.[23] Thus, at least some Indian manufacturing firms may have developed basic and intermediate technological capabilities that were not driven by IAT strategy alone but also by the sector-specific incentives to innovate and adapt previously designed products and processes to the local environment.

The relaxation of patent laws and restrictions on royalty payments led to a marked increase in technology expenditures by firms. According to Athreye and Kapur, the liberalization of importing resulted in lower tariff levels, and the costs of capital goods and embodied technology imports were consequently lowered.[3] In high-technology industries, such as passenger car and ancillary auto parts, technology intensity increased sector-wide after liberalization as firms adopted the latest technology, including modern assembly lines.

Anecdotal evidence from firms such as Coromandel Fertilizer (CFL), Lakshmi Mittal, SCL, Saint Gobain, and Tata Steel indicates that Indian firms attempted to perform major modifications on process technologies to adapt to local inputs and to reduce capital and operating costs post-liberalization. There is a growing evidence that sector-specific incentives might play a larger role in the actual adaptation of technology.

4.1.5. *Process and Product Innovation*

A specific form of incentive is the firm's ability to exploit a given product or process innovation for an extended period of time. In the case of the pharmaceutical industry, the adoption of process patenting in the early 1970s appears to have realized the effects of the IAT strategy. Process patenting was intended to develop an indigenous chemical and pharmaceutical industry to meet the domestic demand for drugs and pharmaceuticals at affordable prices. Since pharmaceutical R&D is capital-intensive, and none of the domestic firms possessed the requisite capital and technical capabilities, firms were allowed to reverse-engineer products that had been invented elsewhere as long as they could invent a new process for production.

The resulting imitative capabilities were expected in the long run to lead to pioneering R&D capabilities, as has been the case for Japan, which began in the 1960s with imitative R&D and within few decades progressed to become a leader in new drug development.[12] Chaudhuri has argued that Indian patent regulations indeed had a positive impact on the in-house technological capabilities of local firms.[8] Consistent with this argument, empirical evidence suggests that innovative activity in the chemical and drug industry has been stimulated by the process-patent policy, which encouraged firms to work out alternative processes for the manufacture of known chemical compounds and bulk drugs.[23] The success of the Indian pharmaceutical industry can be attributed to the presence of a large captive market and the sustainability of process technologies (once developed) due to process patenting.

The competitive pressure generated by liberalization has pushed Indian pharmaceutical firms into more R&D activity to develop new products.[33] At the same time, the strong processing capabilities developed during the process-patent regime have opened up new avenues of growth and opportunities for domestic firms to become a part of global supply chain through contract research and manufacturing operations for global drug majors.[37,38] Since liberalization, product performance improvement has become one of the prime objectives of Indian manufacturing firms, and product and process design issues are gaining more importance as firms are trying to reduce lead times in introducing new products into the market.[28] New product development strategies such as concurrent engineering are not yet attracting enough adherents, however, as they require major investments and structural changes.

In summary, the evidence suggests that India's external policy environment has had a significant effect on manufacturing firms' decisions regarding strategic and operational choices of process and product technologies. While firms in certain sectors such as chemicals and pharmaceuticals took advantage of patent regulations and improved their process capabilities, firms in the electrical equipment, non-electrical machinery, and machine tools sectors developed their technical capabilities to exploit the product adaptation opportunities following the IAT strategy. Technological adaptation, sector-specific incentives, and the sustainability of technological advantage all seem to have influenced the efforts of firms in this policy environment. The drawback of this strategy has been the forced reduction of imported ready-made technologies, which affected high-technology industries for which local enterprises could not master the requisite technology — or which, having mastered it, could not keep pace with its development.

Licensing requirements and restrictions on the importing of technologies appear to have prevented firms in certain industries — particularly those that were already suffering from capacity restrictions — from differentiating themselves through product and process improvements. However, the evidence from the post-liberalization period suggests that, despite operating within a restricted regime for a long time, firms reacted positively to the economic reforms and adapted quickly by upgrading to advanced manufacturing technologies and focusing on new product development.

Current and Future Trends

4.2. Current State of Manufacturing

Economic reforms took place at different times in different industries. For example, the government policy restricting the manufacture of about 800 items to the small-scale sector was not relaxed until 2001. Similar quantity restrictions on importing of consumer goods remained in force until 2001; most of this segment also had been reserved for the small-scale sector. Many of these items, such as garments, shoes, and toys, had high export potential, but investment in plant and machinery for any individual unit producing these items was not permitted to exceed USD250,000, thus precluding firms from taking advantage of scale and potential export opportunities.[1] However, the situation has changed recently, with 64 items having been removed from the reserved list during the period 2000–2002 and many more expected to be removed in the coming years. The investment ceiling for certain items was increased to USD1 million, and quantitative restrictions on the importing of consumer goods were also removed in 2001, increasing competition in the domestic market. Since these changes came into effect only recently, it remains to be seen how firms will react in the long run. Expansion in certain industries, including cotton textiles and brewing, continues to be difficult, as these industries are still subject to capacity regulations, price controls, and small-scale industry reservations. The result of this phased implementation is that different industries today are at different levels in terms of their manufacturing sophistication.

Hayes and Wheelwright have classified manufacturing firms into four stages based on the degree of emphasis a firm places on its manufacturing division in the achievement of its corporate-level strategic objectives.[14] In their framework, the degree of manufacturing effectiveness of each firm is evaluated on a continuum from stages 1 to 4:

(i) Stage 1 firms are described as "internally neutral", with a main focus on minimizing potential negative impacts on manufacturing.

(ii) Stage 2 firms seek to maintain parity with rest of the industry, and hence they are "externally neutral."

(iii) Stage 3 firms are "internally supportive" of the corporate strategy.

(iv) Stage 4 firms are "externally supportive" of the organization in its competitive endeavor.

Hayes and Wheelwright based their classification on various sector-specific factors and organizational characteristics. Although there has been wide acceptance of their framework in the literature and it has been applied to a few developed-country scenarios, it has not yet been applied to manufacturing firms in less-developed countries. We classify Indian manufacturing firms in this framework based on the progress they have made with the choices available to them, given the policy environment and other external constraints. We also trace the developments in Indian manufacturing industries according to the sequence predicted by Rosenzweig and Roth's competitive progression theory (CPT), which holds that sustainable competitive capabilities are built cumulatively, from conformance quality to delivery reliability to volume flexibility to low cost.[35]

4.2.1. *Stage 1 Firms*

Firms in sectors reserved for public-sector units did not face competition, and hence they had limited incentives to modernize, while firms in many private sectors did not have the flexibility to modernize their equipment and process technologies due to the restrictions on importing of technology. The protected regime also meant captive consumers, further reducing the incentives to initiate quality programs or adapt information systems and advanced manufacturing systems.[40] Consequently, the manufacturing functions of most public and private sector firms were in stage 1 of the framework, as they did not seek to upgrade their labor-intensive, low-technology processes when products involving a new generation of technologies appeared on the world market.

Quality, delivery, inventory reduction, and capacity utilization have been identified as the objectives that are most important to manufacturing firms, while manufacturing lead-time reduction and the linking of manufacturing to corporate strategy are of slightly less concern.[39] This highlights the need to align IT initiatives towards agile manufacturing rather than simply automating conventional operations, as many firms have fragmented information management systems that may not allow them to deliver superior value to their customers and achieve world-class status. The majority of Indian firms, except for those in the pharmaceutical and auto-component industries, are still in stage 1 of Hayes and Wheelwright's framework.

4.2.2. *Stage 2 Firms*

The automobile industry obtained the impetus for development in 1982 when the Indian government established a joint venture with Suzuki of Japan (Maruti-Suzuki) with the intention of bringing affordable cars to the masses. During the 1980s, the government carefully protected and supported Maruti by preventing other foreign firms from entering the Indian market and other domestic firms from entering the small-car segment through licensing and policy measures. The entry of Suzuki, a quality-conscious Japanese OEM, gave rise to a strong, customer-oriented auto-component industry in India. Maruti-Suzuki also recruited a considerable number of apprentices each year from the Industrial Training Institutes[f] (ITI) — a two-year vocational school for high-school graduates — which accounted for approximately 15% of its workforce. Maruti trained these

---

[f] According to Okada (1998), along with a number of universities and six Indian Institutes of Technology (IITs) for higher education, the government of India also established a number of Industrial Training Institutes (ITIs), two-year vocational schools for high school graduates all over the country. Delhi alone has 13 ITIs for 8500 trainees in 50–60 different trades.

ITI apprentices at the actual production sites and hired many of them at the end of their training.

Thus, unlike workers in countries such as Mexico, where foreign-owned auto plants and auto component suppliers often rely heavily on poorly paid hourly workers with less educational background, Indian auto workers often are well educated and well trained in their respective fields. The liberalization of 1991, which allowed the entry of multinational enterprises, further encouraged the auto component suppliers to upgrade their quality programs by adapting just-in-time (JIT), total-quality management (TQM), total productivity management (TPM), Six Sigma, etc. The number of ISO, QS and automotive industry-specific TS 16949 certifications, along with quality awards such as the Deming award and the Japanese quality medal, substantiate the achievements of auto component suppliers relative to quality standards.[4]

During the period 1993–1998, the auto-component firms also moved a step ahead and achieved cost efficiency along with technical efficiency gains, which resulted in further productivity growth.[15] Thus, conformance quality and technical upgrades gave rise directly to cost efficiency. Anecdotal evidence suggests, however, that some of the component suppliers were unable to fill the larger standard orders of multinational companies even in the late 1990s. One supplier had to reject half of the 20 requests for price quotations it had received from multinational OEMs because the order sizes seemed colossal.[27] The recent market stability and renewed interest in India as a market and manufacturing base among multinational OEMs such as General Motors, Ford, and BMW are encouraging the auto-component firms to pursue volume flexibility, which represents level 3 in the cumulative capability model of Rosenzweig and Roth.

Overall, a majority of Indian auto-component firms seem to have reached stage 2 of Hayes and Wheelwright's framework by following industry standards in manufacturing practices, while a few firms, such as Sundaram Fasteners, have progressed to stage 3 by upgrading their processes and quality levels and achieving volume flexibilities (for instance, the ability to supply 100% of GM's radiator caps). It is likely that most auto-component firms merely embraced the control systems, without yet having built the supply-chain systems that require more sophistication.

4.2.3. *Stages 3 and 4 Firms*

Process-based industries, such as chemicals and pharmaceuticals, have placed much more importance on manufacturing since the early 1970s. Firms in these industries invested heavily in the R&D of process technologies, as their emphasis was on the low-cost production of bulk drugs and formulations to compete with other domestic low-cost producers.[8,37] The strong manufacturing capability developed during the process-patenting regime thus enabled many Indian pharmaceutical firms to enter export markets before and after the policy restrictions were lifted.[24] The need to obtain approvals of good manufacturing practices (GMP) from international regulatory authorities such as the FDA in the United States, the Medicines Control Agency (MCA) in the United Kingdom, and the Therapeutic Goods Administration (TGA) in Australia, which were mandatory for export contracts, encouraged these firms to further improve their facilities, equipment, and internal processes. Since firms in these sectors derive their competitive advantage from manufacturing capability, the manufacturing functions of some of the leading pharmaceutical firms, such as Aurobindo Pharmaceuticals Ltd., Dr. Reddy's Laboratories, Ranbaxy Laboratories Ltd., Cipla Ltd., Wockhardt Ltd., and Nicholas Piramal Ltd. appear to have reached stages 3 and 4 of Hayes and Wheelwright's framework, by internally and/or externally supporting the corporate-level strategic objectives of the enterprises.

Quality initiatives, technical upgrades, and R&D investments both pre- and post-liberalization have resulted in significant quality improvements in the Indian pharmaceutical industry.[5,34,38] Self-sufficiency in the domestic market, as well as increasing export markets for bulk drugs and formulations, offer proof of the Indian pharmaceutical industry's delivery reliability and volume flexibility, achieved through collaboration between small bulk pharmaceutical product manufacturers and established formulation producers. Finally, cost efficiency can be inferred from the broadly affordable pharmaceutical product prices, which are a fraction of the prices prevailing internationally, confirming the cumulative nature of these competitive capabilities as suggested by Rosenzweig and Roth.

The empirical and anecdotal evidence suggests that post-liberalization process and quality management practices have contributed to the better performance of manufacturing functions at the corporate level in just a few sectors,[8,15,24,38] pushing these firms to stages 3 and 4 of Hayes and Wheelwright's framework. Indeed, a few studies suggest that infrastructural elements such as vendor management, human resource management, and information systems are receiving increased attention in recent times.[28]

4.3. Conclusions

Productivity studies of Indian manufacturing industries reveal that there was significant productivity growth in various manufacturing sectors after policy restrictions were relaxed through economic liberalization in 1991. However, small-scale firms maintain a strong presence in Indian manufacturing, as they generate almost 85% of the manufacturing employment in the country[g] due to a variety of external factors including favorable government policies, dispersed local demand, and poor

---

[g] http://www.unido.org/userfiles/RussoF/Small.pdf.

infrastructure and transport facilities. Firms in medium- and high-technology sectors, those in which there was rapid growth or scope for rapid growth in demand due to more competitive scenarios, and those liberalized early have benefited the most in regard to scale and technical efficiency post-liberalization. However, since the capacity restrictions in the small-scale sector were relaxed only recently, it is not yet clear how firms in this sector will react in the long run. If the reduced import tariffs result in lower domestic output, then local firms will not have the opportunity to exploit the unutilized scale economies to become more efficient. On the other hand, if the structural characteristics of India remain the same — its size, its underdeveloped transportation networks, and the presence of a vast rural population dispersed across small regions that supported the existence of smaller firms to meet local demands in the first place — then industrial liberalization alone may not induce firms to take advantage of scale economies.

Based on the empirical studies, we have suggested that, faced with capacity and other external constraints, firms will follow either a cost-efficiency strategy or a differentiation strategy. The evidence seems to suggest that productivity growth in sectors such as auto components, which were originally reserved for the small-scale sector, is driven by firms that follow a differentiation strategy and is upgraded by the importing of product and process technologies to face increased foreign competition. In sectors such as pharmaceuticals, where since the early 1970s firms have adopted a cost-efficiency strategy and developed strong processing capabilities, firms have benefited by upgrading their facilities and investing in research and new product development to avail themselves of various globalization opportunities.

Although the protectionist trade regime and restrictions on the importing of technologies had discouraged many public and private sector firms from investing in advanced product and process technologies, we find evidence that in some sectors firms have successfully established quality management systems and strong processing capabilities over the years. The economic reforms of 1991 have given these firms further impetus to improve their planning and control systems to compete with global companies and win supply contracts, becoming part of the global supply chains.

Going forward, there is a strong need for infrastructural improvements, support from state and central governments, and export opportunities to compensate for the domestic demand volatility. A recent study by the World Bank and the Confederation of Indian Industry (CII) finds that the more investor-friendly states are attracting higher investments, both domestic and foreign, as investors perceived as much as a 30% cost advantage in some states over others due to the availability of infrastructure and quality of governance. Thus, it is possible that firms would have achieved scale economies more rapidly if the pace of the liberalization had been faster, and had been accompanied by infrastructural, labor, and corporate governance reforms.

As domestic demand for value-focused products increases, Indian manufacturing will need to play an ever more significant role in the economy. Past data suggest that there are manufacturing pockets of excellence that have arisen as a result of the unique development path of the Indian economy. Several of these companies or industries have leveraged their unique mix of resources as well as the opportunities afforded by past laws to maintain high levels of productivity. These companies have also used the new regulatory climate to further intensify their cost-based or differentiation-based strategies. A future in which infrastructure issues, regulatory issues, and energy and financing issues are all synchronized with global realities may well usher in a new phase of globally competitive Indian manufacturing that is more widespread than in the current situation. Industries that leverage a unique capability for value-engineering products and processes along with a mass-manufacturing capability will likely emerge as future winners in Indian manufacturing.

References

1. Ahluwalia, MS (2002). Economic reforms in India since 1991: has gradualism worked? *Journal of Economic Perspectives*, 16(3), 67–88.
2. Alam, G (1985). India's technology policy and its influence on technology imports and technology development. *Economic and Political Weekly*, 20(45, 46 and 47), November.
3. Athreye, S and S Kapur (2006). Industrial concentration in a liberalizing economy: a study of Indian manufacturing. *Journal of Development Studies*, 42(2), 981–999.
4. Balakrishnan, K, A Iyer, S Seshadri and A Sheopuri (2007). Indian auto supply chains at the crossroads, *Interfaces*, 37(4), 310–323.
5. Banker, R and H Saranga (2006). Productivity and technical changes in the Indian pharmaceutical industry, Working Paper.
6. Basant, R and B Fikkert (1996). The effects of R&D, foreign technology purchase and international spillovers on productivity in Indian firms. *Review of Economics and Statistics*, 78(2), 187–199.
7. Bhagwati, JN and TN Srinivasan (1975). *Foreign Technology Trade Regimes and Economic Development: India.* New York: National Bureau of Economic Research.
8. Chaudhuri, S (1999). Growth and structural changes in the pharmaceutical industry in India. In *The Structure of Indian Industry*, Anindya, S, G Subir and V Rajendra (eds.). New Delhi: Oxford University Press.
9. Deolalikar, AB and RE Evenson (1989). Technology production and technology purchase in Indian industry: an econometric analysis. *The Review of Economics and Statistics*, November, 687–692.

10. Fikkert, B and R Hasan (1998). Returns to scale in a highly regulated economy, evidence from Indian firms. *Journal of Development Economics*, 56(1), 51–79.
11. Gang, IN (1992). Small firm "presence" in Indian manufacturing. *World Development*, 20(9), 1377–1389.
12. Grabowski, HG and JM Vernon (1987). Pioneers, imitators and generics — a simulation model of Schumpeterian competition. *The Quarterly Journal of Economics*, 102(3), 491–526.
13. Guhathakurta, S (1994). Electronic policy and the television manufacturing industry: lessons from India's liberalization efforts. *Economic Development and Cultural Change*, 42, 845–868.
14. Hayes, RH and SC Wheelwright (1985). Competing through manufacturing. *Harvard Business Review*, January–February, 99–109.
15. Iyer, A, H Saranga and S Seshadri (2006). Productivity and technical change in the Indian auto component industry, *Proc. of the North American Productivity Workshop,* 27–30 June, 2006.
16. Iyer, A and S Seshdari (2007) Transforming an Indian manufacturing company: the Rane brake linings case. In *Building Supply Chain Excellence in Emerging Economies*, Lee, H and C-Y Lee (eds.), pp. 441–455.
17. Kalirajan, K and S Bhide (2005). The post-reform performance of the manufacturing sector in India. *Asian Economic Papers*, 3(2), 126–157.
18. Katrak, H (1985). Imported technology, enterprise size and R&D in a newly industrializing country: the Indian experience. *Oxford Bulletin of Economics and Statistics*, 47(3), 213–229.
19. Katrak, H (1990). Imports of technology and the technological effort of Indian enterprises. *World Development*, 18(3), 371–381.
20. Katrak, H (1997). Developing countries' imports of technology, in-house technological capabilities and efforts: an analysis of Indian experience. *Journal of Development Economics*, 53, 67–83.
21. Katz, JM (1985). Domestic technological innovations and dynamic competitive advantages: further reflections on a comparative case-study program. In *International Technology Transfer: Concepts, Measures and Comparisons*, Rosenberg, N and C Firschtak (eds.). New York: Praeger.
22. Krishna, P and D Mitra (1998). Trade liberalization, market discipline and productivity growth: new evidence from India. *Journal of Development Economics*, 56, 447–462.
23. Kumar, N and M Saquib (1995). Firm size, opportunities for adaptation and in-house R&D activity in developing countries: the case of Indian manufacturing. *Research Policy*, 25, 713–722.
24. Kumar, N and JP Pradhan (2003). Export competitiveness in knowledge based industries: a firm-level analysis of Indian manufacturing, RIS-DP # 43/2003, New Delhi.

25. Lall, S (1987). *Learning to Industrialize — The Acquisition of Technological Capability by India*. Hong Kong: Macmillan Press.
26. Lall, S (2001). *Competitiveness, Technology and Skills*. UK: Edward Elgar Publishing Ltd.
27. Luthra, S, R Mangaleswaran and A Padhi (2005). When to Make India a Manufacturing Base, Fulfilling India's Promise, Mackinsey Special Edition, 62–73.
28. Nagabhushana, TS and J Shah (1999). Manufacturing priorities and action programs in the changing environment — an empirical study of Indian industries. *International Journal of Production & Operations Management*, 19(4), 389–398.
29. NMCC (2005). National strategy for manufacturing, National Manufacturing Competitiveness Council — NMCC, Udyog Bhavan, New Delhi.
30. Okada, A (1998). Does Globalization Improve Employment and the Quality of Jobs in India?: A Case from the Automobile Industry, Alfred P. Sloan Foundation Project on Globalization and Jobs, Research Note No. 3. Cambridge, MA: International Motor Vehicle Program.
31. Ozawa, T (1985). Macroeconomic factors affecting Japan's technology inflows and outflows: the postwar experience. In *International Technology Transfer: Concepts, Measures and Comparisons*, Rosenberg, N and C Firschtak (eds.), pp. 222–254. New York: Praeger.
32. Pattnayak, SS and SM Thangavelu (2004). Economic reform and productivity growth in Indian manufacturing industry. *Economic Modelling*, 22, 601–615.
33. Pradhan, JP (2003). Liberalization, firm size and R&D performance: a firm level study of Indian pharmaceutical industry. Research and Information System for the Non-Aligned and Other Developing Countries, RIS-DP # 40/2003.
34. Ramaswamy, K (1996). Competitive intensity and technical efficiency in public sector firms: evidence from India. *International Journal of Public Sector Management*, 9(3), 4–17.
35. Ramaswamy, K (2001). Organizational ownership, competitive intensity and firm performance: an empirical study of the Indian manufacturing sector. *Strategic Management Journal*, 22, 989–998.
36. Rosenzweig, ED and AV Roth (2004). Towards a theory of competitive progression: evidence from high-tech manufacturing. *Production and Operations Management Journal*, Winter, 13(4), 354–368.
37. Saranga, H (2006a). Multi objective DEA as applied to Indian pharmaceutical industry. Forthcoming in *Journal of Operational Research Society*.
38. Saranga, H (2006b). Application of super efficiency, RTS and congestion DEA to Indian auto component industry (under review at *European Journal of Operational Research*).
39. Saxena, KBC and BS Sahay (2000). Managing IT for world-class manufacturing: the Indian scenario. *International Journal of Information Management*, 20, 29–57.

40. Seth, D and D Tripathi (2005). Relationship between TQM and TPM implementation factors and business performance of manufacturing industry in Indian context. *The International Journal of Quality & Reliability Management*, 22(2/3), 256–277.

41. Sivadasan, J (2003). Barriers to entry and productivity: micro-evidence from Indian manufacturing sector reforms. University of Chicago: Graduate School of Business. http://bpp.wharton.upenn.edu/Acrobat/Sivadasan_AEW_paper_1_16_04.pdf#search='Barriers%20to%20Entry%20and%20Productivity:%20MicroEvidence' [Retrieved on 24 March 2005].

42. Tybout, J (2000). Manufacturing firms in developing countries: how well do they do, and why? *Journal of Economic Literature*, 38, 11–44.

43. UNCTAD, Trade and Development Report, 2005.

44. UNIDO, Industrial Development Report, 2005.

45. Westphal, LE, L Kim and CJ Dahlman (1985). Reflections in the Republic of Korea's acquisition of technological capability. In *International Technology Transfer: Concepts, Measures and Comparisons*, Rosenberg, N and C Firschtak (eds.). New York: Praeger.

46. Wilson, D and R Purshothaman (2003). Dreaming with BRICS: the path to 2050. *Global Economics Paper 99*, Goldman Sachs.

Case Example

Rane Brake Linings — A Focused Vignette

This focused summary describes some of the changes at Rane Brake Linings (RBL) that enabled it to compete as a globally competitive manufacturer of brake linings. RBL is a division of the Rane Group and won the Deming prize in 2003. The company produces brake linings and is a major supplier to the Indian railways as well as to automotive companies. We provide a brief description of some of the capabilities developed by the company that enable it to be a global competitor. Detailed descriptions are provided by Iyer and Seshadri.[16]

One of the capabilities that RBL developed is the ability to diagnose problems across the supply chain and solve system-level issues rapidly. A typical problem concerns the brake system provided to a two-wheeler company that reported experiencing stickiness in the brakes. RBL was the brake provider that assembled the brake linings to stamped parts provided by a supplier. The resulting brake was assembled by the OEM into their product. Upon hearing about the issue faced by the OEM's customers, RBL installed its own engineers at every step in the supply chain. They then developed four different designs over a 10-day period that carefully identified adjustments to the supplier stampings. They adjusted the brake lining manufacture and assembly and then worked with the OEM to see that the parts were assembled appropriately at the OEM's assembly operation. The net result was an improved brake system that maintained manufacturing productivity. The ability to co-ordinate upstream and downstream, develop multiple designs rapidly, and deploy the resulting designs suggests a unique capability to synchronize across the supply chain. This capability to meld engineering design talent and manufacturing may well represent a competitive capability that enables RBL to compete globally.

Another of RBL's capabilities is their approach to the maintenance of product costs through careful global sourcing. For example, the company was importing chemical inputs from Canada that were priced in dollars. There was an opportunity to compensate for the rising dollar (at that time) by including sources from Russia. The adjustment in product designs and approval would generate a cost reduction. But at the same time, there was another effort to improve productivity through a change in the design of the existing product. The phasing in of the new design change along with the change in sourcing resulted in both product design improvement and a cost reduction.

While total quality management approaches have not been shown to be profitable in many companies in mature markets, their success in emerging and growing markets is a new story. RBL's success after TQM implementation and its associated productivity gains have enabled it to remain a strong competitor in the Indian market and to engage effectively in global markets.

LOGISTICS

Jayashankar M. Swaminathan

While the Indian manufacturing sector has in the past decade picked up its pace, India still lags much behind China when it comes to its role in global manufacturing supply chains. In an earlier piece,[2] I highlighted logistics (defined as the physical movement of items) as one of the major impediments to supply chain management in India. A fundamental difference between China and India in terms of global supply chain management is the physical infrastructure of roads, airports, and ports. For example, while China had 25,000 miles of major expressway in 2006, India had only 3700 miles (the United States had 47,000 miles, by comparison).[1] While there were 56 major airports in China, India had only 17 major airports (and the United States had 189). Similarly, while only 400 million tons of goods went through the ports in India, in the same year China shipped 2.9 billion tons through its ports (the United States shipped 1.4 billion tons). These differences are largely the result of the amount of money that the respective governments have been spending on infrastructure. While China spent roughly 8.5% of its GDP on infrastructure in 2005, India spent less than 4%. Recently, the Indian government has recognized the need to improve the logistics infrastructure in the country.

The following two chapters, the first focused on land logistics and the second on aviation logistics, provide a detailed account of the mind-boggling changes now taking place in India. Just five years ago, traveling from Delhi to Gurgaon, a nearby satellite town where many call centers are located, took two hours. Now one can cover the same distance on the eight-lane highway in one hour on a good day. The grand entry into Gurgaon — via a radio frequency tag-enabled, 32-toll-booth pass-through — speaks volumes of the type of infrastructure expected in the future across the major highways in India. While the roads are congested with traffic even with such changes, thanks to an immense increase in the number of cars on the roads, the situation at the airports is no different.

Fig. E4.1. Rush hour traffic at the toll booth entrance to Gurgaon.

Almost every major city in India is either renovating its existing airport or adding a new one. Earlier this month, as the driver of our shuttle that transported passengers from our incoming Jet Airways plane to the Delhi passenger terminal commented, "There is hardly any time for me to breathe between 8 a.m. and 12:30 p.m., since there are so many planes landing during that time. During this time, the traffic of shuttles inside the terminal is worse than the traffic of cars out on the roads!"

As the logistics infrastructure in the country further develops, the opportunities of doing business in India will improve by leaps and bounds. What are the current impediments to development in the logistics sector? Where is the development planned? What is the future state of logistics in India going to look like? What are the novel logistics paradigms in India that could serve as an example for others? How can firms leverage the logistics developments planned in the new India?

In the next chapter, entitled "The Logistics Sector in India: Overview and Challenges," Prof. Pankaj Chandra, Professor and Director of the Indian Institute of Management, Bangalore, along with Prof. Nimit Jain, Assistant Professor, Indian Institute of Management, Ahmedabad, provide a detailed account of the challenges and opportunities associated with surface logistics. They start by discussing some of the peculiarities of Indian supply chains, which typically have focused on cost reduction rather than speed. Transportation cost represents roughly 40% of the total logistics cost in India, and the use of technology in logistics is fairly limited. The authors highlight manufacturers' efforts to develop a local supply base (a response to the poor infrastructure), which can lead to inefficiencies. They also discuss the changes in logistics needs as well as the changes in infrastructure planned across the country, including the creation of the Golden Quadrilateral expressway, the planned expansion of rail connectivity, and the development of multimodal transportation capabilities. Professors Chandra and Jain then highlight the trends in the industry since liberalization and the need to expand the scale of operations for logistics providers as more multinationals come in. The authors provide a rich set of case examples of innovations in this sector, including those from GATI (a cargo company that transformed itself into an end-to-end solutions provider), AMUL (one of the most successful dairy cooperatives in the country, with numerous logistics innovations), DABBAHWALLAHS (the lunch-box delivery cooperative of Mumbai whose accuracy has been compared to that of FedEx by many researchers), ITC e-choupal (Indian Tobacco Company's agri-business model based on e-commerce), and the auto component replacement supply chains. Finally, they conclude with a brief overview of the major challenges and opportunities for this sector going forward.

In Chapter 6, entitled "India's Aviation Sector: Dynamic Transformation," Prof. John Kasarda, Kenan Distinguished Professor at the Kenan-Flagler Business School and Director of the Kenan Institute of Private Enterprise at the University of North Carolina, along with Mr. Rambabu Vankayalapati from Indo-Asian Infrastructure Private Limited, provide a detailed account of the rapid changes in the aviation sector in India. They discuss the Indian government's Aviation Vision 2020 for expansion of existing airports and creation of new ones. Following this, they present the history of aviation in India, beginning with J.R.D. Tata's first flight from Karachi to Mumbai in 1932 and continuing through the Air Corporation Act of 1953, by which the Indian government took control of all private airlines after independence and created Indian Airlines. The authors go on to describe the period 1985–1995 as one seeing a surge in air traffic, perhaps because this was the time that the software and IT industries were beginning to take off in India (as described in Chapters 2 and 3). They outline the emergence of private airlines during the post-liberalization era that started in 1995 and elaborate on the subsequent successes — including Jet Airways, Air Deccan, Spicejet, and Kingfisher Airlines — and also the failures. Next, they discuss the ongoing privatization of airports, in which the GMR group is playing a major role along with firms such as Malaysian Airport Holdings Berhard and Larsen and Tubro. Finally, the authors describe the concept of the aerotropolis, or airport city, that is being planned near the airports of Hyderabad, Nagpur, and Delhi. They conclude with a discussion of India's aviation future and the challenges therein.

References

1. Hamm, S (2007). The trouble with India (19 March 2007). *Business Week.*
2. Swaminathan, JM (2006). Managing supply chain operations in India: pitfalls and opportunities. In *Supply Chain Management in Emerging Economies*, Lee, H and C-Y Lee (eds.), pp. 137–154. New York, USA: Springer.

CHAPTER 5

THE LOGISTICS SECTOR IN INDIA: OVERVIEW AND CHALLENGES

Pankaj Chandra* and Nimit Jain[†]

The Indian economy has been growing at an average rate of more than 8% over the last four years,[37] putting enormous demands on its productive infrastructure. Whether it is the physical infrastructure of roads, ports, water, or power, or the digital infrastructure of broadband networks and telecommunication, or the service infrastructure of logistics — all are being stretched beyond their capabilities. Interestingly, this is leading to an emergence of innovative practices that will allow businesses and public services to operate at a higher growth rate in an environment in which the support systems are concurrently being augmented. In this chapter, we describe the status of the evolving logistics sector in India and innovations therein through interesting business models, as well as the challenges that the sector will face in the years to come.

Broadly speaking, the Indian logistics sector, as elsewhere, comprises the entire inbound and outbound segments of the manufacturing and service supply chains. Of late, the logistics infrastructure has received a lot of attention both from business and industry and from policy makers. However, the role of the management of this infrastructure (or the logistics management regimen) in effective competition has been somewhat underemphasized. Although inadequate logistics infrastructure has the effect of creating bottlenecks in the growth of an economy, the logistics management regimen has the capability to overcome infrastructure disadvantages in the short run while providing cutting-edge competitiveness in

*Professor and Director, Indian Institute of Management Bangalore, Bannerghatta Road, Bangalore 560076, India. E-mail chandra@iimb.ernet.in.
†Doctoral Student, Indian Institute of Management Ahmedabad, Vastrapur, Ahmedabad 380015, India. E-mail nimitj@iimahd.ernet.in.

the long term. This presents a number of challenges as well as opportunities for the Indian economy. Several models seem to be emerging based on the critical needs of the Indian economy, and these can stand as viable models for other global economies as well.

Two key areas require attention in the management of logistics chains across the Indian business sectors: cost and reliable value-added services.[9] Logistics costs (i.e., inventory holding, transportation, warehousing, packaging, losses, and related administration costs) have been estimated at 13–14% of Indian GDP, which is higher than that of the United States (8%), but lower than that of China (21%).[34] The service reliability of the logistics industry in emerging markets such as India has been seen as slow and as requiring significant engagement time with the customers, thereby incurring high indirect variable costs.[12] However, the Indian logistics story is one of islands of excellence accompanying a general improvement on almost all parameters. It is this aspect that we explore further in this chapter. In the next section, we offer a brief introduction to some of the peculiarities of the Indian logistics sector. Following this, we discuss the determinants of growth in this industry and highlight several interesting initiatives that point toward a renewal of the sector. We close with a discussion of the challenges facing the logistics sector now and in the future.

Historical Development

5.1. Some Peculiarities of Indian Supply Chains

The Indian logistics sector has typically been driven by the objective of reducing transportation costs that were (and often continue to be) inordinately high due to the regional concentration of manufacturing and geographically diversified distribution activities, as well as inefficiencies in infrastructure and accompanying technology. Freight movement has slowly been shifting from rail to road, with implications for the quality of transfer, the timeliness of delivery, and consequently costs — except for commodities, which move over long distances predominantly via the extensive rail network.

The transportation industry is fragmented and largely unorganized. A large number of independent players with regional or national permits carry freight, often with a small fleet of one or two single-axle trucks. This segment carries a large percentage of the national load and almost all of the regional load. It comprises owners and employees with inadequate skills, narrow perspectives, and limited ability to organize or manage their operations effectively. Low cost has been traditionally achieved by employing low-level technology, offering low wages (due to lower education levels), scrimping on equipment maintenance, and

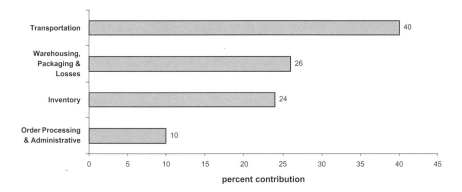

Fig. 5.1. Elements of logistics cost in India.
Source: Sanyal (2009).

overloading trucks beyond capacity. Often, transportation cartels regulate the supply of trucks and transport costs. Price competition among a large number of service providers in the industry also has contributed to lower cost. However, the long-run average cost of transport operations across the entire supply chain may not turn out to be low. Figure 5.1 shows the relative value of transportation costs vis-à-vis other elements of the logistics costs in India.

Logistics spending is increasing, sometimes dramatically, across various industrial sectors in India. Steel, pharmaceuticals, food and agri-business, and automotives are the sectors that have been growing most rapidly in the national economy — and it is no surprise that their logistics costs have been increasing at a faster rate. Table 5.1 gives a breakdown of the logistics costs across different industry sectors and the changes therein over the last five years. A few observations are in order here. The low change in order processing and administrative costs in the cement sector could possibly be due to the use of call centers by various producers for order processing and dispatch planning. The steel and pharmaceutical sectors have seen maximum changes in component costs. The distribution practice of pushing goods down the channel might be responsible for the high increase in inventory and warehousing costs in the pharmaceutical industry. Investments in new cold chains and losses might be the causes of high change in warehousing, packaging, and loss-related costs.

Warehousing has typically been dominated by small players with small capacities and poor deployment of handling, stacking, and monitoring technologies. While warehousing issues have had a detrimental effect on almost all sectors, the food sector has suffered the most, due to low levels of investment in cold chains and allied machinery. Erratic power outages have also required a more manual operation, with less dependence on technology. Another factor that has affected both the location and the cost of operating a warehouse has been the

Table 5.1. Distribution of logistics costs across some sectors (2000–2005).[i]

Sector	Logistics cost components (in USD million)	Transportation	Inventory holding	Warehousing, packaging, and losses	Order processing and administrative	Total logistics cost
Auto	2000–01	285.0	171.0	185.3	71.3	712.6
	2005–06	406.5	243.9	264.3	101.6	1016.4
	Average change	20.3	12.2	13.2	5.1	50.6
Cement	2000–01	50.6	30.4	32.9	12.7	126.5
	2005–06	55.4	33.3	36.0	13.8	138.5
	Average change	4.8	2.9	3.1	1.2	12.0
Consumer durables	2000–01	331.9	199.1	215.7	83.0	829.6
	2005–06	398.9	239.3	259.3	99.7	997.3
	Average change	11.2	6.7	7.3	2.8	27.9
FMCG	2000–01	201.5	120.9	131.0	50.4	503.8
	2005–06	280.7	168.4	182.5	70.2	701.8
	Average change	13.2	7.9	8.6	3.3	33.0
Food	2000–01	398.7	239.3	259.2	99.7	996.8
	2005–06	524.5	314.7	340.9	131.1	1311.2
	Average change	21.0	12.6	13.6	5.2	52.4
Garment	2000–01	337.3	202.4	219.2	84.3	843.2
	2005–06	454.4	272.6	295.3	113.6	1135.9
	Average change	19.5	11.7	12.7	4.9	48.8
Pharmaceutical	2000–01	174.0	104.4	113.1	43.5	434.9
	2005–06	310.0	186.0	201.5	77.5	775.0
	Average change	22.7	13.6	14.7	5.7	56.7
Steel	2000–01	438.3	263.0	284.9	109.6	1095.7
	2005–06	693.6	416.1	450.8	173.4	1734.0
	Average change	42.5	25.5	27.7	10.6	106.4

[i] *Source*: IA, EIS (CMIE databases).

"octroi tax",[a] in response to which firms have been locating warehouses outside city limits and have delayed moving goods into the retail network as long as possible. The tax has also led firms to develop an unholy business-government nexus to avoid the tax and extraction of rents.

The use of technology to increase productivity and service — both IT and engineering equipment — is still quite limited. An inappropriate evaluation of the benefits of technology has led to the higher usage of manual labor across the logistics industry, whether in distribution activities or within plants. Many firms try to compete through the advantage of low wages, which in turn necessitate hiring low-skilled or unskilled personnel, thereby sacrificing the possibility of long-run productivity-related gains.

Understanding the linkage between inventory and transport planning is the key to reduce the operational costs of distribution. In a survey of Indian manufacturing firms, Chandra and Sastry (2004) found that 98% of the firms have a contract with trucking companies for making dispatches, while only 11% own their own fleet of trucks. While 36% of these firms use third-party logistics (3PL) service providers for making dispatches, only about 30% use 3PL service providers for procuring materials from their suppliers. In the survey, only 21% of firms report the use of some software for scheduling dispatches. Somehow, transport planning (e.g., optimal dispatch quantities and frequency of dispatch; vehicle routing; and truck loading patterns) has received little attention within operations despite the fact that about 10% of the cost of sales is associated with physical distribution.[33] Transport planning does not appear to have received the required attention.

An understanding of the overall structure of Indian supply chains will lead to a better appreciation of many of the issues raised earlier. In Chandra and Sastry's survey, about 4% of firms have fewer than five suppliers, about 85% of firms have fewer than five plants, about 14% of firms have fewer than five regional distributors, and about 9% of firms have fewer than five retailers. Similar statistics are obtained for other ranges of suppliers, plants, distributors, and retailers (see Fig. 5.2). It is worth noting that 63% of firms have more than 100 suppliers, while about 39% of firms have more than 100 distributors and 77% of firms have more than 100 retailers. In addition, about 17% of firms claim to have more than 500 suppliers. The corresponding figures for distributors and retailers are 22 and 54%, respectively. This is perhaps where difficulties in managing logistics in India lie: the larger the number of suppliers or distributors, the higher the cost of co-ordination.

---

[a] The "octroi tax" is an entry tax on goods entering a city. This tax is a major source of revenue for city municipal corporations.

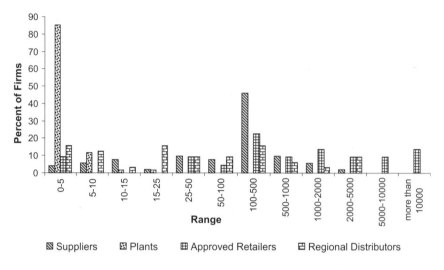

Fig. 5.2.   Structure of the supply chain of sample firms.
Source: Chandra and Sastry (2004).

When we look at the spatial distribution of plants and suppliers, the above statement becomes even stronger. Of the sample firms that operate more than one plant, 48% of these plants are located more than 100 km,[b] apart, 33% of these plants are located more than 500 km apart, and 18% of these plants are located more than 1000 km apart. Similarly, on an average, only 4% of suppliers are located within 5 km of the manufacturing plant, while about 13% are located within 5–25 km of the plant, 16% are located within 25–100 km of the plant, and about 67% of suppliers have facilities that are more than 100 km away from the plants. Past governmental policies may have forced some firms to locate plants further away from each other. However, this may be coming back to haunt these firms today, as the cost of co-ordination increases and the ability to provide a quick response to customer requirements therefore decreases. This problem is exacerbated with suppliers. Manufacturers must either develop suppliers separately for each location (thereby increasing the overall number and affecting consistency in quality, price, and delivery times), or else material has to travel longer distances if the plants all have a common supplier.

The logistics challenge in such an environment is immense: build the infrastructure; manage the requirements of the changing structure of various sectors' supply chains; change industrial policies to facilitate efficient production and movement of goods and services; deploy effective managerial practices and technology

---

[b] 1 km = 0.621 miles.

to enhance competitiveness through better management of logistics networks and develop new models for new sectors, in the service sectors as well as in traditional areas such as agri-business. The logistics industry in India is transforming itself very interestingly despite its peculiarities by developing innovative business models and by chipping away at structural and policy-based rigidities. In a later section, we discuss some of these innovative initiatives that are leading the renewal of the logistics industry in India.

Current and Future Trends

5.2. The Changing Logistics Infrastructure

With rising consumer demand and the resulting growth in global trade, infrastructure support in terms of rails, roads, ports, and warehouses holds the key to the success of the economy. In this section, we provide a brief overview of the status of the logistics infrastructure in India and the current initiatives, both private and public, in this area.

Goods are transported predominantly by road and rail in India. Road transport is controlled by private players, whereas rail transport is handled by the central government. The second largest network in the world, India's roads contribute to 65% of the freight transport.[28] Road is preferred over rail because of its cost effectiveness and flexibility. Rail, on the other hand, is preferred because of its containerization facility and its ease in transporting ship containers and wooden crates. The sea is another complementary mode of transport: 95% of India's foreign trade is by sea.[11] India has 12 major ports, 6 each on the east and west coasts, and 185 minor ports. Table 5.2 maps the various modes on different performance indicators, clearly indicating the vitality and importance of road transport in the Indian economy. There is also evidence of an across-the-board increase in freight traffic for all modes, indicating increased logistics activity. The percentage change in road, rail, air, and sea cargo traffic has increased between 2001 and 2005 from 5% to 14%, 4% to 7.5%, 6% to 20%, and 3.5% to 11%, respectively.[18]

In keeping with the increasing demand for road transportation, the National Highways Authority of India (NHAI) has been strengthening and widening national highways in multiple phases. As part of the National Highways Development Project (NHDP), work on the development of the Golden Quadrilateral (connecting Delhi, Mumbai, Chennai, and Kolkata) and the north-south and east-west links started in 1998. This project will build 13,000 km of expressways that will connect the nation.[38] NHAI is investing about USD650 million towards the development of an Intelligent Transportation System (ITS), which will make transport services on

Table 5.2.   Comparison chart for various modes.[i]

	Rail	Road	Sea
Number (wagons, trucks, ships)	214760	3,487,538[ii]	806
Freight capacity (million ton)	10.66	5.12[iii]	7.9
Route length (million km)/ Number of major ports	0.11	3.34	12
Freight revenue (USD billion)	7.00	38.64	4304
Major products	Coal, steel, petroleum, primary metals	Automobile, electronic items, garments, etc.	Iron ore, coal, petroleum (and industrial and consumer products on the outbound export)

[i] *Source*: IA, EIS (CMIE Databases), 2005–2006 and Financial Express (2006a).
[ii] This figure is for 2002–2003.
[iii] Chandra and Sastry (2004).

the highways (such as congestion reduction, advance signaling, medical assistance, accident management, etc.) efficient and will automate many processes, including toll collection.[32]

Because of the growing opportunity and potential for high revenue, the Ministry of Railways has been taking measures to expand rail connectivity and recapture the market share of freight business. By focusing on improving wagon utilization, the Railways have managed to reduce the freight cost from 61 paise[c] per net ton km (ntkm) in 2001 to 56 paise per ntkm in 2005.[28] At present, freight trains run on the same railway tracks as passenger trains, at an average speed of about 25 kmph.[16] With the proposed dedicated west and east freight corridors, however, the freight trains are expected to run at 100 kmph. The west and east rail corridors of 1469 km and 1232 km, respectively, will be built with investments of USD2.60 billion and USD2.40 billion and will be equipped with the latest centralized traffic control systems.[1] The Indian Railways has also decided to collaborate with bulk users of freight transport to build the rail network in a

[c] 100 paise = 1 INR, 1 USD = 44 INR.

Public-Private Partnership (PPP) mode. The first project on this line comprises nine public and private sector companies that are building an 82 km rail line between Haridarpur and Paradip at a cost of USD120 million.[39] Recently, several steel companies have also shown an interest in linking iron and coal mines in Orissa via a 98 km rail line.[7]

An efficient multimodal transportation system is quite essential for the diverse Indian geography and economy, as it allows players to choose the most economic mode of transport given their product and customer requirements and sourcing location. To allow for the smooth operation of trade through multiple modes, India has a separate governing body, the Director General of Shipping, which works under the Multimodal Transportation of Goods Act of 1993. Its function is to frame rules and grant licenses to operators providing door-to-door service using multiple modes. Multimodal transport in India, through rail, was a monopoly of the Container Corporation of India until 2005. However, with licenses being given to 13 new private players,[2] rail trade should improve considerably. In order to encourage trade by small-scale industries, the Indian Railways has started a "road-railer" system in which container vehicles are capable of running both on highways hauled by trucks and on rail.[17] In 1998–1999, the Konkan Railway (one of the railway zones in southwestern India) pioneered the "roll-on, roll-off" (RO-RO) concept between Mumbai (Kolad) and Goa (Verna). Privately owned trucks are loaded with their goods and are then driven onto a rake of flat cars and carried (trucks and cargo together) to the destination.

In 2005–2006, the ports handled 456.20 million tons of cargo traffic — a doubling of capacity over 2000–2001. This is expected to increase to 700 million tons by 2011–2012. (Consequently, the number of ships berthing at Indian ports has also been growing, from 540 in 2001 to 670 in 2004–2005, and it is expected to increase to 1000 by 2006–2007 with the increase in berthing of larger ships.) To keep pace with the growing demand, the government plans to increase port capacities to about 1 billion tons per annum over the next six years.[27] Under the National Maritime Development Programme (NMDP), the government is encouraging public-private partnership in the building and maintenance of ports. This scheme will cover 276 port-related projects at an investment cost of USD12.40 billion. With the rising congestion levels at major ports and with high average turnaround and waiting times, the government has decided to develop minor ports in seven states to ease the traffic at the major ports.[14] The operational performance of various ports in India is improving (see Tables 5.3a and 5.3b), but the pace is slow, and delays, particularly those due to the port authority, need to be reduced further through better planning, execution, and technology. The estimated cost of the development of these minor ports is expected to be about USD350 million.

In addition to the public-private partnerships, the private sector is expected to invest USD7.67 billion over the next six years. Currently, 15 private-sector

Table 5.3(a).   Average turnaround time at ports (in days).[i]

Port	2000–2001	2001–2002	2002–2003	2003–2004	2004–2005	2005–2006	CAGR
Chennai	6.40	5.80	5.30	3.70	4.60	3.80	(9.90)
Cochin	3.23	3.10	2.37	2.19	2.22	2.33	(6.32)
Haldia	5.21	3.96	4.01	3.02	2.87	3.00	(10.45)
Jawaharlal Nehru	1.72	2.48	2.34	2.28	2.04	1.84	1.36
Kandla	6.15	4.72	6.55	5.94	5.06	4.62	(5.56)
Kolkata	6.59	5.50	4.71	4.47	4.29	4.17	(8.75)
Marmugao	4.30	4.25	2.04	3.86	4.47	4.35	0.23
Mumbai	5.60	5.20	5.47	5.06	4.10	4.21	(5.55)
New Mangalore	3.80	2.89	2.73	1.90	2.35	2.96	(4.87)
Paradip	3.89	4.16	3.99	3.37	3.42	3.41	(2.60)
Tuticorin	6.39	4.10	4.11	3.59	2.59	2.66	(16.08)
Vishakhapatnam	4.75	3.71	3.51	3.72	3.33	3.20	(7.60)
Average	4.84	4.16	3.93	3.59	3.45	3.38	(6.92)

[i] *Source*: IA, EIS (CMIE databases).

Table 5.3(b).   Average pre-berth waiting time — on port account (in hours).[i]

Port	2000–2001	2001–2002	2002–2003	2003–2004	2004–2005	2005–2006	CAGR
Chennai	48.00	38.40	25.92	4.32	0.96	0.96	(54.27)
Cochin	4.80	3.12	4.32	1.68	3.84	4.08	(3.20)
Haldia	14.64	3.60	3.84	3.60	3.36	7.44	(12.66)
Jawaharlal Nehru	15.36	10.08	10.08	11.28	9.36	8.40	(11.37)
Kandla	27.12	8.16	21.36	16.80	10.80	16.56	(9.39)
Kolkata	5.04	1.20	0.24	0.00	0.00	0.00	(100.00)
Marmugao	8.64	12.00	32.16	19.92	26.64	25.20	23.87
Mumbai	6.96	6.72	7.68	3.60	3.60	6.00	(2.92)
New Mangalore	5.04	4.32	6.00	4.32	3.12	2.64	(12.13)
Paradip	6.96	8.88	11.04	10.32	5.04	1.68	(24.74)
Tuticorin	61.20	15.84	10.56	7.20	1.44	1.68	(51.28)
Vishakhapatnam	16.56	6.72	5.76	18.00	1.20	0.96	(43.42)
Average	18.36	9.92	11.58	8.42	5.78	6.30	(19.26)

[i] *Source*: IA, EIS (CMIE databases).

projects are operational at various major ports, and four more are under implementation. One of these aims to build the deepest port in the world, at an investment of USD1 billion.[15] This project is being handled by a three-firm Chinese consortium with a Mumbai-based partner, Zoom Developers. Interestingly, firms like Ambuja Cement have been using barges for the transport of clinkers from their factories to crushing and packaging plants all over the coast, thereby reducing transport costs considerably. The Sethusamudram Ship Channel Project, which is creating a deep-sea channel across the Palk Strait between India and Sri Lanka, will allow for the direct and efficient transport of big ships between the western and eastern coasts of India. Right now, these ships have to sail around Sri Lanka's coast, thereby incurring an additional 30 hours of sailing time. A flurry of activity is underway that is enhancing the infrastructure capacities in the country. It is hoped that these developments will reduce the extent of congestion at the major ports and perhaps lead to the specialization of certain ports, with their accompanying technology and managerial practices; for instance, ports in Gujarat are eminently poised to focus on chemical and textile exports. Improvements in planning, however, through the deployment of IT, advanced planning tools, and better managerial practices, remain largely ignored.

5.3. Determinants of Logistics Growth in India

The Indian logistics business is valued at USD14 billion and has been growing at a compound annual growth rate (CAGR) of 7% to 8%. As mentioned earlier, logistics costs represent 13% to 14% of the country's GDP. The market is fragmented, with thousands of players offering partial services in logistics; it is estimated that there are about 400 firms capable of providing some level of integrated service.[19] The economy is expected to grow about 10% over the next 10 years, and sectors including chemicals, petrochemicals (especially distribution), pharmaceuticals, metals and metal processing, fast-moving consumer goods (FMCG), textile, retail, and automotives are projected to grow the fastest. New business models are emerging as new firms, both domestic and foreign, enter the market. As a result of the ensuing competition, domestic market growth and linkages with global supply chains promise to change the face of the logistics industry beyond recognition. In this section, we examine how these are going to determine the growth of the sector.

The scale of operations in manufacturing is changing, and so are the markets and sourcing geographies. Growth in manufacturing in India has happened across clusters located in different parts of the country, for example, Ludhiana, NCR, Baddi and Dehradun in the north; Rajkot, Jamnagar, Pune, and Mumbai in the west (along with Ankleshwar, Vapi, Aurangabad, and Kolhapur, and most recently Kutch); and Coimbatore, Vishakapatnam, Bangalore, Hosur, Chennai, Puducherry, and Sriperumbudur in the south. Assembly plants at these locations are being fed with raw materials and intermediate products from all over the country and abroad (as well as from these locations). Moreover, distribution networks with emerging hubs in Indore and Nagpur (i.e., central India) supply all of India as well as foreign countries. These networks are going to increase the nature and extent of the movement of goods and services across the country. The growth in the distribution networks has been accompanied by the expansion of domestic production capacity (e.g., ORPAT in Morbi has added capacity to produce 40,000 units of quartz clocks and time pieces at a single location) as well as a big multinational entry into the Indian manufacturing scene (e.g., NOKIA's new factory at Sriperumbudur produces 1 million mobile phones per month). As the volume of production grows, so will the extent of movement of goods either to the ports for export or to the rest of the country. Some of the large players to enter or expand significantly in the Indian market recently have been Reliance Retail, Big Bazaar Hypermart, Pantaloon, and RPG in retail; Nokia, LG, Samsung, Motorola, Sony, and Blue Star in consumer electronics; Bajaj, Hero Honda, Maruti-Honda, Toyota, Audi, Volkswagen, Renault, and Volvo in the automotive sector; and Holcim in cement. We expect that their operations will drive the growth of the logistics industry.

The liberalizing Indian economy is experiencing the entry of large domestic and global firms into new businesses as well as the enlargement of the distribution network of many regional Indian firms. The announcement of large retail projects by Reliance and Bharti (in collaboration with Wal-Mart) will bring new technology, add additional warehouse capacity, and require fast and reliable movement of goods across the country. Reliance is considering establishing large warehouses in Thailand to take advantage of low-cost sourcing from Southeast Asia once the Free Trade Agreement with Thailand (as well as ASEAN) gets finalized. Similarly, regional food and grocery retail leaders such as Subhiksha which are present very extensively in the South Indian market are now entering the rest of the country, with more than 600 new retail stores in 2007. Their logistics strategies and needs are being very significantly transformed by this nationwide expansion. New retail chains are entering the non-metro towns and non-state capitals. The growth of the courier industry post-liberalization has helped change the parameters of service evaluation in the industry from cost alone to cost, time, and reliability. This sector has also seen a number alliances between regional and local players, especially in the small-package (less than 500 grams) market, creating networks of small players that are not only cost-effective but also more flexible than the large national players. This segment of the industry has taken advantage of the plentiful manpower and is gradually moving away from "angadiyas," or manual intercity couriers, to a more organized network that shares transport infrastructure. Courier firms even

Table 5.4.   Investment plans of major 3PL service providers.[i]

Firms	Investment details/ plans, 2007–2008 (in USD millions)
DHL	260
TNT	115
Gati	200
Shreyas Shipping and Logistics	350

[i] *Source*: Baxi (2006) and Sanjai (2006a).

work together to consolidate subpackages from various small couriers into a single large courier bag to be transported by air cargo or road transport rather by several manual couriers via train. This allows small couriers to save on service and share fixed costs.

The entry of large 3PL carriers, including FedEx and DHL, and the expansion of domestic networks of Indian firms such as Gati and Shreyas Shipping is also transforming the nature of services and business practices across the sector. Table 5.4 shows some of the investment plans announced by various 3PL service providers for the coming financial year and gives a sense of their increasing activity.

Another trend driving growth in this sector has been the consolidation among the logistics players. Mergers and acquisitions among Indian and multinational logistics firms are starting to increase the reach of the multinationals' 3PLs in the domestic market while consolidating the business (e.g., DHL acquired Blue Dart, TNT acquired Speedage Express Cargo Service, and FedEx bought Pafex). Consolidation is expected to be beneficial both to the service providers and to the consumers. Initially, multinational 3PL firms provided only customs-clearance and freight-forwarding services to their international clients. With a growing logistics market, however, we should see a shift in this trend. The complexity of managing the supply chain in the pre-consolidation era is illustrated by the experience of Nokia (Fig. 5.3).

Logistics activity for Nokia's India hub was maintained by a large number of service providers, and co-ordination and handover were a problem at times. With its acquisition of Blue Dart, DHL is now able to provide seamless end-to-end integrated supply chain solutions. Downstream distribution channels have also seen some consolidation. Manufacturing firms, particularly in the FMCG sector, have started to reduce the number of wholesalers (and at times distributors) so as to increase the reach of — and consequently the returns to — each wholesaler. This also induces them to invest in new productivity-enhancing technology and effective managerial practices.

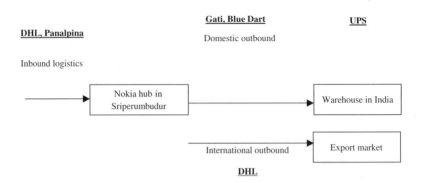

Fig. 5.3. Typical logistics supply chain of Nokia.
Source: Mishra *et al.* (2006).

Technology in the logistics chain is being upgraded, bringing better visibility to customers' skimming (though an absence of cash registers and the accompanying regulatory discipline to avoid tax evasion stand in the way of automated data updating). The introduction of more efficient transport technology and mobile communication has the potential to change the logistics practices in the industry. Increasing competition and the low levels of IT penetration also imply that the scope for change is immense and imminent. The agri-business sector's supply chain, for example, has changed significantly with increasing investment in cold-chains across the country. Through these chains, fruits and vegetables can be transported long distances (often more than 1500 km) and the milk grid is able to pick up liquid milk from, and deliver it to, remote areas more frequently. Here, the role of co-operatives like AMUL (see the case study at the end of this chapter) has been exemplary in increasing the size of the distribution network and reorganizing the supply network very efficiently, which has built up enormous social capital — a pre-requisite for growth in emerging economies.[10] Low levels of penetration of hand-held technologies for order processing and tracking, product tracking, and material handling accessories, as well as IT for improved decision making, can be seen as opportunities for growth. Mobile technologies also hold the potential for the rapid use of information for real-time decision making and for co-ordinating both inbound and outbound logistics. Indian customers exhibit strong value- and variety-seeking behavior; hence, the development of capabilities in the process of product and service delivery will create loyalty (i.e., process loyalty).

For firms entering India, the biggest challenges are to co-ordinate with multiple service providers, understand the regulatory requirements, and establish capacity in the supply chain. One of the key weaknesses in the approach of many new firms is their inability to quickly understand Indian business conventions and market dynamics. Indian product and logistics markets are highly segmented, with growth happening in the low-cost and value-conscious segments. Firms that recognize this cost-conscious environment and deploy technology that will deliver a cost-based advantage will gain in this market. Moreover, firms must be ready to participate in the building of local infrastructure in terms of warehouse capacity and technology networks. This may be seen as a strategic activity. The application of IT in the logistics industry as well as in client industries is an interesting opportunity that is waiting to be exploited. The co-ordination of the logistics markets of the SMEs with appropriate products also represents a valuable area of potential development.

Government policies have been another driver of change in the logistics industry. The trend toward a higher road-cargo traffic relative to rail is going to require better logistics control and co-ordination. The Golden Quadrilateral road project and the East and West rail corridors are expected to change the reactivity of Indian firms through shorter lead times and lower maintenance costs for transport equipment. These projects also have the potential to reduce procedural delays on highways by decreasing the number of checks and related stoppages of vehicles. The impact on perishable goods will be the most significant. Thirteen states and three union territories have already amended the state laws allowing private sector participation in the direct purchase of farm produce from farmers,[4] which is making procurement more efficient and is bringing better technology as well as products into the rural production and distribution network (e.g., see the case study of ITC e-choupal at the end of this chapter). In addition, banks have developed venture capital funds for logistics players. The Small Industries Development Bank of India (SIDBI), for instance, has invested USD2.3 million in the Mumbai-based firm Direct Logistics.[5] The unbundling of the logistics supply chain — including the physical pick-up, storage, and movement of goods, as well as allied services such as invoicing, order management, freight forwarding, customs clearance, and octroi tax management — will lead to new business opportunities and further value-added for the customers. An interesting example is that of the Reliance Connect Service Centers, which have been established on Indian highways by Reliance along with petrol stations. The Connect Centers provide a place for truckers to relax (sometimes with overnight stay facilities); send information (including data) to parent firms on their location, completed transactions, etc.; receive material/instructions; and remit money to the parent firms. They have become a "one-stop shop" helping truckers and their companies to keep in touch. Similarly, once the value added tax (VAT) is introduced, it will simplify the process of goods servicing and will lead to the rationalizing of many operational decisions.

The potential effect of the emergence of a strong service industry on logistics performance is not well understood. Perhaps a new business segment will emerge that is technology-driven and will help co-ordinate activities across business channels. For example, there is a need to integrate the flow of information, goods, and services between medical physicians, diagnostics center, hospitals and nursing homes, and retail medical outlets — all of which are uncoordinated, independent entities at the moment. This could range from the digital transmission of MRI scans from a diagnostics center to a physician's computer, to blood collection and delivery from various city centers to nursing homes and blood banks or directly to dispersed operating rooms. The role of a co-ordinating agency becomes organizationally valuable in such an environment. The need is to link physical logistics processes with communication technologies, building on the strengths of the IT and mobile communication industries.[d]

5.3.1. *Transforming the Auto Components Replacement Supply Chain*

Changing government policies and consumer preferences have significantly affected the distribution supply chain of Indian companies, posing new challenges for various channel partners. We view this transformation process through the lens of the auto components replacement market supply chain and discuss its implications below. In a study of this process, we surveyed 21 manufacturers and 22 channel members (distributors, wholesalers, and retailers) spread equally in northern and western clusters of the auto-components industry in India.

In 2004–2005, the auto-component industry produced parts worth USD6.7 billion, with 57% of the demand coming from the replacement market.[3] Low entry barriers have led to a large number of players in the replacement market: there are about 400 firms in the organized sector and more than 5000 in the unorganized sector. Another feature of this subsector is the long duration of ownership of vehicles in India, which leads to a significant demand for replacement parts. Anecdotal evidence indicates that customers' willingness to pay for parts ecreases with the length of car ownership. This has led to an intense segmentation of the parts market by price.

Pre-1991, this industry was still in a nascent stage. It was characterized by few manufacturers and low demand. Consequently, the distribution network was flat (Fig. 5.4a). Availability of spare parts was a key issue, with long delivery lead-times, and manufacturers sought large order sizes. This also led to the growth of unbranded parts or parts branded by regional producers (often supplied by small firms) in the replacement market. Products were sold chiefly on the basis of the seller's personal relationship with the buyer; quality, brand, and price were not the selling propositions. Maruti Udyog Ltd. created a network of

---

[d] See Chapter 8 of this volume for an in-depth discussion of the growing role of technology in India's health-services sector.

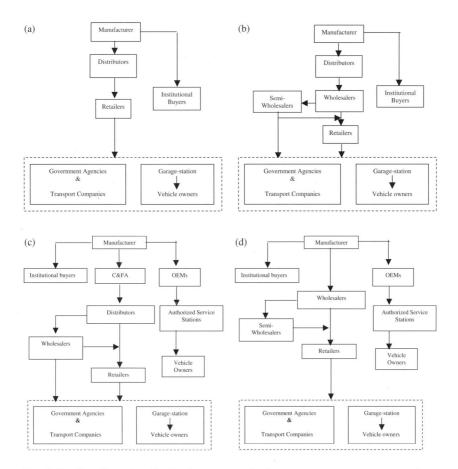

Fig. 5.4(a–d). Changing distribution structure in the auto-component sector over time.

suppliers of quality parts for its vehicles, and Hero Honda did the same for its motorcycles.

Post-1991, the liberalization of the automotive industry led to the entry of many foreign auto players. Because of the impending automobile industry boom and high margins for distributors, the demand for spare auto parts was expected to grow. The distribution channel was modified, with the entry of two more channel members, namely, wholesalers and semi-wholesalers (Fig. 5.4b). The latter were smaller versions of the former and locally oriented.

The period 1994–2007 saw a major transformation of the distribution structure (Fig. 5.4c). OEMs started to operate in the replacement market through a parallel supply chain selling parts through their service stations. Additionally, the entry of a large number of channel members caused semi-wholesalers to move out of the supply chain: they either moved up the chain to become wholesalers or moved down to become retailers. To strengthen the co-ordination of this extended supply chain and to buffer against the differential tax structure across states, companies started to operate with carry and forwarding agents (C&FA). Transportation-related activities were carried out by all the members of the supply chain. Manufacturers used 3PL services for transferring their stock to C&FA and distributor locations. But thereafter, transportation activity was solely managed by the channel members themselves.

An analysis of the available IT infrastructure and its usage pattern for all the channel members in our survey indicates that there is a high variation in the usage of IT in the replacement market supply chain. Among the surveyed firms, 87% use ERP packages, most of which are customized and developed locally. The main impediment to the use of branded packages is the high cost of purchase and implementation. These packages are used to generate sales reports, order from suppliers, account for financial transactions, and track the level of inventory at plants and C&FA. Manufacturers order their stock from suppliers mostly via email. In order to track inventory in the channel, firms also make IT investments both at C&FA and within the firm. Linking the C&FA to the company website enables firms to check stock status at the C&FA and reduce the order-processing and customer-response times. Larger firms are also providing a similar set-up for their distributors. Since the C&FA is mostly owned and managed by the firms, manufacturers are also able to check the inventory status, dispatching status, and customer records. Distributors have invested in computers primarily for keeping track of the inventory and updating accounting details. On the other hand, the rest of the channel partners (wholesalers and retailers) generally do not even own computers. Parts are ordered primarily over the phone. Interestingly, most distributors were found to be following a periodic review policy, while the rest of the channel members were following a continuous review policy because of their low sales volume.

Post-2007, with the implementation of a uniform tax structure all states, there will be some changes in the way firms operate. The C&FA will, perhaps, become redundant, as most manufacturers will prefer to deal directly with distributors. The concept of an exclusive distributor is likely to vanish. It is also expected that with the increase in variety of components, distributors might become wholesalers and will stock multiple brands of the same product. Two parallel distribution channels are expected to be in operation — the OEM chain and the non-OEM chain (Fig. 5.4d). The OEM network will primarily handle passenger-car replacement parts and the non-OEM distribution network will sell parts for light commercial vehicles, heavy commercial vehicles, 2-wheelers, and 3-wheelers, as the car customer is becoming more brand-conscious even when replacing parts (which comes along with superior service). Further, we perceive that more-advanced automobiles, free trade agreements with other Asian countries, and the VAT are going to change the way the replacement market operates. There will be a rationalization of this market in terms of the number of firms competing, thereby leading to an improvement in quality, delivery time, and availability of parts. The size of the firms is expected to increase, with an emergence of large national players (in addition to OEMs). This may reduce the number of producers exclusively focusing on the local markets.

5.4. Challenges Ahead

Several challenges remain in the Indian logistics sector, and its future success will depend on the ability of the industry to overcome these hurdles. Some of these impediments are at the policy level, while others are at the firm level.

At the policy level, the issues of infrastructure and the integration of the nation's logistics network remain the two most critical areas that require attention. The growth of infrastructure since 1991 has been quite extensive (covering a wide geographical area) as well as strategic — linking the key industrial, consumption, and trans-shipment centers. However, some apparent weaknesses need to be addressed. Poor road conditions increase vehicle turnover, increasing operating cost and reducing efficiency. Movement beyond the Golden Quadrilateral is required to bring goods from upcountry production sources to main shipment centers. The growth rate for expressways thus must increase. National highways are being upgraded, but they account for a meager 2% of the total road network.[34] More importantly, due to the non-contiguous development of expressways, truck traffic must frequently move from the expressway onto old national highways and back. This is inconvenient and restricts the utilization of the excellent road network that is being developed. The pricing of the toll on these expressways, especially for cargo traffic, has also been a deterrent to its usage — hence, the price elasticity of this demand needs to be better understood, and appropriate price packages should be developed for heavy users. The role of transport technology is also crucial: once the cost of manufacturing multiaxle trucks comes down, this market will see higher penetration and consequently lower per-unit cost of transportation. Volvo is currently trying to develop this market, but the volume of high capacity trucks continues to be low (about 7% of the total truck production).[18] The East and West bulk rail transport corridor will divert some traffic from the roads, provided that the secondary movement (i.e., from the nearest station to the plant/warehouse) can be minimized and the issue of the security of the goods is adequately addressed. Similarly, river navigation in north and northeastern India may offer useful options for cargo movement in the hinterland, where road congestion is high.

Freight vehicles run only 250–300 km per day in India, as compared to 800–1000 km in developed countries.[35] Interstate checkposts, surprise checks, and unauthorized hold-ups on highways (some due to security reasons, others to establish the authenticity of the cargo as declared) create bottlenecks. Entry taxes into cities for goods also create procedural bottlenecks. The Motor Vehicles Act and the Motor Transport Workers Act that regulate driver licensing and loading norms, and the duty hours of drivers, respectively, require modification to address the quality of services in this sector.[38] Similarly, while the regional permits that allow a truck to ply between certain states come at a lower cost (as compared to a national permit), it limits the flexibility of truckers to convert opportunities. The Indian logistics market remains fragmented on this account, and the national market (as well as the service market) does not appear as one integrated entity. Harmonization of taxes, procedures, and policies across states is required to facilitate a seamless flow of goods and services. For instance, if there were a nationwide broadband logistics IT-network, then a trucker starting in Chennai (in the southern Indian state of Tamilnadu) could file all the required papers in Chennai, get all inspections done there, and move without interruptions to, say, Jammu (in the northern Indian state of Jammu and Kashmir). Each state entry point could have access to these papers, and they could flag the truck through their checkpost as it arrived with no stoppages or delays. Today, it can take anywhere from half-an-hour to several hours to get the papers and goods inspected at each checkpost. The issue of inspections could be taken care of by the use of sealed container carriers. This and similar changes in process technology are needed to increase the effectiveness and responsiveness of the transport network.

In privatizing the operations of railway container traffic, new entrants are expected to face serious problems. Because of limited manufacturing capacity for producing rail cars, these firms will have to import them, at significant expense. Huge investments in storage capacities near railway stations will also add to the cost.[6] All these factors will increase the entry barriers for private operators. Moreover, the tariff structure and revenue sharing will still be a hindrance to the success of public-private partnership projects in infrastructure development.

While the use of IT for logistics management is increasing, it is largely limited to large firms. This represents an opportunity for firms to further improve decision-making abilities across the supply chain and reduce costs further. For instance, order processing and delivery status are two areas that exhibit a certain weakness in servicing.[9] With the growth of the IT sector in India, these are clearly areas that could gain from the IT sector's engagement. Manufacturing firms could collaborate with the extensive network of call centers to manage order processing and the actual integration of order servicing with the physical supply chain. Similarly, there is a role for the emergence of a segment (e.g., a service provider) in the logistics chain that manages dispatch information and performs delivery tracking across manufacturers for their customers. Only a few thousand vehicles out of a total of several million currently have a tracking system.[34] Truck manufacturers could integrate the tracking technology in their products, and IT servicing firms could then provide an information service that would track the movement of these vehicles, providing information to distribution firms that would allow them to track both the consignment and the truck better. Currently, the best service is that provided by Reliance Connect at their petrol pumps on the highways, where truckers can stop and call their firms to inform them of their whereabouts. Such service providers will continue to be valuable to the very small trucking companies that have proliferated in the logistics industry and which do not have the wherewithal to either install or operate their own IT systems. As the concentration in the industry increases, the need to manage a larger number of trucks, routes, warehouses, and customers will require decision-support systems that perform dynamic planning and scheduling. The IT base is indeed at a low level, and firms will need to compete on the basis of actual logistics costs instead of clever accounting practices before the sector will see increased IT penetration. As the need for visibility in the supply chain increases, better technology applications will also appear.

Another area that will see tremendous growth is the outsourcing of logistics services. While logistics outsourcing has been in existence for several decades, it has been limited to transportation and warehousing. Post-liberalization, the country has seen the outsourcing of value-added services such as freight forwarding, fleet management, import/export and customs clearance, order fulfillment, and consulting services such as distribution network planning. These are still the early years for the 3PL service providers, and a recent survey cites a lack of trust and awareness as the key hurdles to its growth.[22] Service taxes on outsourced costs and the need to establish multiple warehousing facilities in order to avoid double taxation (thereby losing the advantage of economies of scale) have also been found to undermine the 3PL business. According to the survey, most of the 3PL service providers offer limited services. In the future, their role as co-ordinators will require that they offer a wider menu of value-added services. They also have the potential to integrate SME channels through a variety of logistics services and technology across a network of small producers.

The logistics industry is evolving rapidly, and it is the interplay of infrastructure, technology, and new types of service providers that will determine whether the industry is able to help its customers reduce their logistics costs and provide effective service. Changing government policies on taxation and the regulation of service providers will also play an important role in this process. Co-ordination across various government agencies still requires approval from multiple ministries and this is a road block for multimodal transport in India.

(Ports, roads, railways, and container freight operations are all currently managed by different ministries in the Indian government.[31] At the firm level, the logistics focus will have to move toward the reduction of cycle times in order to offer greater value-added to their customers. These are just a few of the issues that must be resolved, or at least addressed, before the logistics industry can flourish and grow in India.

References

1. Acharya, RC (2006a). Railways Heavy task (20 November 2006). *Economic Times*.
2. Acharya, RC (2006b). Concor: Miles ahead on multimodal track (18 December 2006). *Economic Times*.
3. ACMA report (2005). Indian auto industry-status, prospects and challenges. www.acmainfo.com [Retrieved February 2005]. New Delhi: ACMA
4. Ahya, C (2006). The retail supply chain revolution (7 December 2006). *Economic Times*.
5. Baxi, S (2006). It's a capital idea (20 December 2006). *Economic Times*.
6. Bhatt, N (2006). Concor: Sailing through (8 September 2006). *Business Standard*.
7. *Business Standard* (2006). SPV for Rs 523 cr Orissa rail link soon (24 October 2006).
8. Chandra, P (2003). Coordinating the dabbawallah supply chain, mimeo, Ahmedabad: Indian Institute of Management.
9. Chandra, P and T Sastry (2004). Competitiveness of Indian manufacturing: findings of the 2001 national manufacturing survey. *Technology, Operations and Management* 1(1), 59–89.
10 Chandra, P and D Tirupati (2003). Managing complex networks in emerging markets: the story of AMUL, *WP 2002-5-1*. Ahmedabad: Indian Institute of Management.
11. *Deccan Herald* (2006). Inter-port connectivity needed (18 November 2006).
12. Dobberstein, N, C-S Neumann and M Zils (2005). Logistics in emerging markets. *McKinsey Quarterly*, 1, 15–17.
13. *Financial Express* (2006a). Freight rates to go up 5–6% (6 June 2006). Mumbai.
14. *Financial Express* (2006b). Smooth sailing for coastal shipping as centre mulls special scheme (17 January 2006).
15. *Financial Express* (2006c). Chinese consortium to partner Kerala in Vizhinjam port (19 January 2006). Mumbai.
16. Gill, PNS (2006). Ludhiana expecting freight corridor boast (19 September 2006). *Business Standard*.
17. Guha, R and P Sinha (2006). Two-way sign: rly ministry plans road-rail cargo system (15 July 2006). *Economic Times*.
18. IA, EIS (CMIE Databases). Industry analysis & economic intelligence service database, Centre for Monitoring of Indian Economy (CMIE), Mumbai, 2000–2006.
19. MBS CS (2006). ITC's e-choupal and profitable rural transformation, ITC-IBD Case Study-Michigan Business School. www.echoupal.com [Retrieved December 2006].

20. Mahalakshmi, BV (2006). M&As boost logistics industry (9 December 2006). *Financial Express.*

21. Mishra, AK, R Pratap and S Baxi (2006). Climb to top in logistics ladder. *Economic Times,* November 29, 2006.

22. Mitra, M (2004). Distribution's disruptive duo (18 January 2004). *Business Today,* Mumbai, pp. 86–88.

23. Mitra, S (2005). A survey of the third-party logistics (3PL) service providers in India. *Working Paper*-WPS NP 562, Calcutta, India: Indian Institute of Management.

24. Mukul, J (2007). Ports told to get their act right (4 January 2007). *Daily News & Analysis.*

25. Prowess (2006). Prowess database, Mumbai: Centre for Monitoring of Indian Economy.

26. Raghuram, G and J Shah (2003). Roadmap for logistics excellence: need to break the unholy equilibrium. *Proc. of the Paper Presented at the CII Logistics Convention,* Chennai, October 2003 and *Proc. of the AIMS International Conference on Management,* Bangalore, December 2003.

27. Raja, STE (2006). Pvt sector likely to invest $7.7 billion in ports (23 November 2006). *Hindu Business Line.*

28. Rastogi, A (2006). India infrastructure report 2006, 9–12. New Delhi: *Oxford University Press.*

29. Reddy, CP (2007). Gati eyes retail market (29 January 2007). *Business Standard,* Ahmedabad.

30. Sanjai, PR (2006a). Manufacturing sector demand attracts global heavyweights (11 December 2006). *Business Standard.*

31. Sanjai, PR (2006b). Shippers want integrated multi-modal ministry (25 December 2006). *Business Standard.*

32. Sanjai, PR (2007). NHAI pens Rs 3000 crore solutions plan (29 January 2007). *Business Standard,* Ahmedabad.

33. Sanjeevi, V (2003). Logistics in a competitive milieu (23 December 2003). *The Hindu.*

34. Sanyal, S (2006a). A guide to global logistics and freight forwarding (11 December 2006). *Hindu Business Line.*

35. Sanyal, S (2006b). Freight hike will not be uniform on all routes (8 June 2006). *Hindu Business Line.*

36. Sharma, H and KK Thakur (2006). Gati-Indian equity research (8 November 2006). *Edelweiss Capital.*

37. Srinivasan, G (2006). Public-private partnership is the way to build infrastructure (7 October 2006). *Hindu Business Line.*

38. Surabhi (2006). From Kashmir to Kanyakumari, by road (24 July 2006). *Financial Express.*

39. *Telegraph* (2006). Dedicated railway link for steel makers (12 October 2006).

Case Examples

The Renewal of the Sector: Some Innovative Experiences

A number of firms have undertaken an innovative redesign of their logistics systems or deployed novel business models to enhance the effectiveness of their networks and deliver greater value to their customers. Sometimes this was done to overcome an inherent disadvantage existing in the supply chain. In this section, we present a few such examples, both at the firm level and at the industry level, through brief caselets highlighting these firms' innovative contributions. These cases also highlight the renewal process that is now transforming the logistics sector and the distribution strategy of firms.

GATI[e]

Established in 1989, at a time when firms in India rarely outsourced their logistics requirements, Gati has transformed itself from a cargo movement company into a leading end-to-end logistics and supply chain solutions provider in India. Continuous innovation and high-end technological investments to improve service quality, speed, and efficiency are ascribed as the reasons for their success. Gati is now starting to connect with the mass retail market in several cities through 1500 Customer Convenience Centers. It is also the first Indian company to operate in the Far East market, with its own subsidiary in Hong Kong. On the service front, Gati has pioneered several firsts in India — a money-back guarantee on cargo services; cash-on-delivery; and a toll-free number for the convenience of customers.

Gati operates one of the largest road networks, linking 594 districts out of a total of 602 districts in India with a turnover of USD104 million in 2005–2006. It covers 320,000 km every day in its fleet of 2000 trucks. Its automated shipment-tracking ability has brought it closer to the customers: for example, the SMS-based tracking system has allowed customers to get continuous updates on the status of their consignments. Another feature enables customers to get email-based confirmation of any delivery.

Gati has also transformed warehouse management practices in India with its modern system WMS, a web-based warehouse management system that provides both functionality and flexibility to customers in managing their warehouse operations. WMS enables Gati and its customers to track inventory status in real time.

---

[e] *Source*: www.gati.com, Sharma and Thakur (2006), Prowess (2006), and Reddy (2007).

Along with its transportation-related capabilities, this has allowed Gati to manage the entire outbound logistics (i.e., warehousing, transport, and dealer/retailer replenishment) of Blue Star for their home air-conditioning division. Order processing times and shipping errors have decreased, and customer service levels have improved as a consequence. Currently, Gati operates with 10 warehouses, and it plans to set up another 25 over the next three years at an investment of USD100 million. It is designing these new warehouses with mechatronic systems that could lead to a paradigm shift in warehouse management in India. It has implemented CRM and ERP systems, using IT to full advantage in delivering value to the customers.

AMUL[f]

The Kaira District Milk Cooperative Union, better known as AMUL, was established in 1946 in Anand in the western state of Gujarat with the aim of removing intermediaries in the milk procurement and distribution process and thereby increasing the return to milk farmers. At the time, milk farmers were mostly marginalized members of society, and most of them poured barely a few liters of milk each day. However, they depended on this for their livelihood, and any money lost to a middleman or to uncertainty in the environment meant a threat to their existence. Thus was born AMUL (which means "invaluable" in Hindi)! The story of AMUL is an extraordinary tale of vision, effort, and the power of networks for the benefit of the poor. From being a net importer of milk in 1947, when India became independent, the country has now emerged as the largest milk producer in the world. This remarkable story has been scripted by a network of co-operatives called AMUL.

The AMUL network is co-ordinated by the Gujarat Cooperative Milk Marketing Federation (GCMMF), which markets the milk and milk products that are produced by 12 Milk Unions (each having several factories), one of which is AMUL at Anand. The Unions are spread out in 12 districts of Gujarat. Each Union collects milk from farmers through co-operative Village Societies. (This structure is now replicated in almost all the states of India.) In 2005–2006, GCMMF had a sales turnover of USD860 million from milk and milk products (its Unions produce 15 categories of milk products, comprising several products each).

The 12 Unions collect about 6.3 million liters[g] of milk every day from 2.5 million farmers through 11,962 Village Societies. The annual collection

---

[f] www.amul.org and Chandra and Tirupati (2003).

[g] 1 liter = 0.264 US gallons.

totaled 2.28 billion liters in 2005–2006. Each Village Society may have 100 to 1000 member farmers, who pour milk twice a day. Twice daily, about 500 trucks collect milk from these Village Societies and bring it either to one of the five chilling centers or to the processing plants (or Unions). The Unions process the liquid milk and produce milk of various types for consumption, convert some to powder as inventory, and use both powder and liquid milk to produce other milk products. These products are distributed to consumers through a channel of 4000 distributors and 500,000 retailers. It is not difficult to imagine the complexity of co-ordinating such a network of perishable products with an explicit social objective in addition to a commercial one. The network realized the need for a unique business model to deliver value to customers, and through that they achieve the key objective of the co-operative — making a producer out of a poor consumer and helping her get better returns.

Briefly, we will illustrate the unique mechanisms used by this network to co-ordinate the complex supply chain through the intervention of a number of third-party service providers (including distributors, retailers, logistics service providers, and IT support groups). The network practices frequent delivery and works with low inventory levels in the chain, supported by an extensive information network and IT kiosks at the milk pick-up locations that provide a variety of services. The Village Society staff pays the farmers for raw milk procurement almost immediately, often during the same or in the next pouring shift. Milk is carried in cans by trucks twice daily or in chilling trucks once a day to the plants. The routes of the trucks are well established and the arrival timetables at each Society well known, and rarely is there any delay. This helps provide visibility to every member of the chain and improves the return on investment in the channel. The network operates with a zero stock-out through improved availability of products and quick delivery. Disciplined planning to reduce variability at each stage helps in maintaining timeliness in the channel. GCMMF co-ordinates the production plan among the 12 Unions and ensures appropriate matching of geographic markets with supplies. TQM and Hoshin Kanri are the key tools used to plan and implement daily production and change programs; these have facilitated a six-Sigma performance throughout the network and have led to a doubling of sales revenue in the last 10 years. Most interestingly, AMUL has the largest market share in every product category in which it competes. Its competitors are both large multinationals and large and small Indian firms.

AMUL illustrates how good managerial practices can help bridge the gap between profits for the supplier and low-cost, high-quality products for consumers, all through exceptional co-ordination of logistics operations across an extensive network. AMUL operates with one umbrella brand for products from all its member Unions, which is a testimony to strong quality and cost co-ordination across all Unions and Village Societies. In addition, it has been singularly responsible for pulling several million of its members out from poverty, ill health, and illiteracy through its business model (called the Anand Pattern) and social programs. For further details on this case study, see Chandra and Tirupati (2003).

The DABBAWALLAHs of MUMBAI [h]

Processes can play an important role in co-ordinating the logistics of service industries in India. The Nutan Mumbai Tiffin Box Charity Trust of Mumbai is an example of a company that has capitalized on processes to simultaneously improve logistics and provide value-added for its customers. This firm was established in 1891 to provide pick-up and delivery of lunch for British expatriates working in Mumbai. Since then, it has become the leading lunch-delivery co-operative in the city, with an annual turnover of about USD12 million. The "dabbawallahs," or lunch box delivery people, of Mumbai pick up 200,000 lunch boxes, in a standard container, from homes and restaurants and deliver them to the customers' offices — all within a specified time frame — and then bring the empty box back to the place of pick-up. The company employs about 5000 delivery people, almost all of them uneducated. However, fewer than 10 boxes are misdelivered or left behind in a month! The operations of the group have attracted global attention and have won many awards. The dabbawallahs represent a growing group of service providers that exist as an element of the logistics network, providing niche service and generating value in return for the customer. We discuss here briefly the processes that help make this logistics network error-proof and enable this firm to deliver such astonishing performance.

The Trust, a co-operative, is operationally organized into hierarchical teams that include pick-up teams, consolidation teams, and delivery teams (with the reverse logistics for empty boxes and corresponding reverse functions for the teams). Typically, each *dabba* (lunch box) passes through more than four pairs of hands and may be transported up to 60 km each way. Pick-ups occur between 7:30–9:00 a.m., delivery between 12:00–1:00 p.m., and returns between 2:00–5:00 p.m. These are very tight windows of time in which a team of 20–25 members (supervised by a team leader who also fills in as a pick-up person in case of an absence) picks up lunch boxes from different homes, at a rate of about 30 pick-ups per person. The boxes are carried in a specialized fixture on a bicycle to the nearest train station, where they are consolidated by destination. A consolidation team performs this task and carries the boxes (which may have been

---

[h] Lecture by Mr. Megde, President of the Nutan Mumbai Tiffin Box Suppliers Charity Trust, at IIM Ahmedabad, 2003 and Chandra (2003).

picked up by members of different teams but need to travel to the same geographic destination) into the train. Often these *tiffin* (lunch boxes) are unloaded at intermediate train stations, reconsolidated with boxes coming from other locations (i.e., they are cross-docked), and carried on a third train to their destination stations. At the end stations, the lunch boxes coming from various origins and/or cross-docking destinations are once again segregated, this time by the building to which the delivery is to be made. Finally, a delivery team picks up the boxes that they will deliver to specific owners in specific buildings, carries them on their bicycles, and delivers them to the office of the owner of the box. Later in the afternoon, the same person picks up the empty box and follows the reverse logistics, and the box is ultimately delivered to its point of origin, either a home or a restaurant. Given this level of complexity, what could be plausible reasons for such a low error rate?

Contextually, the group members see their role as very important: they are responsible for delivering food to their customers. This social factor enhances their commitment to their task and establishes a critical customer-service provider link. Operationally, the hand-off is done successfully through simplification or the breaking down of tasks, codification, and repetition. The designed process is simple and easy for each operator to understand. More important, each operator has a limited yet definite role. This role is one of pick-up, consolidation and transfer, and delivery. Pick-up operators deal with no more than 25–30 boxes each, as that is the number of addresses that they can remember accurately. This helps in avoiding mistakes. The lunch box is enclosed in a standard container that carries a unique code for the destination station, the building to which the box is to be delivered, and the floor where the customer's office is located. The operators each recognize a limited set of codes that are relevant to them, and thus they do not have to learn the entire coding scheme. Finally, the repetition of the task (the same pick-up location, the same place for cross-docking, the same delivery location, etc.) helps to make the task foolproof. Of course, what also helps is the linear geography of Mumbai, the punctuality of trains, the relatively stable demand, and strong interdependence between operators. This industry is an example of how manual logistics systems can be organized to effectively deliver value to the customer.

ITC e-choupal[i]

The e-choupal project was launched in the year 2000 by ITC, a large diversified company with a strong FMCG presence, in the central Indian state of

---

[i] *Source*: www.echoupal.com, Talk by the e-choupal CEO S. Sivakumar at IIMA, 2003, Mitra (2004) and MBS CS (2006).

Madhya Pradesh to reorganize the distribution of soybean in rural markets. Today e-choupal handles a variety of agri-business products and reaches out to more than 3.5 million farmers in 31,000 villages through 5200 Internet-enabled kiosks. The e-choupal is a unique venture that has aimed to eliminate the middlemen from the agricultural commodity supply chain and reduce information asymmetry for the farmers. It is an extremely profitable rural distribution system with unique design features.

Prior to the launch of the e-choupal project, the soybean trade was operating in an inefficient manner. Farmers used to sell their produce through government-mandated markets called *mandis*. Mandi trading was conducted by commission agents, who bought and sold the farmers' produce. As these traders sold the produce by auction, farmers would find out the market price only upon arrival at a mandi. If buyers had already purchased enough for the day at this mandi, then either the auction prices fell dramatically or the farmers had to wait for the next day's auction. Meanwhile, as all this was happening at one mandi, the farmers were unaware of the auction status at other mandis, where there could have been shortages. The decision regarding the quality of the produce was also dependent on the trader. Distortions in price and quality also affected agri-business trading firms like ITC, who were by law required to purchase from the mandi through these traders and not directly from farmers.

Under the e-choupal model, kiosks were set up in villages, providing farmers information in the local language on agricultural inputs, best practices in farming, weather details, the market price realized at various mandi auctions, and so on. This model enabled ITC to purchase products directly from farmers (following a change in the law), enhancing the overall quality of products and offering a significant cost reduction (for instance, it saved USD5.40 per ton on soybean). The e-choupal now has just two service providers in its procurement chain: the *sanchalak*, a person between the kiosks and the farmers who inspects the produce and, based on his assessment of the quality, sets the price of the commodity (he gets a 0.5% commission on the volume sold); and the *samyojak*, a person who manages the ITC warehouses (who gets a 1% commission on transactions). Samyojaks also handle much of the logistics at the procurement hub, including storage management and transportation from the hub to processing factories.

ITC was able to overcome the hurdles posed by infrastructure inadequacy in villages. It uses solar energy to power the batteries of the computer kiosks and has shifted from dial-up connections to satellite-based technology (VSAT). Farmers now understand the market better and are able to make more informed decisions, leading to higher productivity. Various seed and fertilizer companies also are able to reach a wider market, with lower transaction cost. The e-choupal has provided a market for more than 64 companies, including Monsanto and Nagarjuna Fertilizers. This innovative direct procurement channel is a win-win mechanism for all the involved parties. ITC is now building a rural retail infrastructure on the foundation of the e-choupal network that promises to change the rural distribution landscape.

CHAPTER 6

INDIA'S AVIATION SECTOR: DYNAMIC TRANSFORMATION

John Kasarda* and Rambabu Vankayalapati[†]

Introduction

India is no longer a country of promise — it has arrived, and in a big way. Not long ago regarded as a relatively closed and staid demographic giant, the nation has emerged over the past decade as "open for business," quickly joining global leaders in everything from IT and BPO to financial services and medical tourism.

As India's integration into the global economy accelerated, so did its annual GDP growth rate, averaging over 8% since 2003. In the fiscal year 2007, its GDP expanded by 9.4% and was forecasted to remain above 9% for the next three years.[40] Foreign investment concurrently mushroomed, positioning India as number two in the world (behind China) as the preferred location for FDI. Net capital inflows (FDI plus long-term commercial debt) exceeded USD24 billion.

The country's explosive economic growth has yielded a burgeoning middle class in which higher incomes have led to sharp rises in purchases of automobiles, motorbikes, computers, mobile phones, TVs, refrigerators, and branded consumer goods of all types. Rapidly rising household incomes have also generated a burst in air travel, both domestic and international. In just three years from 2003–2004 to 2006–2007, commercial aircraft enplanements in India rose from 48.8 million to nearly 90 million, a growth rate of almost 25% annually.

Forecasts such as those by Boeing[4] and others indicate that India will continue to experience double-digit growth rates in passenger enplanements at least

*Kenan Distinguished Professor, Kenan-Flagler Business School, Director of the Kenan Institute of Private Enterprise, University of North Carolina–Chapel Hill.
[†]Indo-Asian Infrastructure Private Limited.

through 2020. Its major metropolitan regions, including Chennai, Delhi, Hyderabad, and Mumbai, are expected to experience the largest increases in air passenger traffic. Air passenger traffic in the Delhi region, for example, which was just under 20 million in 2006, is forecasted to reach over 63 million by 2020 and 112 million by 2036.[26]

For India as a whole, Boeing is forecasting 20% annual growth in air passengers for the next five years and 12% annually for the following 15 years. This will require almost 1000 new commercial aircraft serving India, according to the 2007 Boeing forecast. It will also require expanded, improved, and new airports and substantially improved surface transportation infrastructure connecting passengers and cargo to these facilities. Estimates are that over the next 10 years, some USD120 billion will be invested in India's aviation sector, creating at least three million new jobs.[18]

The current Minister for Civil Aviation Praful Patel, who comes from a business background, is responding quickly and forcefully to the mushrooming demand, making dozens of additional civilian airports operational by 2010. These will include major new public-private partnerships to construct greenfield (undeveloped site) airports in Bangalore and Hyderabad, as well as smaller airports such as those in Durgapur and Asansol. The country's two largest airports in Delhi and Mumbai have also been "privatized" (through public-private partnerships) to accelerate their modernization and expansion, which will enable them to accommodate substantially greater domestic and international passenger traffic.

A new civil aviation policy entitled "Vision 2020" is scheduled to be approved by the Union Cabinet in mid-2008. This policy is designed to strengthen the recently merged state-owned Air India and Indian Airlines, foster the success of a bevy of new commercial private airlines, and substantially upgrade India's airport infrastructure.

Vision 2020 will encourage greater FDI in airlines, airports, and ground handling services; support the expansion of domestic and international service (including the entry of new airlines); and foster public-private partnerships to improve existing airports and build new ones. The policy will also encourage the incorporation of "Airport City" and "Aerotropolis" models (discussed below) to generate commercial development at and around India's airports, increasing their non-aeronautical revenues and further boosting passenger and cargo flows. Preliminary releases (under review at this writing) additionally recommend the development of "Merchant Airports" built and operated on a for-profit basis primarily by private-sector entities, and "Cargo Villages" to promote India as a regional air cargo hub.[29] India, in short, is in the "take-off" stage of an aeronautical revolution, establishing new models for commercial aviation, airport infrastructure, and airport-driven business development.

To establish the background for the current and likely future evolution of India's airlines and airports, the following section provides a brief history of aviation in India. Next, we describe India's modern civil aviation era, including the factors giving rise to the recent surge in passenger traffic and the boom in India's private airlines. We then examine how this is affecting airport development, concluding with a description of the way that India is incorporating Aerotropolis (airport-driven development) principles to help achieve the Ministry of Civil Aviation's goal of India's becoming not only the world's largest aviation industry, but also its most entrepreneurial and progressive.

Historical Development

6.1. India's Aviation History

Civil aviation in India is among the oldest in the world. The present-day business giant The Tata Group was its pioneer, with the founding of Tata Airlines in 1932. Tata's inaugural flight was piloted by the indefatigable founder of the empire, J.R.D. Tata. On October 15, 1932, J.R.D. (as he was affectionately known) piloted a de Havilland Puss Moth aircraft between Karachi, Pakistan, and Bombay (now Mumbai).[34] By 1935, there were nine airfields in India — Bombay, Delhi, Ahmedabad, Hyderabad, Bellary, Nagpur, Madras, Calcutta, and Bhuj — handling an average of seven unscheduled domestic flights a day.

Tata Airlines in its early years served primarily as a feeder airline to the Imperial Airline of Great Britain (British Imperial Airlines), carrying mail and luxury items to British rulers. In 1946, it became a scheduled commercial airline under the name Air India Ltd., and in 1948 Air India launched its first international flight from Bombay to London via Cairo and Geneva and was incorporated as Air India International. By 1952, Air India was the nation's near-exclusive international air carrier, operating flights to London, Nairobi, Düsseldorf, Tokyo, Hong Kong, Bangkok, Singapore, and Darwin, Australia, while a number of smaller private airlines provided domestic service.

Soon after India emerged as a sovereign state in the late 1940s, a significant socialist movement commenced. The federal government appropriated (nationalized) all of the country's airports and began the process of nationalizing its nine private airlines, as well. Through the Air Corporation Act of 1953, India's government took over all domestic private airlines and merged them into a newly created government entity, Indian Airlines Corporation Ltd., to operate the domestic routes. The predominantly international carrier Air India was likewise taken over by the government, which then mandated that the two airline corporations separately operate domestic and international segments.

By 1980, Indian Airlines was offering 79 flights to 27 destinations using 21 aircraft, while Air India was providing 41 flights to 14 destinations with 19 aircraft. Thus, a total of just 40 India-based commercial aircraft (mainly aging Fokker and Boeing planes) were handling all of India's domestic and international traffic. These were supplemented by approximately once-daily flights by foreign-flag carriers to 10 international destinations.

To manage the development of domestic and international air service, the government established independent authorities: the National Airports Authority (NAA) and the International Airports Authority of India (IAAI). The four major metro gateway airports at Delhi, Bombay, Madras (now Chennai), and Calcutta (now Kolkata) were managed by IAAI, the rest of the nation's commercial airports by NAA. This arrangement continued until April 1995, when the government merged both entities under the name Airports Authority of India (AAI) in its new civil aviation policy.

6.2. The First Surge of Passenger Traffic

The period 1985–1995, ushered in by the Rajiv Gandhi era, witnessed the initial surge in India's civil aviation sector. This boom was propelled by:

- New, larger jet aircraft acquired by India's airlines from Airbus and Boeing (42 in all)
- Expanded routes and more convenient schedules
- India's first telecom revolution
- The emigration of millions of skilled and semi-skilled Indian workers to the Gulf countries of the Middle East and to the booming TIGER economies of Southeast Asia

6.2.1. *The Kerala Factor*

Interestingly, the small state of Kerala — about the geographic size of Maine in the United States — played a key role in India's first civil aviation boom. The state had few natural resources, so its large population had to depend primarily on the tourism sector centered around the famous backwaters of the Arabian Sea. With tourism-related employment stagnating in the mid-1980s and with limited agricultural jobs available, huge numbers of workers became unemployed. It was at this time that the oil sector in the Persian and Arabian Gulf region took off, requiring mass numbers of immigrant workers for the oil, construction, and service sectors.

Recognizing this opportunity, hundreds of thousands of Kerala's unemployed flocked to the Gulf region for jobs. This mass emigration from Kerala exposed a major flaw (and an opportunity) in India's aviation infrastructure. Desiring to exploit major movements to and from the Gulf, the Indian government passed a law restricting airline operations to India's state-owned carriers (Air India and Indian Airlines), thus creating a monopoly for these carriers to serve the lucrative region. Existing bilateral air agreements with other countries were bypassed in order for India's flag carriers to retain exclusive Gulf market operations. Likewise, Gulf-country airlines were denied entry to India, a restriction which was held until 1997. By this time, there were 3.2 million non-resident Indians (NRIs) from the state of Kerala (the equivalent of one in four Kerala citizen workers) employed in the Gulf region. To handle emigrant worker flows, there were 27 daily flights from three Kerala airports, making up 11% of India's international air passengers.

Mushrooming emigration to the Gulf region and protected aviation markets not only resulted in a windfall for India's airlines but also generated large net positive foreign exchange via worker remittances. These remittances remained the biggest portion of India's foreign exchange, even surpassing the export revenue from its former dominant export industries of textiles and apparel. Indian Gulf worker remittances served as a foreign exchange leader until the year 2001, when they were overtaken as a source of foreign exchange by the export of software services as well as by the dollar remittances of IT and other professionals who had emigrated from India to the United States.

The surge in aviation traffic between Kerala and the Gulf countries posed major infrastructure hurdles. Initially, every Gulf-bound passenger from Kerala had to travel to the southern tip of the state to its only international airport, Trivandrum, resulting in serious airport congestion and frustrating many. Congestion and other infrastructure problems stimulated the state government to actively lobby the federal Ministry of Civil Aviation to build a new airport.

Simultaneously, the state began wooing a growing number of Kerala's affluent NRIs working in the Gulf to invest in the airport. After years of intense lobbying with the federal government and Kerala's NRIs, India's first private airport was born in 1999: Cochin International Airport Limited (CIAL). This greenfield airport at Nedumbassery — 28 km from Cochin City — was constructed to modern international airport standards at a cost of USD68.5 million (Cochin International Airport Ltd., 2007). Given the large movements of Kerala workers to and from the Gulf, CIAL became profitable in the second year of its operations, a remarkable accomplishment in airport privatization.

Subsequently, the airport at Kozhikode, formerly called Calicut, was upgraded to handle the international traffic. The vibrant trio of Trivandrum, Cochin, and Kozhikode international airports in this tiny state of Kerala dramatically showcased the transitioning face of emerging India, laying the foundation for airport privatization.

6.3. India's Modern Civil Aviation Era

The third-largest job creator in the nation's new line of economic activities since 2001 (after IT and surface transportation infrastructure), India's civil aviation has become one of the fastest growing in the world, whether measured in terms of airport infrastructure, aircraft, or passenger traffic. Its main institutional pillars include the following:

*   The Ministry of Civil Aviation, the federal ministry formulating and controlling aviation policy at the highest level, headed by the Minister of State for Civil Aviation.
*   The Director General of Civil Aviation (DGCA), equivalent to the U.S. Federal Aviation Administration (FAA), the nodal unit within the Ministry administering, monitoring, and evaluating the civil aviation policy of the government.
*   The Airports Authority of India (AAI), the federal government agency that owns and operates most of the airports in the country.
*   Airlines anchored by the national flag carriers Indian Airlines (the domestic and neighboring-countries route operator), Air India (operating international routes), and Jet Airways (the most consistent world-class private airline in the country). These are complemented by a new generation of private low-cost carriers such as Air Deccan, SpiceJet, Indigo, and GoAir, along with the premium-class private airline Kingfisher.

India's dynamic private airlines have been overtaking the market share of the once-proud Indian Airlines. The Ministry of Civil Aviation is tackling this problem through major reorganization and business restructuring of this carrier, starting with the merger with Air India. We illustrate the enormity of the Ministry's task by briefly describing the conditions faced by the Indian Airlines.

6.4. Mediocrity — Thy Name is Indian Airlines

With its new aircraft, the surge in passenger traffic, and the monopolistic position in the domestic sector during the second half of the 1980s, the state-owned Indian Airlines became lethargic and operationally ineffective. Its staff mushroomed as each successive government since 1985 pampered the airline, which recruited personnel far in excess of its operational requirements through political patronage and personal affiliations. Governed by a board composed of a mix of bureaucrats and political appointees, the airline evolved into an entity essentially accountable to no one, including its passengers.

With India's air traffic growing more than 20% annually from 1985 to 1992, the airline could not beef up its routes sufficiently, and mismanaged its schedules. This resulted in passengers who flew the trunk routes (Bombay-Delhi, Delhi-Chennai, Delhi-Kolkata, and Bombay-Chennai) frequently having to wait 30 days or more to obtain reservations on these flights. Since there were no airline alternatives, eager passengers resorted to all means to obtain tickets, fostering corrupt practices. Travel agencies hoarded tickets and sold them at exorbitant prices, frequently in collusion with airline staff. Influential businessmen often procured tickets through the intervention of high-level government officials or executives of the airline, as the demand and supply gap further widened by 1990.

Financial woes created through mismanagement were compounded by the fact that the airline never shied away from its social responsibility of flying to remote, unprofitable locations, which it considered part of its mandate.[34] Yet, significant changes for India were in the wind that would reshape Indian Airlines along with the entire nation.

Current and Future Trends

6.5. The Economic Reforms — Paradigm Shift

The year 1991 was momentous in the history of India for a number of reasons:

- Rajiv Gandhi was assassinated.
- The nation's BOP (balance of payments position) was nil, with zero foreign exchange reserves. Foreign currency remittances by expatriate workers, about USD1.89 billion annually, were not sufficient to meet India's oil import bill and other import needs.
- International lenders were unwilling to extend the nation's credit line.
- For the first time in India's history, 100 tons of gold reserves had to be air-expressed to Switzerland to UBS and other banks in order to raise about USD4 billion to meet the BOP crisis.
- Amidst all this, a minority government headed by Mr. P.V. Narasimha Rao took the reins of federal power.

In response to the financial crisis, Mr. Narasimha Rao initiated the first economic reforms of independent India, moving away from the socialist approach to running the economy and the country in general. He partnered with the present-day Prime Minister Mr. Manmohan Singh, formerly RBI Governor (equivalent to Chairman of the Federal Reserve Board) and subsequently Finance Minister,[33] and with the current Finance Minister, Mr. Palaniappan Chidambaram, formerly Commerce Minister.

The renowned trio ably commenced the trajectory toward a more modern India by initiating numerous economic and financial reforms with a passion. These reforms paved the way for substantial investments that breathed new life into a sluggish economy. Virtually all important sectors were opened for investment by entrepreneurs, corporations, and investment bankers from India and abroad. Trade and financial services were liberalized and tariffs reduced, while numerous public sector enterprises were privatized.[28] Such reforms were carried out while keeping the rupee's foreign exchange convertibility essentially stable, thereby protecting the newly opened economy from speculation by currency traders. The result was huge increases in FDI across the sectors, tens of millions of jobs created, rising personal incomes, and new waves of air travelers in the domestic segment.

Civil aviation likewise became open to the private sector. This, along with a new civil aviation policy in 1995, paved the way for the reblossoming of private airlines serving the domestic sector and, eventually, international routes.

6.6. The Era of Private Airlines

Taking immediate advantage of economic reforms, the new aviation policy, and the lure of the robust economy, aviation companies launched seven private airlines by 1995. This process was far from smooth, however; we briefly summarize their entrepreneurial risks and a number of failures below.

East-West Airlines: East-West Airlines, a division of Bombay-based East-West Travel and Trade Links, started in 1992 as an air taxi service. However, following policy reform, it was converted into a scheduled airline with the leasing of four Boeing aircraft. Founded and managed by the Wahid family, the airline's initial success could not withstand a flailing business strategy and funding difficulties. With all the hiccups in its operations, the airline lasted only four years, and after the sudden assassination of the airline's head, Thakiyudeen Wahid, it was liquidated.[16]

ModiLuft: ModiLuft was promoted by the well-known industrialist family Modi, in association with Lufthansa German airline. It began its operations in 1993.[25] This full-service carrier was positioned to offer premium service to its passengers, well above what Indian Airlines had been providing at that time. However, it also could not sustain its expenses and capital requirements, due largely to the government-mandated 26% ceiling on the foreign holding of any India-based airline.

In 1997, after Lufthansa pulled out of its partnership with the Modi Group over charges of breach of contract and nonpayment of fees, ModiLuft went dormant.[32] It remained as such until 2005, when Royal Airways (formerly ModiLuft) revived it as budget carrier SpiceJet in the wake of the post-2003 second phase of India's civil aviation resurgence.

Damania Airways: This airline was promoted by then poultry farmer Mr. Parvez Damania in 1993 and started with just two aircraft. It ran a highly efficient operation, with on-time departures and arrivals, which was a rarity in India at that time. NEPC Airlines purchased Damania Airways in 1995 and renamed it Skyline NEPC.[36] Yet, Skyline/Damania also went bust in late 1997 when it could no longer raise sufficient capital for its operations. Mr. Damania became an aviation industry expert, later serving with Sahara Airways and Kingfisher.[3,6]

NEPC Airlines: The Khemka family of Chennai, which accumulated its wealth producing windmills and packaged goods, jumped onto the private airline bandwagon with enthusiasm in 1995. Like their peers, they too drowned in red ink caused by operating losses and the high cost of borrowing from Indian financial institutions. The Khemkas had diverted a substantial portion of the revenues from their other group businesses to NEPC, leading many of these companies to go down with the airline in 1997.

Jagson Airlines: This limited-sector scheduled airline began as a charter operation in 1991 before going regional a few years later. Its parent company, Jagson International, is in the oil industry. Jagson Airlines ran into financial difficulties and also stopped service for a time, emerging later as a regional airline and abandoning its plans to expand to national service.[38]

Air Sahara: Air Sahara (formerly Sahara Indian Airlines) was started by the Sahara Group in 1993, mostly with leased jets.[34] Through shrewd business planning, the airline survived and was only one of two private airlines of the 1990s to withstand the vagaries of changing government policies and difficult funding mechanisms. In early 2007, Air Sahara changed hands when it was bought out by rival Jet Airways in a bitter takeover battle spanning 18 months. Today, the airline is operating under the new brand name JetLite.[9] The Jet-Sahara deal was the initial consolidation in the Indian aviation sector and was later eclipsed by the Air Deccan and Kingfisher merger in the second half of 2007.

Jet Airways: Jet Airways is by far India's biggest airline success story in recent times, becoming a world-class domestic and international airline. This premium-service airline was launched by airline veteran Mr. Naresh Goel in 1993, and it survived having its first flight land at the wrong airport.[27] Mr. Goel worked in an array of international airlines in various capacities, ranging from travel agent to country manager for Royal Jordanian Airlines and Philippine Airlines, among others. His niche market strategy, shrewd selection of partners, and professional management allowed Jet Airways to grow and prosper throughout a tumultuous period that included the onslaught of India's budget airlines and cut-throat competition. Jet Airways is only the second airline from India to fly international routes, joining national flag carrier Air India.

Air Deccan: India's modern economic and demographic context sets the stage for the rise of this initially successful low-cost airline. The year 2003 saw a peak of the IT and infrastructure sectors in the country, creating millions of new jobs and raising the level of disposable income for India's rapidly growing middle class. This 100-million-strong middle class, with a disposable income of more than USD1000 per month on average, was the major force underlying a second recent boom in air travel in India.

Until the year 2000, air travel in India was largely limited to business and political travelers whose travel costs were paid by the company or the government. The growing middle class had not been seen as a potential market by India's airlines and hence was not targeted in their business plans. Around this time, an inspiring entrepreneur named Capt. G. R. Gopinath developed the idea of creating an airline with the goal of allowing every Indian to fly at least once in their lifetime. Inspired by Henry Ford, who once said, "I want every American to be able to own an affordable motor car," Capt. Gopinath launched the airline Air Deccan with the slogan "Simplify", targeted to the vast emerging Indian middle class, many in the nation's hinterland regions.

The airline, modeled after JetBlue in the United States and Ryanair in Ireland, was formed in 2003.[14] It soon became the darling of the middle class, with its low fares and deep connectivity to remote cities, which previously could only be reached by long hours of train journey. Air Deccan utilized various innovative business strategies to attract passengers and raise revenues while cutting the cost of operations. It advertised extensively in the middle-income media, established fares that competed with the cost of train travel, and expanded routes. To generate non-ticket revenues, the airline introduced in-flight advertising and shopping along with the sale of food and beverages to passengers. As it added more aircraft and expanded routes across India, the airline became an even greater hit with the middle class.

Air Deccan quickly revolutionized India's air travel market. As a result, a number of competitor low-cost airlines soon started operating using the same model. Air Deccan also successfully tapped capital markets to raise funds for its expansion as well as the maintenance of operations. Yet, in the process of creating its extensive domestic route connectivity, the airline started bleeding heavily. By the end of 2006, despite its popularity, an infusion of IPO funds, and its profitable routes on some sectors, the airline was on the financial ropes.

In an effort to stay afloat, Air Deccan pursued consolidation by merging with another high-profile airline, Kingfisher, in the second half of 2007.

There were several reasons that Kingfisher jumped at the merger opportunity:

- Air Deccan was ready to fly international routes starting in March 2008, after completing the mandatory five years of domestic operations with a minimum of 10 aircraft. Kingfisher was still another three years away from meeting the requirements for serving the lucrative international routes.
- The combined entity of Deccan and Kingfisher would be mightier than the monolithic Indian Airlines in the domestic sector, offering more flights and destinations with newer aircraft whose average age was one-half that of Indian Airlines' equipment.
- The merger was completed through an equity investment, which meant that whatever Kingfisher invested became its equity stake, thereby adding considerable short- and long-term value to its investment.
- Kingfisher could transfer its high-profile — and high-quality — brand to Air Deccan, providing luster to the low-cost carrier.

This novel consolidation of a premium luxury airline with a budget airline was among the smoothest mergers and acquisitions in Indian corporate history. By early 2008, its benefits were already becoming manifest.

SpiceJet: Taking a cue from the initial success of Air Deccan, a bevy of other low-cost airlines began creating highways in India's skies. SpiceJet arose out of the defunct Royal Airways and Modiluft, commencing operations early in 2005 and launching flights in May 2005.[30] Using a mix of its own and leased new aircraft, it has become one of the more profitable budget carriers in the country.

IndiGo: IndiGo, another successful budget carrier modeled after Air Deccan, started its operations toward the end of 2005 and its flights in early 2006. As of early 2008, it has 16 aircraft offering 112 flights every day with 17 destinations.[17]

GoAir: This airline was started by the scions of the Wadia Group (whose holdings include Bombay Dyeing and Britannia Industries) as a budget carrier offering efficient service with eight new aircraft in the Boeing and Airbus family.[39] Launched in 2005, GoAir (Go Airlines) is adding to its weekly operations and its aircraft fleet, with plans for 561 commercial flights per week in winter 007–2008 and 41 aircraft by March 2012.[11]

Paramount Airways: In this age of rising budget carriers in India, it took substantial fortitude for Mr. M. Thiagarajan, a pilot and business management graduate, to start a business-class airline with premium quality service and impeccable service schedules. Mr. Thiagarajan followed novel methods to launch this airline in September 2005, choosing new Embraer jets from Brazil instead of the typical Boeing or Airbus.[31] Limiting operations to eight cities of South India and only offering full-service business-class travel, his strategy paid off. Today, Paramount is one of the most profitable small airlines in India, attracting both passengers and investors. The company ended 2007 with five aircraft and 52 daily flights to eight domestic locations. Paramount is purchasing additional aircraft; setting up maintenance, repair, and overhaul facilities with Embraer; and looking to become a strategic partner with an existing airline such as GoAir.

Kingfisher: A summary of contemporary Indian civil aviation would not be complete without a discussion of Kingfisher Airlines. The airline was promoted in early 2005 by Dr. Vijaya Mallya of the United Brewery Group (famous for Kingfisher beer) to offer luxurious domestic travel to a niche segment of Indian travelers. Modeled on Virgin Atlantic Airlines, Kingfisher made aviation history by successfully taking over another major airline (Air Deccan) within 18 months of entering the business. The firm is eagerly waiting to give the established international airlines a run for their money starting in 2008 under the merged brand Deccan, with the proposed utilization of up to 10 new super-jumbo A380 aircraft in 2011–2012. Air Deccan's Capt. Gopinath will become the newly merged airline's vice-chairman, under Dr. Mallya's continuing leadership.[2]

With India's forecasted strong economic growth and likely continuing boom in domestic and international passenger demand, numerous other new air carriers are expected to enter the nation's skies in the years ahead. How many will financially make it, nobody can guess. Suffice it to say that turbulence and intense competition will likely shake out many of these new entrants, as well as possibly some of those that are current successes. Such is the nature of a dynamic economic environment.

6.7. Burgeoning Air Infrastructure — Airport Privatization

The sudden boom in passenger traffic posed a serious challenge to India's existing air infrastructure. The nation was simply not equipped to meet the burst in aircraft movements and terminal passenger handling. This was particularly telling at the five major metro airports of Mumbai, Delhi, Chennai, Bangalore, and Hyderabad, which were already saturated to near capacity.

To address the problem, the government of India convened the EGoM (Empowered Group of Ministers) of the federal cabinet to assess the issue and suggest ways to markedly upgrade the nation's airport infrastructure. The group studied the privatization option in detail, including the case studies of the first private-sector airport in the country, CIAL, and the possible sanction of public-private partnership greenfield airports at Bangalore and Hyderabad.

The new Bangalore International Airport near Devanahalli-Bangalore was approved in 1998 but was progressing quite slowly. In contrast, the new Rajiv Gandhi International Airport (RGIA) at Shamshabad, near Hyderabad, which was approved in 2001, was making much quicker progress. Both airports are scheduled to be operational by March–April 2008.

The Bangalore International Airport is being built by a consortium of partners led by Siemens Projects Ventures (40% stake), Unique Zurich Airport (17%), and Larsen & Toubro (17%). The remaining 26% of the equity is split between the AAI and the state government of Karnataka (Bangalore International Airport Limited, 2006). The new RGIA in Hyderabad is being built by a GMR Group-led consortium. GMR holds a 63% stake, with the AAI and the state government of Andhra Pradesh holding 13% each and Malaysia Airports Holdings Berhad holding 11% (GMR Hyderabad International Airport Ltd., 2005).

Encouraged by the success of India's CIAL and the progress made at the new private sector-led airport at Hyderabad, EGoM recommended the privatization route for Mumbai and Delhi airports to create world-class passenger facilities and expand their aeronautical infrastructure. The group submitted its recommendations to the government in May 2005, and the federal cabinet approved the proposal to "privatize" the commercial airports at Mumbai and Delhi but asked to make AAI a minority partner.

While AAI's union strongly opposed airport privatization, the federal government defended its decision on the grounds that AAI could not raise the equity for the ambitious modernization and expansion program, as it was operating with a very thin bottom line. Moreover, the federal government said it could not provide the necessary resources either, since it had to allocate available resources to higher-priority sectors such as highway infrastructure and health services.

The 20,000 unionized employees of AAI protested the privatization move mostly because they feared that many would lose their jobs under the new management. Despite continuing protests and opposition to the privatization move, the federal government announced an international competitive bidding process to select the partners for airport development at Mumbai and Delhi in August 2005. After a four-day strike by airport workers in early 2006, the government made a provision in the privatization document that more than 60% of the workforce at the privatized airports would be absorbed by the new management and the remainder would be accommodated at the other airports operated by AAI.[15] With this issue resolved and much scrutiny and due diligence of the bids, the government awarded 30-year renewable management contracts to the private-sector-led consortiums.

India's GMR Group, in association with AAI, Fraport AG, and Malaysia Airports Holdings Berhad, won the bid to modernize and expand the airport at Delhi, while the GVK-SA Consortium of GVK Group, in association with South African companies Airports Company South Africa Limited (ACSA) and the Bidvest Group Limited won the bid to manage and modernize the airport at Mumbai. In both consortiums, AAI retained about 25% of the equity for revenue sharing.[7] After the completion of the formalities, both of the airports were handed over in May 2006 to the newly formed public-private consortiums Mumbai International Airport Limited (MIAL) and Delhi International Airport Limited (DIAL).

6.7.1. *Mumbai and Delhi Airport Progress*

6.7.1.1. *MIAL*

At the time of handover, MIAL at Sahar in suburban Mumbai was India's busiest airport, handling almost 20 million passengers per annum on over 160,000 air traffic movements. Immediately after assuming control, the GVK-led consortium laid out expansion and modernization priorities. This occurred in advance of the preparation of the long-term master plan for development with the assistance of Changi Airport of Singapore.

GVK and its partners rapidly implemented interim airport upgrades to handle more aircraft and passengers and to improve passenger amenities. These included a new taxiway system to allow better use of the main runway, a new departure terminal with 60 check-in counters, upgraded retail and restaurant offerings, and a new parking facility.

By the late 2007, interim improvements were completed and the long-range master plan was approved by India's Ministry of Civil Aviation. This plan includes the development of a new integrated passenger terminal to initially handle 40 million domestic and international passengers annually and further upgrades of existing terminals; a new integrated cargo complex to handle one million tons of cargo; a hotel and entertainment complex; substantially more parking and new road links.

The approved plan has a budget of approximately USD1.2 billion, with the construction contract awarded to Larsen & Toubro (L&T), India's largest engineering and construction company, which is also building the new Hyderabad

Airport and modernizing Delhi International Airport. With the expansion work set to commence, MIAL is still facing problems in reclaiming airport land from slum squatters who are demanding exorbitant relocation costs.

MIAL is actually spread over 2900 acres,[a] but 1000 of these acres have been occupied by slum dwellers on the east and south side of the airport. The consortium has submitted a generous compensation package with the help of the state government of Maharastra to move the dwellers from the property and relocate them onto land to be purchased by the GVK group. Yet, as of January 2008, efforts to take back the land for airport infrastructure and facility expansion have been rebuffed.[24] With annual passengers exceeding 25 million at MIAL in 2008, a new Mumbai airport site at Navi (on the outskirts of Mumbai) is being pursued to meet strong future aviation growth in the metropolitan region, which is expected to surpass 100 million passengers annually by 2030.[35]

6.7.1.2. *DIAL*

Delhi's International Airport spans a more substantial 5000 acres. Though part of the airport site was occupied by the Ministry of Defense, reclamation of this land from the Ministry posed little problem for the GMR Group. In short order, plans were implemented for a new runway (the third) at DIAL and a new integrated passenger terminal, Terminal 3, initially capable of handling 30 million passengers annually and expandable afterwards. The third runway is expected to be operational by late 2008, and the integrated (domestic and international) passenger terminal by 2010.

Terminal 3 will be state-of-the-art in every respect, providing modern passenger amenities and services along with 55 aircraft terminal gates and 20 remote stands. Departing and transferring passengers will have available a significant complement of retail and service options that will measure up to the leading terminals at Singapore Changi, Frankfurt, and Hong Kong International airports, including a 300-room, four-star passenger transit hotel connected to the terminal. The terminal and adjacent infrastructure are being designed in a modular, expandable fashion, allowing the airport to serve up to 100 million passengers annually by 2036.

In addition to the above new infrastructure and terminal, GMR has provided interim facelifts to the existing domestic and international terminals and has improved their operations. The modernization and expansion work, with a budget of USD1.2 billion, was awarded to L&T after a competitive bidding process.

---

[a] 1 acre = 43,560 square feet.

GMR has developed a plan to utilize much of its available land for commercial development at both DIAL and the new Hyderabad airport following the Aerotropolis model. Since this new business model is being implemented so extensively across India, it is useful to summarize its general principles before illustrating ways in which it is being implemented in Delhi, Hyderabad, and Nagpur.

6.8. Aerotropolis: Airport-Driven Business Development

Fueled by an integration of globalization, digitization, aviation, and time-based competition, the roles and commercial impact of major airports are dramatically changing. No longer are airports simply transportation infrastructure where aircraft operate and passengers and cargo transit. Rather, they have become complex, multimodal, multifunctional enterprises driving substantial commercial development within and well beyond their boundaries.

In addition to incorporating shopping mall concepts into passenger terminals and developing airside logistics facilities, landside areas near passenger terminals are seeing hotels, office and retail complexes, conference and exhibition centers, free trade zones, and time-sensitive goods processing facilities emerge. The bottom line is that, today, many major airports receive greater percentages of their revenues from non-aeronautical sources than from aeronautical sources such as landing fees, gate leases, and passenger service charges.

The expansion of non-aeronautical activities at airports is favorably affecting their financial performance, better allowing them to meet their modernization and infrastructure expansion needs. Rapid commercial development is also making airports leading urban growth generators as they become significant employment, shopping, trading, business meeting, and leisure destinations in their own right. The evolution of these new functions and commercial land uses has transformed many city airports into airport cities.[12,23]

Even greater aviation-centric commercial development is occurring beyond airport perimeters. With the airport itself serving as a region-wide multimodal transportation and commercial nexus (analogous to the central business districts of the 20th century metropolis), strings and clusters of airport-linked business parks; information and communications technology complexes; retail, hotel, and entertainment centers; industrial and logistics parks; wholesale merchandise marts; and residential developments are forming along airport arteries up to 20 miles outward. This more dispersed airport-linked development is giving rise to a new urban form, the Aerotropolis.[19–22] Figure 6.1 presents the basic Aerotropolis model, derived from longitudinal case studies of 12 new and evolving international airports around the world.[b]

---

[b] See http://www.aerotropolis.com for elaboration.

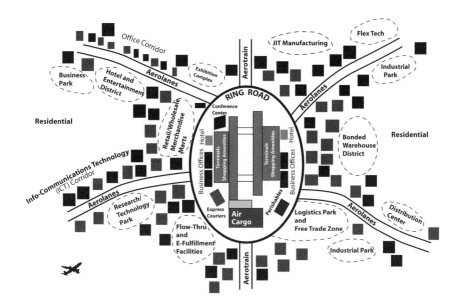

Fig. 6.1. Basic aerotropolis schematic.

Source: Dr. John D. Kasarda © Aerotropolis schematic.

India is at the forefront of Aerotropolis implementation, led by private-sector management consortiums around the country. Aerotropolis case examples for Delhi, Hyderabad, and Nagpur presented after the References section illustrate this new phenomenon.

6.9. Challenges for India's Aviation Future

While the increase of passenger travel and air cargo handling hold great opportunities for India, the country faces several significant challenges in capitalizing on this growth. Losses for domestic airlines totaled USD580 million for 2006–2007 as a result of intense domestic competition, restrictions on flying overseas routes, increased operating expenses due to high fuel costs and taxes, and continuing airport infrastructure and facility constraints.[37] For instance, Deccan Aviation has suffered from a lack of aircraft hangar space at most airports in India, forcing the airline to spend additional funds to rent space from competitors. A lack of night landing facilities also caps airlines at or near current flight levels.

As previously discussed, the government and its private-sector partners are working to meet these challenges by upgrading India's aviation infrastructure, with the modernization of almost 70 airports expected by 2009–2010, along with the construction of a plethora of new commercial airports. To increase capital flows to airports and airlines, FDI limits are being raised as follows:

- FDI of 100% is now allowed in maintenance, repair, and overhaul facilities, up from the previous cap of 49%.
- Up to 100% FDI is also allowed for helicopter and sea-plane services, as well as flight training organizations for pilots, cabin crews, and ground crews.
- FDI of up to 74% is permitted in cargo airlines and non-scheduled airlines, as well as ground-handling services following acquisition of required security clearances.
- FDI remains capped at 49% for scheduled domestic airlines.[13]

Perhaps the greatest challenge to India comes from the rapid expansion of airports and air routes in nearby countries in the Gulf region. For example, Dubai, only a two- to four-hour flight from most Indian cities, is expanding its airports and international aviation network at a breathtaking pace. Dubai already offers convenient air service to all major destinations in Asia and Europe, and it is in the process of adding service to the United States. It is not implausible that Dubai could become India's gateway to Europe and possibly to much of Asia, thereby limiting India's centrality in global aviation networks. This is all the more reason to remove the current limitation that India's airlines must operate domestically for at least five years before receiving the right to fly internationally.

6.10. Conclusions

Three basic words characterize the dynamic transformation of India's aviation sector: growth, privatization, and innovation. Together, they are generating an entrepreneurial spirit that is changing the face of the nation's airlines and airports.

India's aeronautical revolution shows no signs of slowing as it seeks to keep pace with, and further enhance, the nation's rapid economic trajectory. Both business and government recognize that the country's competitive future rests on the development of world-class airlines, airports, and aviation systems, enabling it to succeed in an increasingly integrated, speed-driven global economy. They also realize that the surface transportation infrastructure connecting India's larger airports to major commercial, production, and residential nodes in their metropolitan regions requires significant upgrading to fully unleash the potential of airport-driven economic development.

In the eyes of many, the 21st century is fast becoming "the aviation century." India is positioning itself to fly high and be an important contributor to this dynamic new era.

References

1. Bangalore International Airport Limited (2006). Shareholders. http://www.bialairport.com/about_bial_shareholders.htm?cid=topmenu&ses=bial [Retrieved on 7 February 2008].
2. Bhargava, A (2005). Airborne. *Businessworld (India)*. http://www.businessworldindia.com/jun2705/coverstory01.asp [Retrieved on 7 February 2008].
3. Bhargava, A (2007). The death of a dream. *Business Standard.* Factiva databse [Retrieved on 7 February 2008].
4. Boeing Current Market Outlook 2007 (2007). http://www.boeing.com/commercial/cmo/pdf/Boeing_Current_Market_Outlook_2007.pdf [Retrieved on 17 December 2007].
5. Cochin International Airport Ltd (2007). FAQs. http://www.cochin-airport.in/Faq/Faq.aspx [Retrieved 4 February 2008].
6. Damania takes a flight to fantasy World (2001). *The Times of India.* LexisNexis Academic database [Retrieved 7 February 2008].
7. Dennis, W (2006). India awards contracts that will privatize Delhi, Mumbai airports. *Aviation Daily.* Factiva database [Retrieved 7 February 2008].
8. Friedman, TL (2005). *The World Is Flat: A Brief History of the Twenty-first Century.* New York: Farrar, Strauss and Giroux.
9. Ghosh, R (2007). Jet sets Air Sahara among budget players. *DNA — Daily News & Analysis.* Factiva database [Retrieved 7 February 2008].
10. GMR Hyderabad International Airport Ltd (2005). About us: public-private partnership project. http://www.newhyderabadairport.com/airport/partnership.html [Retrieved 7 February 2008].
11. GoAir Receives 2nd A320 Aircraft (2007). *Business Line (The Hindu).* Factiva database [Retrieved 7 February 2008].
12. Güller, M and M Güller (2001). From airport to airport city. *Proc. of the Airports Regions Conference.* Barcelona, Spain.
13. India Eases Norms on Foreign Direct Investment (2008, January 30). *CNBC.com*, http://www.cnbc.com/id/22912327 [Retrieved 11 February 2008].
14. India's First Low-Cost Airline Takes off Today (2003, August 27). *Business Times Singapore.* Factiva database [Retrieved 7 February 2008].
15. Indian Airport Workers Call off Anti-Privatisation Strike (2006, February 5). *AFX Asia.* Factiva database [Retrieved 7 February 2008].
16. Indian Police Hunt for Airline Chief's Killers (1995, November 14). *Reuters Limited.* Factiva database [Retrieved 4 February 2008].
17. Indigo Air Service (2008, January 30). *The Statesman (India).* Factiva database [Retrieved 7 February 2008].
18. Ionides, N (2007). Reforming India's skies. *Airline Business*, 23(12), 34–37.
19. Kasarda, JD (2000). Aerotropolis: airport-driven urban development. In *The Future of Cities*, pp. 32–41. Washington, DC: Urban Land Institute.

20. Kasarda, JD (2001). From airport city to Aerotropolis. *Airport World*, 6(4), 42–45.
21. Kasarda, JD (2004). Aerotropolis: the future form. *Just-in-Time Real Estate*, Frej, A (ed.), pp. 92–95. Washington, DC: Urban Land Institute.
22. Kasarda, JD (2007). Airport cities and the Aerotropolis: new planning models. *Airport Innovation*, 1(1), 106–110.
23. LeTourner, C (2001). The bricks and mortar of global commerce. *Airport World*, 6(6), 26–40.
24. Mishra, V (2008, January 25). Mumbai: airport rehabilitation plan: a confusing case. *DNA: Daily News & Analysis*. Factiva database [Retrieved 7 February 2008].
25. Modis Launch Airline (1993, April 18). *Khaleej Times*. LexisNexis academic database [Retrieved 7 February 2008].
26. Mott MacDonald Group (2006). Delhi airport traffic forecasting report, Final Report. Delhi International Airport Limited.
27. New Indian Airline's First Flight Lands at Wrong Airport (1993, May 5). *Agence France-Presse*. Factiva database [Retrieved 7 February 2008].
28. OECD Economic Surveys: India (2007). Organisation for Economic Co-operation and Development (OECD), Vol 14.
29. Planning Commission, Government of India (2006). Working groups/steering committees/task force for the eleventh five year plan (2007–2012). http://planningcommission.nic.in/aboutus/committee/11strindx.htm [Retrieved 16 January 2008].
30. Royal Airways becomes SpiceJet (2005, May 5). *The Economic Times*. Factiva database [Retrieved 7 February 2008].
31. Shankar, TS (2005, June 23). Paramount to launch low-cost air service. *The Hindu*. Factiva database [Retrieved 7 February 2008].
32. Sharma, S and P Waldman (1996, May 31). Charges fly over soured Lufthansa deal; Indian partner in ModiLuft denies breach of contract and accuses German carrier of exploitation. *The Globe and Mail*. LexisNexis Academic database [Retrieved 7 February 2008].
33. Singh, M (2007). *Curriculum Vitae*. http://pmindia.nic.in/meet.htm [Retrieved 4 February 2008].
34. Singh, P (2003). *History of Aviation in India: Spanning the Century of Flight*. New Delhi: The Society for Aerospace Studies.
35. Singhal, M (2008, January 30). Navi Mumbai airport to be ready by 2012. *Business Standard*. Factiva database [Retrieved 7 February 2008].
36. Skyline NEPC to Buy Two More Boeings (1996, February 17). *Business Standard*. Factiva database [Retrieved 7 February 2008].
37. Subramanian, S (2008, January 14). High Flyer. *Open Sky*. http://bsopensky.com/opensky/wcms/en/home/take-off/Praful-Patel-080114.html [Retrieved 5 February 2008].

38. Talreja, V and S Chauhan (2008, January 28). Jagson airlines to fly as regional carrier. *The Economic Times*. Factiva database [Retrieved 7 February 2008].
39. Wadia Group (2008). *Wadia Group Companies*. http://www.wadiagroup/ Grp_Cmp/grp_index.htm.
40. Zainulbhai, A (2007). Securing India's place in the global economy. *The McKinsey Quarterly*. http://www.mckinseyquarterly.com/article_abstract. aspx?ar=2058 [Retrieved 29 November 2007].

Case Examples

The Aerotropolis

The Delhi Aerotropolis: Despite having a 5000-acre property, DIAL is currently restricted by federal law to the commercial development of only 250 acres of its airport land. It is, therefore, doing this wisely based on best use and highest value, following Aerotropolis principles.

The first major Aerotropolis component to be developed is a hospitality and retail district located adjacent to DIAL's planned new private jet facility and National Highway 8 (NH-8). The district will be composed of six land parcels: (a) 5.5 acres for a five-star plus deluxe hotel and premium apartment hotel with a maximum built-up area of 590,000 sq. ft.; (b) a 4.7-acre parcel for another luxury hotel and apartment hotel of maximum 625,000 sq. ft.; (c) 7.1 acres for a business and mid-market hotel, a mid-market condo hotel, and office and retail space with a maximum 970,000 sq. ft. build-out; (d) a 140-acre "high street" style pedestrian arcade surrounded by luxury, business, and mid-market hotels and condo hotels plus office and retail space and a hotel convention facility, including metro station access, with a maximum gross build-out of 1.9 million sq. ft.; (e) an 8.7-acre parcel for luxury and business hotels, luxury apartment hotels, and office and retail space, with a maximum build-out of 1.2 million sq. ft.; and (f) a five-acre parcel with a proposed boutique, luxury resort hotels, spas, and hotel villas.

The above six parcels will each be designed to have a distinct thematic identity, yet be integrated functionally. All will be architecturally appealing, with green spaces and a perimeter road network for vehicular access. Internal pedestrian routes lined with upscale retail shops will give the feel of a high-quality urban experience.

The hospitality and retail district has the potential to become the Aerotropolis core and second central business district (CBD) of the Delhi metropolitan area, serving an accelerating number of passengers expected to pass through DIAL as well as destination visitors. DIAL hotel development will also help reduce a serious deficit in Delhi hotel space, currently estimated to exceed 30,000 rooms.

DIAL's hospitality and retail district will be complemented and reinforced by the Delhi Development Authority's (DDA) planned International Convention and Exhibition Center, Hotels, and Allied Commercial Facilities Complex in Dwaraka, just two miles from DIAL. This 30-acre parcel will house an 86,400-sq.-meter convention and exhibition complex, a 60,000-sq.-meter hotel complex, and a 36,600-sq.-meter[c] commercial complex, all built to top international standards. With both the DIAL hospitality district and the DDA convention and exhibition/commercial complex serving as major Aerotropolis clusters along nearby NH-8, this area is expected to evolve into India's primary Aerotropolis corridor.

The NH-8 corridor also continues to Gurgaon near the airport which is developing into a major southern Delhi IT, office, and retail mall cluster housing such multinationals as Adobe Systems, General Electric, Hewlett-Packard, Nokia, and PepsiCo Holdings. The burgeoning Gurgaon area is attracting thousands of young professionals who also regularly shop at the many large malls being developed there.

There will no doubt be other major commercial complexes attracted to the NH-8 corridor and around DIAL in the not-too-distant future. DIAL itself still has two other substantial land parcels of a combined 220 acres reserved for future commercial development along with the several other small parcels of land adjacent to new Terminal 3. These offer immense potential for DIAL to become the functional core of a world-class Delhi Aerotropolis.

The Hyderabad Aerotropolis: What was originally conceived by the AAI as an airport to reduce congestion at the existing Begumpet Airport near the center of Hyderabad City has become a bold experiment in Aerotropolis development. A visionary and ambitious master plan has been prepared by CPG Consultants under the direction of the GMR Group. If implemented, the plan will transform the new 5500-acre international airport with state-of-the-art infrastructure and facilities into a leading Aerotropolis and driver of economic development throughout a broad Hyderabad Airport Development Area.

Phased market-driven infrastructure and facility development is planned, with a capacity at opening in March 2008 of 12 million passengers and 100,000 metric tons of cargo. Expansion will occur in phases, rising to a target of more than 40 million passengers and up to one million metric tons of cargo by 2038. Modular design of facilities will enable incremental expansion to meet growing aeronautical demand and associated commercial opportunities. The plan is for the

---

[c] 1 sq. meter = 10.7639 sq. ft.

new airport (HIAL) to evolve into a full-blown Aerotropolis, complete with business parks, hotels, shopping malls, convention centers, and exhibition halls as well as an air cargo/industrial complex, the latter anchored by logistics hubs and special economic zones (SEZs).

In the first phase, HIAL will house 4300 sq. meters of airside retail (3000 sq. meters in international and 1300 sq. meters in domestic) and 500 sq. meters of landside retail. In addition, there will be a 2500-sq.-meter landside "Airport Village" where passengers and meeters-and-greeters can shop and dine in an aesthetically pleasing Indian ambiance. There will also be a four-star terminal-linked business hotel for transit passengers.

At later phases of development, numerous commercial, logistics, and industrial facilities are planned. These are organized into three zones: Zone West, Zone Core, and Zone East. Zone West (landside) is envisioned as a core 250-acre multiproduct SEZ with an affiliated 17-acre logistics hub near the airport's air cargo terminal. In addition, Zone West is designated to house a 57-acre business park, 22 acres of which will be mixed commercial; a 2.5-acre hospital and a 71-acre recreational golf course. The multiproduct SEZ can be built out to a maximum of 3.4 million sq. ft., the logistics hub to 723,000 sq. ft., the business park to 3.4 million sq. ft., and the mixed commercial space to nearly seven million sq. ft.

Zone East (airside) will have a 125-acre aviation support SEZ with an affiliated 39-acre logistics hub in close proximity to Terminal 2; a 67-acre business park; a 25-acre corporate office complex; 313 acres of commercial and mixed commercial development; a 104-acre aircraft maintenance zone; a 5.2-acre business hotel; and 3.7 acres for service apartments. Together, the commercial and mixed commercial parcels can support an office parcel of 1.9 million sq. ft. of buildings, the logistics hub of 1.7 million sq. ft. of facilities, and the business park (including IT offices) of 5.3 million sq. ft. Health, wellness, and medical tourism facilities are also being contemplated.

The Core Zone will house the passenger terminal complex (89.5 acres), hotels (13 acres), a convention center (16 acres), and the GMR corporate office (19 acres), along with a 104-acre commercial parcel supporting nearly seven million sq. ft. of additional commercial facilities. Iconic aviation-themed architectural design, public art, and sculptures will enhance HIAL's Aerotropolis image and brand.

Nagpur: A Multimodal Logistics Aerotropolis

Driving much of the airport-linked business development around the world is fast-cycle logistics, especially that which utilizes air cargo. In fact, in many goods-processing sectors, the 21st century is becoming known as the "Fast Century." Customers in both India and international markets are demanding speedy and reliable delivery of products, often with distinctive features. An industrial advantage is thus being gained by firms that respond flexibly and rapidly to their domestic and global customers, delivering lower-cost, higher-quality (often customized) products quickly and efficiently over great distances (Friedman, 2005).

For example, high-tech manufacturers must be able to access national and global networks of suppliers of materials, components and sub-assemblies in order to obtain the best-quality components at the lowest possible price. Likewise, contract drug and medical testing often requires a 24- to 36-hour turn-around from potential source to distant test site and often back to source, the latter usually done electronically.

The above business requisites underlie plans by India's Ministry of Civil Aviation to build a multimodal logistics-driven Aerotropolis at and around Nagpur Airport. A center point of India situated in the state of Maharashtra, Nagpur Airport is one of the nation's oldest airports, developed by the British in the early 1930s.

It was selected for air cargo and logistics-driven development for a variety of reasons. It has a strategic location below the international air corridor connecting Asia-Pacific to the Middle East and Europe, with almost 300 international flights crossing its skies daily. It is also at the center of the Indian subcontinent, which offers logistical access advantages. It is the meeting point of the major national highways and rail systems in India linking the north-south and west-east corridors, which provides for seamless connectivity of road and rail linkages. In addition, there is ample land surrounding the airport that is available for commercial development.

Capitalizing on these factors, the Vidarbha Economic Development Council (VEDC) — the regional development forum — started pursuing an ambitious project to develop a multimodal cargo airport at Nagpur in 1987. After a 10-year hiatus, efforts to develop this multimodal logistics airport gathered momentum. In addition to linking air, road, and rail in a seamless fashion, a master plan was created that included: (1) special economic zones to attract and foster high-tech and other time-sensitive industries, (2) improved and expanded airport infrastructure to accommodate wide-bodied cargo aircraft and to provide MRO services, (3) an ICT and software development zone, (4) a commercial district, (5) a health and allied medical services complex, and (6) residential, recreation, and shopping parcels.

Taking advantage of the Nagpur airport development area, scores of real estate entrepreneurs have commenced outside-the-airport-fence ventures to meet anticipated growing housing and commercial demands. As of late 2007, these include an 800-acre IT and jewelry park adjacent to the commercial district and a hotel and entertainment complex, as well as Boeing's proposed MRO facility. It was estimated that as of early 2008, Nagpur's airport-linked development has also attracted at least 100 smaller entrepreneurs, generating approximately 3000 additional jobs.

Connecting Wave

HEALTHCARE

Jayashankar M. Swaminathan

While most of its previous developments have focused on products, services, and infrastructure, India is also beginning to play a major role in healthcare. On a recent business visit to Apollo Hospitals[1] in Delhi, an MBA student commented that she was surprised at the level of healthcare technology available in India. I replied, "Me too." In 1982, I had to be rushed to a small private hospital with minimal amenities for emergency surgery after I was told I would have to wait at least 72 hours for the procedure at the large and very popular government hospital. It turned out that most of the doctors were on leave to celebrate the opening ceremony of the Asian Games in Delhi. A lot has changed in India in terms of the availability of medical care in urban areas in the last 25 years. Medical tourism — in which foreign nationals come to India to get various types of surgeries performed at a lower cost than in their home countries — has played a major part in this development. A liver transplant might cost USD45,000 in India, as compared to USD140,000 in Europe or USD280,000 in the United States, while heart surgery that costs about USD5000 in India would be close to USD30,000 in the United States. It is expected that by 2012 medical tourism will become a USD2.1 billion industry in India.

Firms such as Apollo Hospitals have facilitated this growth by providing high-quality care at low cost. Further, a burgeoning middle-class population that is more aware of preventative healthcare is demanding better standards and is willing to pay for them. Healthcare in India is for the most part a "pay as you need" system, and the concept of health insurance and preventative care is relatively new. The healthcare delivery system in India can be described in terms of a simple two-by-two matrix. There are four types of facilities: high-quality, state-of-the-art private facilities (such as Apollo or Escorts); high-quality government

---

[1] Apollo is the largest group of hospitals in Asia today.

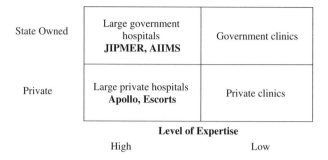

Fig. E5.1.   Healthcare facilities in India.

facilities such as the All India Institute of Medical Sciences (AIIMS) or JIPMER, which are the most similar to research hospitals in the United States; smaller private clinics and hospitals; and small government-run clinics and facilities. Most of the high-quality hospitals (both private and government-run) are located in the major cities such as Delhi, Chennai, Mumbai, Bangalore, and Hyderabad. Much of the population that lives in rural areas (accounting for more than 60% of the overall population) has limited access to good quality healthcare, which is one of the prime reasons that India as a country lags behind the rest of the world in this area. A recent WHO report indicates that India as a whole has only 1.5 beds, 1.2 doctors and 2.6 nurses per 1000 people. These numbers are far lower than those in the developed world. But the real problem lies in the acuteness of the situation facing the rural population. For example, the averages for some rural districts in India are as low as 0.2 hospital beds, 0.06 doctors, and 0.3 nurses per 1000 people. These statistics highlight the skewed development that India has witnessed in the last two decades. While all kinds of amenities (including healthcare) have improved by leaps and bounds in urban areas, rural families — often the poor — have been left behind. Why did this happen? How is India going to cope with this crisis? What are the upcoming changes on this front?

In Chapter 7, entitled "Healthcare Delivery Models and the Role of Telemedicine," Prof. Ravi Anupindi, Mike and Mary Hallman Fellow and Associate Professor at the Ross School of Business, University of Michigan, along with Prof. Madhuchanda Aundhe, T. A. Pai Management Institute at Bangalore and Prof. Mainak Sarkar, International Management Institute at New Delhi, focus on the inequity and inadequacy of India's healthcare infrastructure and the role that technology can play in ameliorating this situation. They describe the three main problems related to healthcare delivery in India: access, quality, and affordability for the rural population. These authors then focus on the use of IT for healthcare, often termed "telemedicine," describing the basic telemedicine architecture in terms of the hardware, communication, and service delivery outlets that successful telemedicine programs require. In the process, they describe five detailed cases and successful strategies adopted for the delivery model by Sankara Nethralaya and Aravind Eye Hospitals (ophthalmic care) Narayana Hrudayalaya (cardiovascular care) and Apollo Hospitals and Byrraju Foundation (comprehensive care). Finally, they conclude with a discussion of the major challenges facing this sector, including telecommunications connectivity, logistics, low utilization, payment schemes, and liability issues.

CHAPTER 7

HEALTHCARE DELIVERY MODELS AND THE ROLE OF TELEMEDICINE

Ravi Anupindi*, Madhuchhanda Das Aundhe[†]
and Mainak Sarkar[‡]

The last decade has seen dramatic improvements in India's economy. India's growth in the past four years (2002–2006) has averaged 8.6%, the fastest growth since the country's independence in 1947. More recently, India's economy grew 9.4% in 2007,[1] the fastest pace since 1989. Most of this growth has come from the liberal policies adopted by the government and triggered largely by the manufacturing and service sectors. The services sector constituted close to 62% of GDP in the fiscal year 2007 (FY07) and contributed to two-thirds of average real GDP growth for the period FY02 to FY07.[13] The most visible area of growth within the service sector was fueled by business services dominated by IT.[15] In fact, India has become the destination of choice for IT services: more than 50% of the Fortune 500 companies have outsourced software development to India.

Two major issues have been identified in regard to the sustainability of this growth rate. The first issue concerns the major bottlenecks in infrastructure, both physical (e.g., transportation and power) and social (e.g., education and health). Second is the issue that the growth achieved so far is heavily lopsided. It is safe to state that majority of the growth is coming from the manufacturing and services sector, which is primarily urban-oriented. Thus, the approximately 70% of India's population who live in rural areas are largely untouched by this phenomenon. Only recently, the government of India and leading thinkers have begun to embrace the idea of *inclusive growth* under the premise that India's past

---

*Stephen Ross School of Business, University of Michigan, Ann Arbor, Michigan, USA.
[†]T.A. Pai Management Institute, Bangalore, India.
[‡]International Management Institute, New Delhi, India.

achievements may not be sustainable unless it begins to include its vast majority living in rural areas.

There are several issues and challenges involved in inclusive growth. The focus of this chapter is on the health infrastructure in India, its inequity and inadequacy, and the role information and communication technology (ICT) can play in improving the healthcare delivery systems. It is rather well understood that health is one of the key components of human development. Empirical evidence, however, also shows it to be closely intertwined with other economic variables such as growth, productivity, and employment.[a] This is true across much of the world and in particular for developing countries. It has been established that better initial health status leads to faster economic growth rates.[6] In the Indian context, economic growth is correlated with health status, and the causality is bi-directional; furthermore, while economic growth reduces poverty, the impact is stronger when health status is better.[16] Finally, poor health is associated with large losses in labor productivity among working adults.[5] Given the crucial role played by health in the well-being of the population both directly and also via economic opportunities and outcomes, this chapter sets out to examine some of the challenges, achievements, and shortcomings in this sector with regard to India.

Access, quality, and affordability are the three main problems facing the healthcare sector in India. While India is the second most populous country in the world, there is a tremendous geographical dispersion of the population, especially in the rural areas, where the average population density is about 300 people per square kilometer. Consequently, while the country has a large public health infrastructure, it is not accessible to a large proportion of the population. The problem of access is further exacerbated by two factors: (a) the skewed nature of infrastructure, with more than 70% of the infrastructure (including healthcare personnel and hospital beds) located in urban areas and (b) the rampant understaffing and absenteeism in healthcare facilities in rural areas. The gap created by the lack of an adequate number of appropriately trained personnel is being filled by unqualified rural medical practitioners, resulting in significant quality degradation. To seek better quality healthcare, patients visit privately operated medical facilities, incurring huge expenses. The lack of any significant health insurance mechanism means that most health expenditures are an out-of-pocket expense, inflicting a huge burden on the poor. Evidence shows that health expenditure is the second largest cause of indebtedness in rural India.[12] Furthermore, out-of-pocket spending on healthcare drives over 20 million Indians below the poverty line every year.[11]

---

[a] Recent findings by the Commission on Macroeconomics and Health (CMH) (2001) set up under Prof. Jeffrey Sachs by the World Health Organization (WHO) (CMH, 2001).

The application of ICT to healthcare delivery holds great promise for ameliorating the issues of access, quality, and cost. ICT for healthcare is a very broad area and includes applications in clinical practice, health information systems, medical education, and technology for healthcare delivery and the dissemination of health information. In this chapter, we limit our attention to the role of technology in healthcare delivery. In particular, we focus on the role of *telemedicine*, which is the use of telecommunications technology to deliver healthcare services. Specifically, we consider the potential for using telemedicine to address the issues of access, quality, and cost in healthcare delivery. Our observations are based on field studies of five sites in India undertaken in 2006–2007 covering a broad spectrum of single- and multispecialty care as well as primary care. The sites include Sankara Nethralaya and Aravind Eye Hospitals (AEH) in ophthalmology, Narayana Hrudayala in cardiology, Apollo Hospitals in multispecialty care, and the Byrraju Foundation in primary health. Our study of telemedicine is not exhaustive; in fact, there are several notable and exciting projects in telemedicine being implemented by various organizations across the country. Significantly, the Indian Space Research Organization (ISRO) has played a pivotal role in the spread of telemedicine in India. Nevertheless, we hope that our study is a representative of the role of telemedicine in healthcare delivery in the Indian context.

In the following section, we outline the current healthcare infrastructure, briefly discuss some of the healthcare outcomes, and discuss the critical issues facing healthcare delivery. The next section introduces the concept of telemedicine and highlights how it can address some of the critical issues in healthcare delivery. Subsequently, we describe a basic telemedicine configuration and various delivery models, outline the structure of a telemedicine network for healthcare delivery, articulate the value proposition for various stakeholders, and conclude with challenges in implementation. These observations are drawn from our research as well as field studies. A brief description of each of the five case studies appears in the Appendix.

Historical Development

7.1. The State of Healthcare in India

India boasts a large public as well as private healthcare infrastructure. We begin with a description highlighting the state of the current public-private infrastructure, its usage, and the resulting healthcare outcomes, and conclude the section by highlighting the critical issues in healthcare delivery.

168 R. Anupindi et al.

7.1.1. *Healthcare Infrastructure*

India's vast multitiered public healthcare system is equipped, at least in theory, to handle a variety of medical conditions in ascending order of complexity. Primary healthcare is provided through a network of subcenters (SC), primary healthcare centers (PHC), community health centers (CHC), and district hospitals. These facilities are structured as per an administrative unit of the government. In rural areas, most primary healthcare is provided either by subcenters or primary health-care centers, whereas in urban areas it is provided via health posts and family welfare centers. Table 7.1 summarizes the organization and availability of the tiered public healthcare infrastructure in India.

A recent rural health service bulletin of the government of India put the number of beds in government hospitals (including CHCs) at 470,000, of which only 23.8% were in rural areas.[8] Further, based on the data collected by the National Family Health Survey II 1998–1999 (NFHS II), only 33% of rural residents (in terms of population coverage) had access to a subcenter, 28.3% to a clinic, 13% to a primary health center, and 9.6% to a hospital.

A significant shortage of qualified manpower in the health sector further exacerbates the problem. India has about 229 medical colleges, with an annual admission capacity of 25,600. A large majority of graduates, however, choose to

Table 7.1.   Public healthcare infrastructure in India[i]

Agglomeration	Village level	Block level	Sub-district[ii] level
Name of Facility	Subcenter (SC)	Primary health center (PHC)	Community health center (CHC)
Coverage	—	—	—
Population	5000	32,000	220,000
Avg. area (sq. km.)	21.35	134.2	931.95
Radial distance (km)	2.61	6.53	17.22
No. of villages	4	27	191
Facilities	1 trained male and female healthcare worker	Out-patient; 1–2 general practitioners	50–60 bed hospital offering curative services
Referral Unit		Up to 6 SCs	Up to 7 PHCs

[i] *Source*: Data from Bulletin of Rural Health Statistics in India (2006) and authors' analysis.
[ii] India has 28 states with a total of 593 districts. Average district size is 5340 sq. km., and average population per district is 1.73 million.

live and practice in urban areas. It is estimated that close to 75% of the nearly 1.1 million medical practitioners are located in urban areas. Consequently, the existing CHCs have a high shortfall of specialist manpower, such as obstetricians and gynecologists (56%), pediatricians (67%), surgeons (56%), and medical specialists (59%), and no provision of anesthesiologists. Furthermore, nearly 700 PHCs are without a doctor. The public health system in India faces a critical problem of staff shortage, especially in rural areas, as medical personnel in general do not want to locate to rural or remote areas. As a result, many posts in sub-centers and PHCs in rural areas remain vacant. For example, in 1996, as many as 4281 of the 29,699 sanctioned doctors' posts remained unfilled in rural health institutions.[19]

The urban concentration of qualified practitioners and facilities and the limited spread of the voluntary sector (non-governmental organizations [NGOs]) has given rise to unqualified rural medical practitioners (RMPs). It is estimated that there are about one million unqualified RMPs in India. They manage about 50–70% of primary consultations, mostly for minor illnesses, comprising the de facto primary curative healthcare system of rural India.[b] These unqualified RMPs offer convenience and lower (effective) costs by providing the service closer to the patient. This appears to be more important to their clientele than the fact that they are unqualified. This system has proliferated despite government attempts at licensing and regulation.

Public perception of government-provided health services, based on people's experiences with the system, is that of low quality. This leads to gross underutilization of free care. In general, Indians have come to depend more on the private sector for healthcare. The National Sample Survey Organization estimates that between 1986–1987 and 1995–1996 the utilization of government sources of treatment (including public hospitals, PHC/CHC, public dispensaries, Employee State Insurance [ESI] doctors, etc.) declined from 26% to 19% in rural India and from 28% to 20% in urban India.[25] For hospital-based treatment, the decline in utilization of government medical sources was from 59.7% to 43.8% in rural areas and from 60.3% to 43% in urban areas.

The state of the public health infrastructure is not surprising when one considers the meager financial resources devoted to health. India's public expenditures on health are a relatively low 1.0% of GDP, considerably below the average of 2.8% for low- and middle-income countries and the global average of 5.5%.[28] The government's fiscal effort, measured as the proportion of total government

---

[b] The overwhelming majority of them have some form of diploma in healthcare that allows them to prescribe medication for basic illnesses. They need to register with the government to be able to practice their trade; however, monitoring is virtually non-existent, and fraudulent behavior is rampant (Banerjee and Duflo, 2005).

expenditure on health, again identifies India as a low performer. In a global ranking of the shares of total public expenditures earmarked for health, only 12 countries in the world had lower proportions spent on health.[30] Overall, India spent about 5.2% of GDP on health, or about USD23 per capita in 2000, below the average of 5.6% for low- and middle-income countries.

Limited government spending, the liberalization of the health sector, and the overall significant economic growth that created a large middle class have spurred huge investments by the private sector in healthcare. These investments include multispecialty hospitals and secondary hospitals, as well as private clinics. The infrastructure, however, is largely concentrated in the urban areas. The larger, better-equipped hospitals have also tended to focus on providing specialized medical care for the middle- to upper-income segment of India's population and on supporting medical tourism for international patients.[c] Thus, the overall health infrastructure has become significantly skewed towards urban areas catering to urban populations. By 2001, the total number of hospital beds in India was about 810,000,[25] of which 32% belonged to corporate private hospitals. The remaining beds were at government hospitals and private clinics. A preliminary analysis reveals that 72% of all hospital beds are in urban areas, and consequently the population-to-bed ratio is about 520:1 in urban areas but only 5200:1 in rural areas.[d] While detailed data on occupancy rates of hospitals are not available, limited studies indicate that they are quite low, especially in public sector hospitals. For example, Nandraj and Duggal (1996) found occupancy rates of about 51% in their sample study of private hospitals in part of Maharashtra; Prahalad (2004) makes a similar observation for the ESI hospitals in that state.

7.1.2. Health Outcomes

Despite its myriad shortcomings, the healthcare sector in India has shown significant improvements in certain aspects. Life expectancy has increased from 49 years in 1970 to 63 years in 1998. Similarly, infant mortality has dropped from 146 deaths per 1000 births in the 1950s to only 70 per 1000 births in 1999, while the total fertility rate fell significantly from 6.0 in the 1960s to 3.3 in 1999. The progress, however, has been much slower in certain other areas, such as malnutrition.

---

[c] Furthermore, over the past few years, medical tourism has gained momentum. For example, in 2004, approximately 180,000 patients visited India for medical care, a significant growth over previous years. The medical tourism market in India is estimated to be a US$2 billion per year opportunity (Indian Healthcare).

[d] This assumes that the corporate private sector hospitals are in urban areas, that 70% of private clinics are also in urban areas, and that the urban population is 30%. For government beds, we use estimates from the 2006 rural health survey.

Although Indians no longer suffer from the waves of famine that marked earlier periods in the nation's history, recent surveys show that 47% of all children under three are underweight, down from 52% six years previously. In addition, nearly three-quarters of children are anemic, which has a significant impact on their cognitive development.[29] The average figures for India hide a great deal of variation in the performance of different states. Recent evidence shows that some states such as Kerala, Maharashtra, and Tamil Nadu are much further along in the health transition trajectory, whereas the densely populated states of Orissa, West Bengal, Bihar, Rajasthan, Madhya Pradesh, and Uttar Pradesh are still in the early part, with the other states falling in-between.[29]

India carries a large burden of the world's disease, as one would expect given its large population and high levels of poverty (Table 7.2). The country experiences a major portion of the world's child and maternal deaths, as well as a disproportionate amount of the disease burden due to tuberculosis, leprosy, and immunizable diseases. Thus, worldwide progress against these conditions will depend on India's achievements. Similarly, India needs to play a central role in preventing the further spread of the HIV/AIDS pandemic.

Another critical concern is equity in healthcare outcomes. Both the quantity and quality of healthcare provision varies widely across states, reflecting their widely varying levels of economic development, their health sector priorities, and their current and past investments in health. Similarly, there are wide variations in health outcomes across socioeconomic groups and also across rural and urban areas. Consider, for example, infant mortality. In 2002, infant mortality rate varied from a low of 14 per 1000 live births in the state of Kerala to 97 per 1000 live births in the state of Orissa. The rural infant mortality rate was 75 per 1000 live births in 2002, as compared to 44 per 1000 live births in urban areas.[22]

Table 7.2.   India's share of the world's health problems (percentage)[i]

Population	17
People living in poverty (<USD 1/day)	36
Total deaths	17
Child deaths	23
Maternal deaths	20
Disability-adjusted life years lost (DALY)	20
Childhood vaccine preventable deaths	26
Persons with HIV	14
Tuberculosis cases	30
Leprosy cases	68

[i] The World Bank, 2000.

7.1.3. *Critical Issues in Healthcare*

There are three major problems with the healthcare scenario in rural India, namely, the access to, quality of, and affordability of healthcare. The problems faced by the urban poor are similar, except that access to healthcare is less of an issue: public facilities tend to be overcrowded but are available to all. Despite concerted efforts by the government, the availability of healthcare at a reasonable proximity is unattainable for most villagers in India. What is available is also of questionable quality both in terms of infrastructure and the competence of the medical professionals concerned. While public healthcare is mostly free for patients, given its poor quality and lack of availability they typically have to go to private medical facilities, which charge market rates that can be significantly more expensive. To the extent that local facilities are inadequate to handle more complicated cases, patients may also need to travel to the nearest district hospital or nearby town, which entails a loss in earnings as well as transportation costs. This additional hurdle is a major reason that patients are often reluctant to seek medical care when sick.

The access issue is further exacerbated by high rates of absenteeism of healthcare workers in public health facilities. According to one study, absenteeism among doctors was as high as 43% and among other health workers 39% in government healthcare facilities across the Indian states.[9] A survey conducted in Udaipur in Rajasthan found greater absenteeism in PHCs and CHCs than in sub-centers.[3] Moreover, the absenteeism did not display any regularity with respect to the time of the day or day of the week. This meant that for people seeking healthcare services from these facilities, there was considerable uncertainty attached to a visit that was costly in terms of time and money: they would not be sure whether they would find the facility open, and, if open, whether they would find a medical professional there. Such uncertainty further attenuates people's incentives to make use of public health resources. Furthermore, as alluded to earlier, there is a serious shortage of manpower in terms of physicians, nurses, and midwives at the public facilities. Doctors have little incentive to locate in rural areas or work for the public healthcare system.

Quality of healthcare services is a complex variable, encompassing as it does such tangibles as the availability of drugs and equipment and such intangibles as the courtesy and respect shown to patients by providers during visits. In India, the quality of healthcare services provided by the public healthcare system is extremely low along almost all the criteria on which quality can be judged — infrastructure, availability of drugs and equipment, regular presence of qualified medical personnel, and treatment of patients. One of the major lacunae in India's health system is the lack of quality control. There is little public enforcement of appropriate standards of care in clinical practices. This is true for both the public sector and the private sector, which is largely unregulated. The Medical Council of India, the main body overseeing standards of care, has no process in place to assess doctors as to their competence with respect to current standards of care when they renew their registrations. While this is the overall situation, judging by where patients seek care, the hospitals in the private sector offer better quality than those in the public sector. Nationwide, the private sector accounts for 82% of all outpatient visits.[19] Further, studies conducted by the National Sample Survey of India shows the following reasons that patients seek the private sector for care: doctor more readily available (44%), dissatisfied with treatment in public sector (36%), medicines not available (7%). Distance and long waiting times were also quoted as reasons for poor use of public health facilities.[19]

With more than 80% of healthcare expenditure being financed privately, India has one of the highest levels of out-of-pocket expenditure for healthcare in the world. Moreover, it is the poor who suffer the most as a result, since they have to bear the double burden of poverty and ill health. With thin and/or missing health insurance markets, illness can result in chronic poverty as households bear the costs of illness by selling off productive assets or taking on debilitating loans (actions that finance about 40% of costs for all quintiles of income). Other sources of funds are current income or savings, which form a lower share of total expenditure on health for lower income quintiles, for obvious reasons. Only about 10% of Indians have some form of health insurance; these fortunate few are mostly employed in the formal sector and the government. One conservative estimate finds that one quarter of hospitalized Indians fall below the poverty line because of hospital expenses, with the risk varying greatly from state to state.[29] Even at public hospitals intended to protect the poor from financial risks, the poor are vulnerable to health costs. This is also a dominant reason for not seeking care, as seen in Table 7.3. We see that there is significant income-based variation in access to healthcare: the poor are 2.6 times more likely not to seek care when sick. Similarly, they are likely to be living in areas where adequate medical facilities do not exist, and they also are reluctant to seek medical care due to the costs involved. Furthermore, because the poor rely so widely on untrained health practitioners, the medical care they receive is of much lower quality.

In summary, the issues of access, quality, and affordability plague the healthcare system in India. Surmounting these challenges is essential to the attainment of the goal of inclusive growth, and yet the task is monumental. Quality of healthcare services is an issue of prime importance but also the hardest to solve. Various approaches have been undertaken across the world, such as monitoring (via cameras) to stop absenteeism and the provision of incentives (allowing doctors to charge market rates, to be reimbursed by the government), with only limited success. In addition, the government can partner with private healthcare providers to manage the public healthcare facilities, under what can be called public-private partnerships.

Table 7.3.   Percentage of Indians reporting an illness within last 15 days who did not seek care, and reasons for inaction, by poverty quintile, 1995–1996[i]

Reasons	Poorest quintile	Second quintile	Third quintile	Fourth quintile	Richest quintile	Total	Poorest to richest ratio
Did not seek care	24.3	20.9	16.1	17.8	9.2	16.7	2.6
Among those not seeking care:							
Illness not considered serious	42.4	52.2	54.7	57.3	59.8	52.7	0.7
Financial reasons	32.9	23.0	21.0	21.9	15.2	24.0	2.2
Medical facility not available in area	11.1	10.0	7.2	5.1	3.3	7.8	3.4
Other reasons	13.6	14.4	16.6	15.2	21.7	15.6	0.6

[i] World Bank Report, 2001.

The issue of affordability can be solved through some provision of community health insurance. Various initiatives across India, such as the Yeshaswini project in Karnataka and SEWA in Madhya Pradesh, have shown great promise in pooling risk for the rural poor, particularly for high-cost healthcare items such as hospitalization and surgery that can bankrupt poor households.

Finally, at first glance the issue of lack of access may signal inadequate infrastructure in terms of hospitals, beds, and personnel. According to an NCAER study, India needs to invest approximately INR250 billion (USD6.25 billion) every year to build 750 hospitals, each with a capacity of 250 beds, to meet the basic medical support recommended by the WHO. This goal is unattainable in the near future. At the same time, several studies point to the low utilization of facilities — both public and private — that are already available, albeit in urban areas. Several experiments in India and other countries are demonstrating that access to quality healthcare for the vast majority of underserved can be improved, if not solved, through the application of the latest ICT technology via what has come to be known as telemedicine. We take up the potential for telemedicine to make a dent in India's healthcare needs in more detail in the remainder of this chapter.

Current and Future Trends

7.2. ICT for Healthcare Delivery

7.2.1. *What is Telemedicine?*

At a very basic level, telemedicine is often defined as the use of audio/video telecommunication technology to deliver healthcare services. Under this characterization, telemedicine uses technology to effectively substitute for face-to-face encounters between a patient and a healthcare professional, thereby transcending geographical boundaries in the delivery of healthcare. To the extent that diagnosis does not involve touching and feeling a patient directly, telemedicine is a feasible proposition to bring high-quality care closer to the doorstep of the patient. The potential of telemedicine is, however, even greater than this. When viewed as an integrative network, it has a larger role to play as an "innovative system of care that can provide a variety of health and educational services to its clients unhindered by space and time".[4] Thus, not only does telemedicine aid in diagnosis of patients, but it can be effectively leveraged to provide continuing medical education to healthcare providers, patient education, and so on. Often the term "tele-health" is used to signify these broader applications of telemedicine.

The basic concept of telemedicine has been around for about 40 years. Early efforts in telemedicine were spearheaded by the NASA in the United States in the 1960s as humans began flying into space. One of the earliest endeavors was STARPAHC,[e] which delivered medical care to the Papago Indian Reservation in Arizona from 1972–1975. The project was designed by NASA in partnership with Lockheed and implemented by the Papago people with assistance from the Indian Health Service and the Department of Health, Education, and Welfare.[7] Since then, telemedicine programs have proliferated across the world. While no consolidated figures are available, several telemedicine projects have registered with the Telemedicine Information Exchange (TIE),[f] which maintains a database.

---

[e] Space Technology Applied to Rural Papago Advanced Healthcare.
[f] http://tie.telemed.org/.

Presently, there are about 213 telemedicine projects registered with TIE spread across North America (156 projects, 151 of which are in the United States), Europe (21), Australia and New Zealand (19), Asia (10), South America (4), and Africa (3). TIE, along with the Telemedicine Research Center, also conducts a bi-annual survey of telemedicine projects in the United States. Of course, this database only contains projects registered with TIE and therefore represents an underestimate of the extent of worldwide telemedicine activity.

The focus of this chapter is to explore the role of telemedicine in healthcare delivery in India. We limit our discussion to the role of telemedicine in diagnosis and consultation rather than its broader applications under telehealth. Since the basic premise of telemedicine is to break the distance barrier in delivering health-care, it can help bridge the gap between the service provider (doctor or hospital) located in cities and towns and the patient living in a remote village. To the extent that the more urban facility may have better qualified doctors, the quality of healthcare available to rural folks can improve significantly. Further, if through an appropriate screening mechanism only the most complicated cases are referred to the main hospital, other patients avoid the opportunity cost of seeking care (lost earnings as well as travel costs). Thus, improving access within the current healthcare infrastructure has the potential to partially improve both the quality of available services as well as reduce its cost burden on sections of the population thus increasing the consumption of healthcare.

7.2.2. Basic Telemedicine Configuration

A basic telemedicine set-up provides connectivity between an agent who wishes to obtain medical consulting services and the provider of these services. The former is called the Telemedicine Consult Center (TCC), and the latter is the Telemedicine Specialty Center (TSC). A TCC could be a kiosk, clinic, diagnostic center, or hospital. A TSC is usually a hospital with an appropriate specialty, typically at the secondary or tertiary care level. Figure 7.1 illustrates typical telemedicine connectivity between a TCC and a TSC.

The technology infrastructure of a TCC or TSC consists of certain choices regarding hardware, software, and connectivity. A minimal hardware configuration will consist of a computer, fax machine, printer, and scanner or digital camera. Beyond this basic configuration, equipment requirements will depend on the clinic's needs. For example, if a TCC wants to examine the eyes, they will need a high resolution camera. In general, a telemedicine set-up may require special clinical devices to be interfaced with the computing system. These include ultrasound scanners, a digital ECG, an X-ray digitizer, tiny cameras used in arthroscopic surgeries, special fundus cameras used in ophthalmology, and other imaging technologies. These devices facilitate the capture of diagnostic images

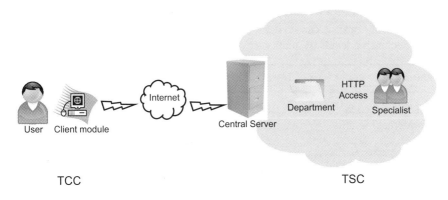

User   Client module

Central Server

Department   Specialist

HTTP Access

TCC   TSC

Fig. 7.1.   A typical telemedicine set-up.

in a digital format and allow for their storage, processing, compression, and efficient transport through a wired or wireless environment without loss of crucial information.

Finally, there are several options for video conferencing, depending on need and whether the clinic is a TCC or TSC. Figure 7.2 illustrates some video conferencing technology options. The choice among these alternatives will depend on the stream of medicine in question (e.g., ophthalmology requires greater clarity during real-time examination) and the investment decision. Video conferencing is the primary requirement for telemedicine, and this normally needs higher bandwidth connectivity for better quality of service. At the primary healthcare level, a low bandwidth of 128 kbps may provide adequate connectivity quality for normal video conferencing. However, the availability of higher bandwidth can enhance the quality of video conferencing.

Software for telemedicine should be capable of the capture, storage, display, and transmission of patient medical records consisting of text, images, and audio across a diverse set of platforms. Ideally, the software application package will support electronic medical records of patients created as part of the data acquisition process. It may also involve different types of files, including audio, video, graphics, and text. The typical data captured as part of the patient medical records are shown in Fig. 7.3.

There are four possible solutions for connectivity: ISDN,[g] broadband, VSAT,[h] or wireless. Figure 7.4 shows the various connectivity options.

---

[g] Integrated System Digital Network is a later telephony technology that is wholly digital and is used with a terminal adapter instead of a modem.
[h] Very Small Aperture Terminal.

The following options can be deployed at decreasing costs but with correspondingly decreasing levels of quality.

Option	Description	Bandwidth
Stand-alone video conferencing unit	A stand-alone box with a network interface and a camera, microphone, and display (usually a video monitor or TV). May share the same communication channel as the computer.	About 2 Mbps
PC add-on card with codec[i]	The card is plugged into the computer with appropriate software for configuration and control. An external CCD camera and a microphone are connected to the card provided, with video and audio input connectors.	Up to 768 kbps
Small camera with built-in encoder	The camera connects to the computer through a USB, requires software for configuration and control, and uses the desktop display.	Up to 512 kbps
Software-based desktop video conferencing	Uses a web camera and a microphone.	Up to 64 kbps

[i] A "code/decode" electrical device that converts an analog electrical signal into digital form for transmission purposes and then converts it back to analog at the other end.

Fig. 7.2.   Video conferencing technology options.

Depending upon the needs of the TCC, an appropriate connectivity platform can be chosen. These needs will depend on the nature of teleconsultation desired, as well as the mode of data transfer to be used for the teleconsultation. The type of consultation could range from a simple audio (telephone) consultation to video conferencing involving the transfer of a wide range of voice/data (including text, verbal commentary, and graphic and microscopic images) from a remote location to a specialist. In general, there are two modes of data transfer. The first is *real-time* (live) data transfer. This is often used for pathology, ECG, color doppler, endoscopy, and angiograms. The second type of data transfer is called

- PATIENT DEMOGRAPHICS such as name, patient ID, address, etc.
- PATIENT HISTORY such as past illnesses, present illnesses, treatment details, etc.
- Details of EXAMINATIONS, INVESTIGATIONS, and DIAGNOSES conducted so far, including general/physical examination and systemic examination (as relevant).
- ATTACHMENT OF AUDIO FILES. This allows the facility to both record and play and is in popular formats such as .mp3 or .wav.
- ATTACHMENT OF VIDEO/IMAGES. Images captured from various imaging sources — e.g., directly through medical equipment, scanned images, etc. These are either DICOM images or non-DICOM images.
- ATTACHMENT OF FILES (other than audio and video images) related to patient examination and history. These may be in various formats, such as Word, Excel, pdf, etc.
- REPORT(S) based on examinations.

Fig. 7.3. Patient medical record.

store and forward, typically used for X-rays, CT scans, ECG, MRI, etc. While high bandwidth connectivity becomes essential for real-time data transfer, it is not critical for a store-and-forward setting.

Beyond the hardware connectivity infrastructure, it is imperative that all communication adhere to any legal regulations and patient security laws and ensure patient confidentiality. Furthermore, the telemedicine set-up should use standard terms, procedures, and protocols within telemedicine. DICOM10[i] standards are used for exchange of clinical information and diagnostic data such as X-rays, CT scans, and ultrasounds between disparate telemedicine systems. HL7[j] is the recommended standard for messaging between telemedicine systems.

Telemedicine unit configuration costs can widely vary depending on the needs of the client, but they typically fall anywhere between INR[k] 300,000 and 3 million. There is no single standard model for a TCC; the technology set-up will

[i] DICOM (Digital Imaging and Communication In Medicine) is a standard for communications among medical imaging devices.
[j] HL7 (Health Level-7 Data Communications Protocol) defines standards for transmitting billing, hospital census, order entry, and other health-related information. These messages are used for interchanges between hospital and physician record systems and between electronic medical record (EMR) systems and practice management systems. HL7 Clinical Document Architecture (CDA) documents are used to communicate documents such as physician notes and other material.
[k] 1 USD = 44 INR.

	Option	Description	Bandwidth
Terrestrial	PSTN/ POTS[i]	Standard telephone line; dial-up modem needed to connect.	33.6 kbps–56 kbps
	ISDN[ii]	Set of protocols that allow higher bandwidth levels over standard telephone lines.	128 kbps
	Broadband	Higher speed connectivity achieved either over standard telephone lines (e.g., via DSL or cable modem) or fiber optics.	Greater than 1 Mbps
Wireless	VSAT	Connectivity through a satellite link; ideally suited for remote locations with no land line connectivity.	Depends on agreed-upon service level; up to 4 Mbps.
	Wi-Fi	Provides connectivity of devices to a local access point.	Depends on the bandwidth provided by the access point; maximum 54 Mbps.
	CDMA/GSM		Up to 2 Mbps

[i] Public Switched Telephone Network / Plain Old Telephone Service.
[ii] Integrated System Digital Network.

Fig. 7.4.   Telemedicine connectivity options.

be needs-based. Needs assessment should take into account disease demographics of the catchment area of a TCC, which will then determine the kind of equipment needed. For example, ECG equipment is only needed if one is treating or screening for cardiac cases. The second issue concerns the location of the TCC. In a small town, the range of medical expertise needed may be relatively limited. However, if a hospital in Hyderabad wants to connect to Chennai in order to do a bone marrow transplant, this hospital will need the technology to look at a pathology slide under a microscope. For a lower-level center, such equipment may be unnecessary.

Finally, protocols for service delivery need to be developed at both the TCC and TSC, but especially at the TCC. Protocols specify the various steps to be followed from patient entry at the TCC leading up to the consultation with the TSC, along with any follow-up action to be taken. Since the specialist at the TSC is not physically present with the patient, structured protocols promote a methodical approach to service provision. It also allows the staff to maintain and track telemedicine activities. Most of the sites we visited have developed structured protocols.

7.2.3. *Last Mile Delivery Models*

One of the issues crucial to the success of telemedicine in India is the reaching of the proverbial last mile. Broadly, there are two ways to achieve this. One is through a fixed infrastructure, in which a brick and mortar structure with the appropriate human, medical, and technological capability is set up as close to the needs of the population as possible. We call this the *fixed-node delivery model*. The other alternative is to have a mobile infrastructure in which the needs of the population are served by a mobile unit with the appropriate human, medical, and technological capability. We call this the *mobile delivery model*. Interestingly, healthcare delivery experiments using both models are being carried out today. We illustrate each of these below with examples.

7.2.3.1. *Fixed-node delivery model*

The fixed node can take two generic forms, differentiated primarily by whether or not the node that is initiating the consultation is a healthcare facility. *Internet kiosks* are facilities that offer Internet access with a primary focus on non-health services; health services can be part of the value proposition mix for such kiosks. In contrast, *clinics* — either general or specialty clinics — are primarily healthcare facilities; they employ a healthcare worker to mediate in the tele-consultation as appropriate.

7.2.3.1.1. Internet Kiosks

An Internet kiosk is a physical infrastructure set up to provide public Internet access, including e-mail and web browsing. The typical technology infrastructure will include a multimedia personal computer with power back-up, a printer, and Internet connectivity. Equipment to enable video conferencing could include a web camera, telephone connectivity, and video conferencing software. Some kiosks may also have Indian language software support. Kiosks can provide a variety of non-health related services, including e-governance applications, education, and entertainment.[l] To be able to provide health-related services, the kiosk needs to be part of a healthcare provider network that will provide the consultation. Two types of service can be provided through a kiosk, depending upon whether the service requires a live consultation. For services that do not require live consultation, patients send their documents to the healthcare provider via e-mail or browser-based software for diagnosis and consultation. The healthcare provider then responds with his or her opinion. Live consultation service can be arranged via the use of a web camera, video conferencing software, and telephone connectivity. When the kiosk is not staffed by a healthcare professional (as is usually the case), the interaction occurs directly between the patient and the remote healthcare consultant.

One of the earliest examples of the use of kiosks for healthcare services arose from the partnership between a rural service provider, n-Logue, and AEH at Madurai. n-Logue Communications Limited was established in 2000 with the support of the Telecommunications and Computer Networks Group (TeNet) at the Indian Institute of Technology, Madras, to offer connectivity solutions to rural India.[m] n-Logue offers kiosks in rural areas that provide simultaneous telephone and 35/70 kbps Internet connections. The connectivity is provided via a corDECT[n] wireless system. While the kiosk itself is owned by a local entrepreneur, n-Logue provides the connectivity backbone. Under this partnership, visitors to n-Logue kiosks can avail themselves of the ophthalmic care services of AEH. Rural patients visit the kiosk to obtain a preliminary diagnosis of their eye condition through remote consultation; if it is deemed that further treatment is required, they are directed to the nearest Aravind hospital or to a free eye camp. Each kiosk serves approximately 800 people. At present, there is no fee charged for the consultation. However, the user pays the kiosk operator for the connectivity time.

The Byrraju Foundation operates in the eastern and western Godavari districts of Andhra Pradesh. Healthcare is one of its focus areas. Primary healthcare is delivered through several rural health centers (RHC), each of which has a resident auxiliary nurse midwife (ANM) practitioner. She assists a medical doctor who visits a RHC daily for a 2-hour period. In addition to the

---

[l] See the ITC e-choupal case study in Chapter 5 of this volume for an example of the use of kiosks in agri-business.

[m] Also see http://www.n-logue.com/ (accessed on May 15, 2007).

[n] corDECT is an advanced wireless system developed by Midas Communication Technologies and IIT, Madras, in association with Analog Devices, USA.

RHCs, the foundation has several Ashwini centers equipped with information and communication technology. The Ashwini centers are connected to the Alluri Sita Ramaraju Academy of Medical Sciences (ASRAM), a medical school located in Eluru, in order to provide specialist consultation with cardiologists, gynecologists, and pediatricians. The consultations are provided on a scheduled basis; that is, doctors from the medical college make themselves available for a few hours on certain days of the week. Each village within the catchment area of an Ashwini center is scheduled for a specific day. Patients needing teleconsultation with a specialist are bused to the Ashwini center by the Foundation. The interaction between the patient and the specialist is mediated by the ANM at the Ashwini center. Consultations are presently offered free of charge.

The delivery of healthcare services through kiosks poses a few challenges. Often, the connectivity provided is of low bandwidth, affecting the quality of images transmitted and making diagnosis difficult. Further, without a healthcare professional to mediate the conversation between the specialist and the patient, there is significant hesitation in the use of these facilities, especially in rural areas. The Ashwini centers of the Byrraju Foundation are an exception here: the consultation at the TCC is mediated by the ANM and appropriate guidance is given. Regardless, kiosk-based consultations presently function primarily as screening mechanisms to determine whether a patient needs to visit the specialist at the remote hospital. Another challenge faced is that remote specialists are often unable to provide reasonable diagnoses in the absence of measurable basic physiological parameters. A number of telemedicine solutions companies[o] have developed a low-cost remote diagnostic kit to measure four primary parameters, namely, temperature, blood pressure, ECG, and heartbeat (via stethoscope) for teleconsultation. n-Logue proposes to deploy this kit in select locations to facilitate remote telemedicine services.[23] It is, however, unclear whether rural customers will be able to use these diagnostic kits themselves without assistance from a healthcare provider at the TCC.

7.2.3.1.2. Clinics

Another example of the fixed-node delivery model is a clinic. Unlike the kiosk, a clinic is a healthcare facility providing either general primary healthcare or specialty care. Examples of such clinics include primary healthcare clinics (typically with a trained nurse or a general practitioner) or specialty clinics such as vision centers providing eye screening and corrective lens services or coronary care units for cardiac services. While several such primary and specialty facilities

---

[o] For example, Neurosynaptic Communications Pvt. Ltd., Bangalore, India.

Screened by paramedic at Vision Center	Wireless connectivity @ 4 Mbps	Consultation by Ophthalmologist at AEH, Theni

Fig. 7.5.   Teleophthalmology from a vision center, AEH.

exist throughout the country, they function as a node in the telemedicine network only when they are connected to a secondary or tertiary care hospital for remote diagnosis and consultation.

Aravind Eye Hospitals started setting up remote vision centers to provide basic ophthalmic services closer to the patient population. After an examination is performed by a well-trained ophthalmic assistant, as necessary, a remote consultation is initiated to a base hospital. Figure 7.5 shows patients who are being examined at a vision center discussing their case with the ophthalmologist at AEH, Theni, via video conferencing. Typically, the technological infrastructure is of higher quality, facilitating better image capture and higher-quality connectivity. The connectivity technology for the vision centers is provided by the TIER group of the University of California, Berkeley, and Intel Corporation; the bandwidth provided is about 4 Mbps for up to a distance of 50 miles (line of sight) using wireless antennas.[p] The vision center itself is meant to be self-sustaining, through revenue generated by the dispensing of corrective lenses to incoming patients.

Apollo Hospitals has started setting up primary healthcare clinics, called Apollo Clinics, in urban areas. These clinics are staffed by medical doctors who attend to the basic health needs of the patients. They can also be telenetworked to a secondary/tertiary care hospital for specialist services. Presently, Apollo has about 54 clinics, with plans to grow to 250 clinics. The company has recently partnered with ITC Limited to provide health services through their e-choupal[q] network. Under this scenario, Apollo will provide primary healthcare services at the Choupal Sagar hubs of ITC, and these clinics will also be connected to secondary and tertiary care hospitals within the Apollo network.[r]

[p] http://tier.cs.berkeley.edu/wiki/Aravind (Accessed on May 15, 2007).
[q] ITC's e-choupal initiative is discussed in Chapter 5 of this volume.
[r] Recently, ITC has initiated similar pilot programs with the CARE Hospitals group.

Typically, these clinics cater to a larger population (e.g., a typical Aravind vision center serves a population of 35,000–50,000) and tend to be located a little farther away from remote areas requiring the rural population to travel for care. However, the travel for the patient is still shorter compared to visiting a tertiary care center in a metropolitan city. Furthermore, the larger geographic aggregations that such centers are designed to serve make it viable to invest in more sophisticated equipment, which facilitates better teleconsultations for specialty services. For the tertiary care provider, a fraction of the investment needed for a full-fledged hospital allows these centers to provide outpatient care as well as acting as demand generation points. Since these centers are staffed by a healthcare professional, teleconsultation with the specialist is more productive.

7.2.3.2 *Mobile delivery model*

Historically, healthcare camps have been used by all health providers as a means to reach out to the rural population in remote locations. In a healthcare camp, a health service provider, typically a hospital, collaborates with an NGO working in the area to organize a temporary camp to provide health services to the surrounding populations. These camps require that healthcare professionals travel to the remote site with their staff and equipment. Camps differ in terms of services offered, which range from screening and diagnostics to on-site surgery. The services are usually provided at a public facility such as a school or a community center. Often a fully-equipped mobile unit is used for the delivery of services. Under this model, the range of services delivered is limited by the expertise of the healthcare providers available at the camp site.

A mobile unit equipped with teleconnectivity is able to deliver telemedicine by connecting to a specialist in a tertiary hospital. This potentially reduces the need for specialists to travel to remote locations. The on-site healthcare provider operating the mobile unit can, as needed, connect to a remote specialist and provide a wide variety of services to the target population. Figure 7.6 illustrates one such mobile telemedicine unit.

Among the case study sites we have researched, mobile telemedicine has been widely practiced by both Sankara Nethralaya (SN) and AEH in the field of ophthalmology. Their vans are typically used for comprehensive eye examinations and eye screening camps, including screening for diabetic retinopathy. The van of the health provider travels to remote places and takes fundus images of known diabetic patients. The patients' digital case sheets are then sent from the mobile terminal via special software to the reading and grading center and on to a hospital. At the hospital, all the digital images and information are graded and an opinion is relayed back to the mobile terminal in the van, with real-time consultation carried out if necessary.

Fig. 7.6. A mobile teleophthalmology unit (Sankara Nethralaya).

In the experimental period, these mobile units needed the capabilities of both healthcare and connectivity. The resulting mobile unit was a large vehicle that was difficult to navigate in rural areas. In addition, the connectivity equipment set-up was often non-trivial, with considerable need for technical assistance. Furthermore, these mobile units were primarily used for screening and had little independent value as a viable business proposition. Given the increasing proliferation of Internet kiosks, aided by a big thrust by the Indian government,[s] several rural areas will soon have Internet connectivity. This has allowed SN to experiment with mobile units that are equipped with only medical capability with connectivity provided by partnering with the kiosks. The newer vans are smaller, require less investment, and are more easily navigable in rural areas. Under this arrangement, the SN van will conduct the medical camp in the vicinity of the kiosks and use their connectivity as needed during the camp. Another innovation seeks to make the mobile unit self-sustainable. By equipping the van with a refractive lens-making unit that can dispense corrective glasses to the patients, SN created a continuing source of revenue. The funds generated through the sale of these lenses will allow the company to

---

[s] Under the National e-Governance Project (NeGP), the government plans to roll out 100,000 common service centers (CSC), which are Internet kiosks designed to deliver various services to remote rural areas. The teleconnectivity for these centers is to be provided by the ISRO.

recoup its investments in the van as well as to cover the daily operating costs of conducting the camps.

7.2.4. *Telemedicine Network*

In the previous sections, we have described a basic two-way telemedicine configuration including hardware, software, and connectivity options as well as the various delivery modes (fixed and mobile) for a TCC. This basic two-way configuration can be expanded to cover a larger healthcare network. The healthcare infrastructure (see Section 7.2) is really a healthcare network catering to the health needs of the population at different levels of sophistication. Each of these healthcare provider levels can be linked using telecommunications to form a telemedicine network. We suggest the following classification for the various layers of the telemedicine network, adapted from the recommendations of the Ministry of Communication and Information Technology:[26]

(1) **Kiosk telemedicine center (KTC)**: A KTC is simply an Internet kiosk[t] with at least the minimal infrastructure to act as a TCC, allowing a patient to connect to higher levels in the network to seek consultation. A KTC has the potential to serve populations of 5000–6000.

(2) **Mobile telemedicine center (MTC)**: An MTC is a mobile van equipped with teleconnectivity and the capability to deliver health services. While stationed at a given location, the population coverage will likely be at the same level as a KTC. However, an MTC moves from location to location. The total population coverage of an MTC can thus vary depending on the distance the unit covers, which in turn depends on the frequency of services provided at a given location.[u]

(3) **Primary telemedicine center (PTC)**: A PTC is usually a primary health center or a clinic staffed by a trained healthcare professional that can connect to higher levels in the network to seek consultation. The telemedicine sessions are mediated by the healthcare professional at the PTC. In the context of rural India, a PTC could be located in a primary health center catering to an approximate population of 30,000.

(4) **Secondary telemedicine center (STC)**: An STC will be most likely a 100–250 bed hospital located at district headquarters and staffed by several healthcare professionals. Several PTCs can be connected to an STC. An STC

---

[t] A kiosk may offer several services other than health.

[u] Emergency management services can be delivered through ambulances equipped with teleconnectivity, which can also be considered mobile telemedicine units.

should be able to handle most of the medical service needs of a PTC, including specialty services such as neurology, oncology, cardiac surgery, etc. The population coverage of an STC would be similar to that of a district hospital, ranging from 100,000 to two million.

(5) **Tertiary telemedicine center (TTC)**: A TTC is located at a specialty hospital. A TTC could be a single-specialty hospital, e.g., an eye or cardiac care hospital, or a multispecialty hospital located in an urban center that offers specialties such as ophthalmology, neurology, cardiology, and oncology, among others. A number of STCs would be connected to a TTC. Typically, a tertiary care hospital is located in a large metropolitan area; increasingly, however, we see that such centers are being opened in the Tier II cities.

Table 7.4 gives some examples of the modes of telemedicine delivery in primary and specialty healthcare.

Since KTC and MTC both function at the same geographic aggregation levels, we essentially have a telemedicine network with four layers. While the above descriptions appear to indicate a hierarchy in connectivity from KTC or MTC to PTC to STC to TTC, this is not necessarily the case. In theory, any lower-level node can function as a TCC (clinic initiating the consultation) and any higher-level node can function as a TSC (clinic providing the consultation). So, for example, a KTC or MTC could connect to a STC/TTC, or a PTC to a TTC. However, more often than not we will see the following configurations: KTC/MTC/PTC to STC, or TTC/STC to TTC. Figure 7.7 depicts a telemedicine network.

Healthcare delivery through a telemedicine network requires a web of partnerships between private parties, public institutions, NGOs, and charitable organizations. As mentioned before, healthcare infrastructure is spread across public and private (i.e., for-profit and not-for-profit) entities. These hospitals should be co-ordinated as part of a telemedicine network at all levels, from primary to

Table 7.4.   Modes of telemedicine delivery

	KTC	PTC	MTC
Primary care	Byrraju–Ashwini Center	Apollo	
Specialty care	AEH	Apollo, AEH, Narayana Hrudayalaya	Sankara Nethralaya, AEH

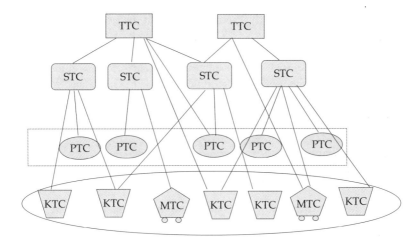

Fig. 7.7. A representative telemedicine network.

secondary to tertiary care. For example, Narayana Hrudayalaya (NH) has part-nered with state governments to set up coronary care units (CCUs) at the (public) district hospitals that are telelinked back to NH. Connectivity is one of the biggest challenges in facilitating telemedicine. The government can play a major role in providing the necessary telecommunications network infrastruc-ture, especially in remote areas. In fact, the ISRO has already helped to pro-vide satellite connectivity to several telemedicine projects, including both connectivity between hospitals and connectivity between kiosks/mobile units and a hospital. Under the recently launched National e-Governance project, the government plans to set up 100,000 kiosks called Common Service Centers. However, with the private telecommunications network spreading quickly, connectivity may be a moot issue except for the most remote areas. Beyond connectivity infrastructure, the government can also play an important role in encouraging telemedicine either by providing subsidized health insur-ance schemes for users or by funding the telemedicine activities of the various healthcare institutions.

NGOs and charitable organizations can help in two ways. First, they can encourage active participation in a telemedicine network by connecting their hos-pitals to the network. Secondly, given the high cost of healthcare, charitable organizations can step in to provide treatment to patients who cannot afford it. At several of the sites we studied, telemedicine referrals leading to surgeries have been provided free of charge by the specialist hospitals largely because charita-ble organizations have offered to pay for the procedures. NGOs can also spread health awareness and increase the availability of telemedicine through camps conducted in rural areas. Finally, private parties that are non-healthcare institutions can play an important role as a platform provider. Today several private initiatives are using ICT to deliver a range of services in rural and urban areas. Notable among these is ITC Limited's e-choupal initiative.[2] These companies can partner with healthcare providers to set up primary care clinics and deliver specialist services through telemedicine, expanding the service value proposition to their clientele. Ultimately, however, there must be a clear value proposition not only for the healthcare consumer, but also for each of these partners.

7.2.5. *Stakeholders and Value Proposition*

In the delivery of telemedicine, one can clearly identify three key stakeholders. First and foremost is the *client* or the *patient*. Next is the *provider*, of which there are two types. The first is the *healthcare provider* at various levels in the telemedicine network. In addition, there is the *platform provider*, who owns and/or operates the telecommunications network that carries the telemedicine services. The platform provider can be an entrepreneur operating a kiosk, or a large organization (public or private, for-profit or not-for-profit) that offers the appropriate technology for delivering telemedicine. These platform providers usually partner with one or more healthcare providers to deliver health services through their network. A healthcare provider, in contrast, can develop its own infrastructure to deploy telemedicine or partner with a platform provider, or both. In the case studies we have researched, healthcare providers include Sankara Nethralaya, Apollo Hospitals, AEH, and Narayana Hrudayalaya; platform providers include n-Logue, Dhristi Foundation, M. S. Swaminathan Research Foundation, ITC e-choupal, and the National e-Governance Project (NeGP). Finally, the third stakeholder is the *society at large*.

While clients are concerned about out-of-pocket expenses and quality of care, in the introductory stages, healthcare providers might consider telemedicine as a form of corporate social responsibility and not concern themselves with return on investment (ROI). In this case, the providers' goals are in alignment with societal concerns, which include equitable distribution of health resources, improved access to healthcare, and decreased total cost. This view, however, is inadequate to support the widespread adoption of telemedicine. For telemedicine to be successfully implemented on a wide scale, providers must ultimately be concerned about revenue generation and ROI.

The value proposition for the client needs to be evaluated along the dimensions of *access*, *cost*, and *quality*. With telemedicine, the patient, especially one in a rural area, benefits along all three of these dimensions. Healthcare is now available closer to the patient's doorstep, thus improving access. Since the patient can avoid traveling to the distant healthcare provider unless absolutely necessary, there is significant cost savings in terms of travel costs[v] for the person and at least one family member in terms of lost wages, board, and lodging while visiting the distant hospital. Cost is indeed a big factor in healthcare consumption, especially in rural India and telemedicine, with its potential to significantly bring down the cost of care, can relieve a severe financial burden for the rural poor. Finally, we argue that the overall quality of care also improves. Quality must be evaluated along the two dimensions of clinical and health services, where the potential outcomes of the current system (without telemedicine) and the proposed system with telemedicine should be compared for all cases. In the current system we observe the following types of outcomes:

(1) Patients get care from a local source, often of questionable quality.
(2) Patients seek care from a quality healthcare provider at a distance. Often this entails a significant cost burden due to non-medical expenses.
(3) Patients forgo care, either due to the poor quality of care available locally or due to financial constraints preventing the patient from seeking higher-quality care at a distance.

Let us see how telemedicine has the potential to address each of these issues. Telemedicine provides a higher quality healthcare alternative by bringing a better qualified professional service (albeit remotely) to the patient. With the option of utilizing telemedicine at a reasonable cost, the cost burden is reduced. This is particularly significant when the trip to the distant healthcare facility is deemed unnecessary. Then, given the more convenient access and more reasonable cost, patients may decide to avail themselves of health services instead of forgoing care. Finally, the availability of a lower-cost, higher-quality option allows clients to take advantage of health services in a timely fashion, reducing the chances that a health situation will reach a critical stage requiring urgent care at a distant facility. Thus, it is clear that the quality of healthcare improves significantly with telemedicine. There is sufficient research now to suggest that, clinically, little is sacrificed in the delivery of care through this medium.[4]

To consider the value proposition from the perspective of the healthcare provider, we need to consider both the specialty center providing the consultation (TSC), and the consult center (TCC) when TCC is also a health center. Telemedicine can be a very important tool for demand management by a TSC. Demand for healthcare is affected by various factors, primary among these being cost, quality, and distance. Telemedicine allows a firm to break the distance barrier and thus enables a TSC provider to increase its demand through the referral service. Overall increase in volume will allow the provider to bring down the cost

---

[v] These could be significant, as often at least one additional family member travels with the client, with associated costs for board and lodging.

of care through better utilization of its infrastructure. This is particularly the case when certain areas of the specialty are very capital-intensive and sufficient volume is essential to keep the cost of healthcare at a reasonable level. Furthermore, by expanding its geographical reach, the specialty provider gets access to a more diverse set of clinical cases, enriching the experience of healthcare personnel and allowing them to build further expertise. There are indirect benefits to a TSC as well. In the present context in India, patients often show up at a specialty center and after a brief examination it is determined that the travel was unnecessary. Such cases are today overcrowding the specialty centers. By utilizing telemedicine, the TSC will be able to screen out these unnecessary cases, thus relieving capacity and allowing the TSC to focus its assets on the cases in which care is most needed. In this role, telemedicine is an effective triage tool. Finally, once a patient receives care at the specialty center, hospitals need to effectively manage their average length of stay (ALOS). Consider the case in which the TSC is a tertiary care hospital and the TCC is a secondary hospital. Instead of having a patient stay at the tertiary care hospital during the entire post-care period, it is possible to move the patient to the secondary hospital after a few days, with the remainder of the recovery period managed by the TCC hospital in teleconsultation with the TSC. Such an arrangement would improve the effective utilization of scarce tertiary care hospital beds as well as providing greater volume to the secondary care hospital.

For the healthcare provider acting as a TCC (whether it is a secondary hospital or a primary clinic), reliance on the expertise of the TSC is a double-edged sword. On one hand, it allows them to increase the quality of care they can deliver to their local population. In certain cases, this may even be a matter of saving lives: in cardiac care, for example, timely intervention is critical. With teleconnectivity, even a local general practitioner, guided by a remote cardiologist, can help save lives. The telecardiology network of Narayana Hrudayalaya, which has telelinks to cardiac care units located at district hospitals, exemplifies this. On the other hand, TCCs may fear of losing their client base to the specialty provider if the consultations create a perception that the local healthcare provider is incompetent. Of course, in life-threatening cases this is a non-issue, as timely intervention is critical and the patient might not survive the travel. In other cases, however, we believe that this fear is unfounded, since a client, when making healthcare decisions, has to weigh the utility of additional travel inconvenience and costs in choosing between the remote vs. the specialty location for *all* types of care. In fact, connectivity with a specialty hospital should allow the TCC hospital to expand the types of clinical specialties it can attend to and thus enhance its reputation. Furthermore, regular consultations will enable the TCC to upgrade its skill set. Finally, a TSC may shift patients back to the TCC in order to better manage its ALOS, and this would be a source of revenue for the TCC hospital.

A TCC can also be managed by a platform provider. This is usually the case when the TCC is a kiosk. As mentioned earlier, a kiosk delivers a variety of services, including some that are health-related. Typically, the TCCs charge healthcare patients only for the connectivity. Thus, the greater the variety of services a kiosk can offer, the higher its revenue stream will be.

The value of telemedicine to society is obvious. The network allows more equitable access to healthcare at a reasonable cost and higher quality. Widespread use of telemedicine also has the potential to fundamentally restructure how healthcare is delivered. The first issue is resource positioning in a country like India, where 70% of the population lives in rural areas. It is difficult to position specialty services in these areas, and perhaps unnecessary, too, because telemedicine allows a society to bring specialty services to the remote corners of the country. Since the infrastructure required at the TCC is minimal, access to healthcare increases dramatically with lower investments. The experience of the Byrraju Foundation demonstrates that with some basic ICT and an ANM, it is possible to bring specialty services to rural areas. In the area of more sophisticated care (e.g., cardiology), the experience of Narayana Hrudayalaya shows how the delivery of cardiac services can be reengineered into two sets of components — one that requires a trained cardiologist and another that requires emergency medical intervention that can be carried out by a general practitioner. The first set of activities, including diagnosis and surgery, can then be concentrated at the tertiary care center, while the second set of activities can be administered under guidance at the remote location, closer to the population.[24] This reorganized system has the potential to reduce the overall cost of healthcare through better utilization of scarce resources and the provision of appropriate and timely care at the doorstep of the patient.

7.2.6. *Challenges*

Despite the tremendous interest in and expansion of telemedicine activity in India today, a number of challenges remain. These include:

(1) *Connectivity*: In spite of the expansion of telecommunications in India, connectivity is cited as the biggest problem for telemedicine. This is especially true in regard to the connection of remote rural areas to the network. While ISDN/VSAT connectivity is being made available, the quality and reliability of the communication is often not very good.

(2) *Logistics*: Typically, a specialist hospital locates its entire telemedicine infrastructure in one room, primarily due to concerns about cost. This, however, means that specialists must leave their offices and travel to the telemedicine room to do teleconsultations. The need to physically move to a different location is an interruption in the doctors' routines and creates a barrier to the acceptance of telemedicine. Ideally, if the doctors could do teleconsultation from their offices, then it could become part of their routine. Some of the providers are exploring the use of desktop conferencing systems to address the issue.

(3) *Low utilization*: The utilization of the current telemedicine infrastructure at TSCs is abysmally low and highly variable. For example, on a typical day in one of the hospitals we studied, the number of daily consultations ranged between 2 and 25. However, as the telemedicine network expands, it is expected that TSCs will be able to increase their level of utilization.

(4) *Fees and payment*: There are two aspects of the fee structure. The first involves fees for a specialist. Typically, this is determined by the TSC hospital (network), but until now, this has been heavily subsidized, as most of the telemedicine consultations are with patients in remote rural areas where there is little ability to pay. The charges to the patient are determined by the TCC. At Apollo Hospital, Aragonda, for example, there is no charge. Under the kiosk model, however, the kiosk operator may charge either a flat fee or a fee based on the usage time of the equipment/infrastructure. In rural areas, again there is very little ability to pay for these services, mostly due to the lack of any form of health insurance. Thus, the adoption and spread of telemedicine will be closely linked to the availability and adoption of health insurance. Presently, the unrecoverable costs of most telemedicine activity have been a hindrance to its spread. If and when effective health insurance takes hold in India, it will provide a strong impetus to the various healthcare providers to expand their use of telemedicine.

(5) *Cultural issues*: While some specialists are enthusiastic about telemedicine and its potential, there remain some who are uncomfortable diagnosing and treating a patient remotely. These doctors still prefer to see patients in person.

(6) *Liability issues*: There is fear among some healthcare workers about medical liability issues related to telemedicine. Therefore, many doctors are unwilling to give an opinion without physically examining the patient. Doctors have to diagnose and recommend treatment based on facts that the patient reveals. So without seeing patients in person, the doctor may not be fully aware of all of their conditions. In a face-to-face encounter, a doctor can pick up other cues — body language, facial expressions, etc. — and it is harder

for patients to willfully and deliberately conceal things. To provide some protection against such deception, the conversations in a teleconsultation may need to be recorded. It is unclear, however, exactly how important the legal liability issue really is, because the risks of telemedicine are also tied to compensation. While similar risks exist for in-person consultations as well, at least doctors are appropriately compensated. Given the appropriate incentives, then, doctors may be willing to take on greater risk for some event that may be of low probability. In a similar fashion, appropriate compensation for telemedicine services may partially offset the potential risk of liability.

7.3. Conclusion

India has demonstrated tremendous economic growth in the past decade. Sustaining this growth rate into the future will require addressing both hard and soft infrastructure bottlenecks. It is well known that health is one of the key components of development, and it is closely intertwined with economic progress. India, unfortunately, has lagged behind in delivering effective healthcare to the masses. While the public infrastructure is large, it has not been effective in servicing the health needs of the population. Government spending as a fraction of GDP lags behind even several low-income countries. Simultaneously, increased demand and a demographic shift from infectious to lifestyle diseases have led to increasing and robust private-sector activity in healthcare. The overall health infrastructure, however, remains significantly skewed towards urban areas even though a large majority of the population still resides in the rural heartland. The poor quality of the public healthcare is forcing more citizens to seek private care at higher cost. Access, quality, and affordability have become the three main issues facing India's healthcare sector.

Advances in medical technology and significant developments in the telecommunications infrastructure have opened the possibility of leveraging information and communication technology, via telemedicine, to improve healthcare delivery in India. In this chapter, we have used five case studies to articulate the potential of telemedicine to improve delivery of healthcare in specialty and primary care. Telemedicine, or broadly ICT, can be exploited to fundamentally alter the process of healthcare delivery through unbundling diagnosis and (critical) care, allowing for more effective patient triage and — when matched with appropriate resources based on skills — reducing the cost of care. Obviously, at this nascent stage of adoption there exist some challenges, which range from connectivity and logistics to payment and legal issues. Healthcare delivery through a telemedicine network will require a web of partnerships among private parties, public institutions, NGOs, and charitable organizations. While telemedicine has been shown to be quite effective clinically, it is crucial to identify all the stakeholders and articulate a clear value proposition for each, which should be rigorously evaluated. Such an articulation will enable the various parties to focus on the role that each might play in the network and how they can derive value, leading to a much wider adoption of telemedicine. Without this, telemedicine cannot become a mainstream healthcare delivery mechanism.

There is room for tremendous growth in telemedicine. A USD10 billion industry globally, it is a key consumer of broadband in countries that have been able to offer the bandwidth. But in India, at an industry size of USD50 million, it has yet to reach the masses. According to a FICCI study, the Indian telemedicine business has a market potential of USD500 million.[14]

Telemedicine is not a panacea for the healthcare delivery problems of India. Significant infrastructure investment is needed at all levels — primary, secondary, and tertiary — to improve the overall quality of healthcare. The key challenge will be to orient the infrastructure towards primary health in rural areas. Appropriate healthcare professionals are required, including rural health workers in the villages, general practitioners in primary clinics close by, and doctors and specialists in secondary and tertiary care hospitals. The existing government infrastructure can be better managed through public-private partnerships that could be deployed to facilitate the interaction of telemedicine across these levels.

While we have focused on the potential of telemedicine for the clinical delivery of diagnosis and care, in its broader manifestation, known as telehealth, it can be leveraged to increase collegial support to medical personnel working in remote areas and provide improved teaching and learning opportunities, leading to increased job satisfaction.

Acknowledgments

We would like to thank Prof. C. K. Prahalad for introducing us to the topic of telemedicine at a bootcamp organized by the Ross School of Business's Center for Global Resource Leverage: India in December 2005. There are many people who have assisted our understanding of telemedicine as it is practiced in India. We would particularly like to thank Ms. Sangita Reddy, Dr. K. Ganapathy, Dr. Vilvanathan, Mr. Ashvani Srivastava, and Ms. Sangita Durbha of Apollo Hospitals; Dr. Aravind Srinivasan, Dr. R. D. Thulasiraj, Dr. R. Kim, and Ms. Sashi Priya of AEH; Dr. Rama Raju, Dr. Sudhakar, Dr. Akshay, Dr. Ratna Devi, and Mr. Verghese Jacob of the Byrraju Foundation; Dr. Devi Shetty, Dr. Bommiah, and Dr. Vijay Singh of Narayana Hrudayalaya; and Dr. S. S. Badrinath and Mr. V. Murali of Sankara Nethralaya.

References

1. Agencies (2007). What's fueling India's growth story? *Economic Times Online* [Retrieved 10 June 2007].
2. Anupindi, R and S Sivakumar (2006). ITC's e-Choupal: a platform strategy for rural transformation. In *Business Approaches for Helping the World's Poor: Solutions that Create Social and Economic Value*, Barton, B, H Gustavo, J Quelch and K Rangan, CA, USA: Jossey-Bass, December 2006, pp. 173–182.
3. Banerjee, A and E Duflo (2005). Improving healthcare delivery in India, mimeo, MIT: Department of Economics.
4. Bashshur, RL (1997). Telemedicine and the healthcare system. In *Telemedicine — Theory and Practice*, Bashshur, S *et al.* (eds.), Springfield, IL: Charles C. Thomas Publisher Ltd, pp. 5–35.
5. Behrman, JR and AB Deolalikar (1988). Health and nutrition. In *Handbook of Development Economics Volume 1*, Chenery, H and TN Srinivasan (eds), Amsterdam: Elsevier Science Publishers, pp. 633–704.
6. Bloom, DE, D Canning and DT Jamison (2004). Health, wealth and welfare. *Finance and Development*, 41(1), 10–15.
7. Brown, N (1995, May 30). A brief history of telemedicine, *Telemedicine Information Exchange*. http://tie.telemed.org/articles/article.asp?path=articles&article=tmhistory_nb_tie95.xml [Retrieved 15 December 2007].
8. Bulletin of Rural Health Statistics in India (2006). Ministry of Health and Family Welfare, Government of India.
9. Chaudhury, N and J Hammer (2003). *Ghost Doctors: Absenteeism in Bangladeshi Health Facilities*, mimeo, The World Bank: Development Research Group.
10. Commission on Macroeconomics and Health (CMH) (2001). *Macroeconomics and Health: Investing in Health for Economic Development.* Geneva: World Health Organization.
11. Deogaonkar, M (2004). Socio-economic inequality and its effect on health-care delivery in India: inequality and healthcare. *Electronic Journal of Sociology* [Retrieved 15 December 2007].
12. Duggal, R (1997). Healthcare budgets in a changing political economy. *Economic and Political Weekly*, May 1997, 17–24.
13. Equitymaster.com (2007, June 1). YV Reddy on India's growth story, June 1. http://www.rediff.com/money/2007/jun/01india.htm [Retrieved 15 December 2007].

14. Ghosh, K (2007, November 5). Telemedicine: an answer to ailing India. *Financial Express*, http://www.financialexpress.com/printer/news/236263/ [Retrieved 15 December 2007].

15. Gordon, J and P Gupta (2004). Understanding India's services revolution. *IMF working paper* WF/04/171, September 2004.

16. Gupta, I and A Mitra (2004). Economic growth, poverty and health: an exploratory study for India. *Development Policy Review*, 22(2), 193–206.

17. India Healthcare (2006). *IBEF Report*, www.ibef.org, Gurgoan, India.

18. Menon, J (2005, September 7). Telemedicine puts AP village on health map. *Indian Express*. http://www.indianexpress.com/full_story.php?content_id= 77670 [Retrieved 15 December 2007].

19. Misra, R, R Chatterjee and S Rao (2003). *India Health Report 2003*, New Delhi, India: Oxford University Press.

20. Nandraj, Sunil and R Duggal (1996). Physical standards in the private health sector. *Radical Journal of Health*, 2(2/3), 141–184 (New Series, April–September 1996).

21. Narayanan, PR, T Santha and P Kumaran Paul (2003). Tuberculosis control strategies: challenges to health management research. *Health Administrator*, 15(1,2), 113–117.

22. National Health Policy (NHP) (2002). New Delhi: Ministry of Health and Family Welfare, Government of India.

23. Paul, J (2004). What works: n-Logue's rural connectivity model. A Digital Dividend Study by the World Resources Institute.

24. Prahalad, CK (2004). *World-Class Technology for the Rural Poor: Tele-cardiology at Narayana Hrudayalaya*. University of Michigan: Ross School of Business (preliminary draft).

25. Purohit, B (2001). Private initiatives and policy options: recent health system experience in India. *Health and Policy Planning*, 16(1), 87–97.

26. Recommended Guidelines and Standards for Practice of Telemedicine in India (2003). Technical working group for telemedicine standardization. Department of Information Technology, Ministry of Communication and Information Technology, May 2003.

27. The World Bank (2000). *World Development Indicators 2000*. USA: Oxford University Press.

28. World Bank (1997). *India: New Directions in Health Sector Development at the State Level: An Operational Perspective*. Washington: World Bank, Report No. 15753-IN.

29. World Bank Report (2001). *India Raising the Sights — Better Health Systems for India's Poor*, World Bank Health, Nutrition, Population Sector Unit, India.

30. World Health Report (2000). *Health Systems: Improving Performance*. Geneva: World Health Organization.

Case Examples

A. Appendix: Case Studies

A.1. *Sankara Nethralaya*

Sankara Nethralaya (SN) was established in September 1978 with the aim of providing world-class eye care at an affordable cost. Today, it is a super-specialty institution for ophthalmic care and serves patients from all over the country as well as from abroad. SN has over 1000 employees, including 85 ophthalmic consultants. Each day, an average of 1200 patients walk in and 100 surgeries are performed. SN has been judged "The Best Eye Hospital in India" by *Outlook* magazine (July 2002) and *Week* magazine (April 2005, April 2007).[w]

In the light of the poor doctor-patient ratio and lack of fully equipped medical facilities in rural areas, SN launched its first teleophthalmology initiative in 2002 using three ISDN lines (384 Kbps) between Bangalore and the Central Hub at Chennai. Subsequently, in 2003 ISRO provided the satellite link between the Bangalore unit and the main hospital in Chennai. The satellite link set-up consisted of two mobile buses/vans with satellite connections and other screening/imaging equipment (e.g., a slit lamp, a fundus camera, and an indirect ophthalmoscope). The vans are staffed with two optometrists and four social workers. This team is backed by an ophthalmologist for teleconsultation from the central hub of SN at Chennai or sometimes from Bangalore. The images of the patients' eyes are forwarded to the consulting hub in two modes: (i) store and forward, and/or (ii) real time, depending on the case requirement. In the first mode, which is more often used, images of the eye are forwarded to the specialist in advance, and based upon the latter's reading of these images, he or she advises the patients during the live consultation. However, in certain situations, the consultant at the hub may ask for a real-time view of a patient's eye. In either case, the clarity of the image is very important to ensure a correct diagnosis. In an effort toward achieving excellence in image quality and its transmission, the software and hardware have gone through a lot of modification, including changes in the video camera for the slit lamp and fundus camera. Besides direct consultation, teleopthalmology is also used in many cases for seeking a second opinion from an expert — the seeker being either the patient or an ophthalmologist.

The mobile vans of SN travel to several remote villages, and teleophthalmology camps are held in these locations. The various kinds of teleophthalmology camps conducted include comprehensive eye examination camps, eye

---

[w] http://www.sankaranethralaya.org/.

screening camps for school children, and diabetic retinopathy screening camps. Presently, the teleophthalmology initiative is in the pilot stage, and hence most of the consultations are being provided free of charge. This initiative is being supported by other sources of hospital income. However, SN's management hopes to be able to eventually charge an amount between INR30–150 ($0.75–$3.75), based on the nature of the teleconsultation.

SN provides teleophthalmology services in seven districts around Chennai. Between October 2003 and September 2006, SN conducted a total of 957 camps benefiting 80,861 patients. Of these patients, approximately 25% needed teleconsultations. SN has also conducted satisfaction studies for its camps and teleconsultations. These studies show that while satisfaction levels are very high (close to 70% for camps and above 85%–90% for teleconsultations), many patients fail to follow up with hospital visits as recommended. Financial problems, lack of transportation, and lost wages constitute about 80% of the reasons for lack of follow-up.

In the early experiments, the mobile units needed the capabilities of both healthcare and connectivity. The resulting mobile unit was a large vehicle that was difficult to navigate in rural areas. In addition, the connectivity equipment set-up was often non-trivial, with the need for technical assistance. Furthermore, these mobile units were primarily used for screening and had little independent value as a viable business proposition. SN has brought two innovations to this early model. With the increasing proliferation of Internet kiosks, aided by a big government initiative in that area, there are several rural areas that now have Internet connectivity. This has allowed SN to focus its mobile unit solely on medical capability. The newer vans are smaller, require less investment, and are more easily navigable in rural areas. SN is partnering with the kiosks to provide connectivity. Specifically, under a recently launched initiative, SN is partnering with the M. S. Swaminathan Research Foundation to avail itself of the connectivity provided by the Village Resource Centers operated by the foundation. Under this arrangement, SN van will conduct medical camps in the vicinity of the kiosks and use their connectivity as needed during the camps. The second innovation is intended to make the mobile unit self-sustainable. These vans now have a refractive lens-making unit to dispense corrective glasses to patients. The revenue generated through the sale of these lenses will allow SN to recoup its investments in the van as well as the covering the operational costs of the camps.

A.2. *Aravind Eye Hospitals*

Established in 1976 with the mission of eliminating needless blindness, AEH[x] is the largest and most productive eye care facility in the world. The Aravind Eye

---

[x] http://www.aravind.org.

Care System consists of five eye hospitals owned and operated by Aravind as well as two Aravind-managed hospitals. Together they examine over 1.7 million patients and perform over 250,000 surgeries annually. With less than 1% of the country's ophthalmic manpower, Aravind accounts for 5% of the ophthalmic surgeries performed nationwide. Its hospitals have well-equipped specialty clinics with comprehensive support facilities.

Aravind embarked on telemedicine initiatives starting in 1998. At the beginning, the initiative was funded by ORBIS International and the Acumen Fund. Presently, telemedicine links have been established between AEH at Madurai, Coimbatore, Theni, Tirulnelveli, and Pondicherry. In addition to the hospitals, the Aravind telemedicine network includes kiosks, a mobile van unit, and several vision centers that deliver eye care to remote places.

The village Internet kiosks are used by AEH to extend the reach of quality eye care to remote villages in Madurai district. These kiosks were set up by n-Logue,[y] and in addition to eyecare they provide other services. The villages are connected by wireless local loop (WLL). The kiosks, which cater to approximately 800 people each, are run by kiosk-owners, and AEH has no management role in their operations. Teleophthalmology through kiosks largely involves primary eye care consisting of screening for cataracts, diabetic retinopathy, and other eye diseases.

Besides Internet kiosks, Aravind conducts diabetic retinopathy (DR) camps using the mobile VSAT van (provided by ISRO) to provide retinal diagnostic services to rural patients. The van goes to remote places and takes fundus images of known diabetic patients. The patients' digital case sheets are then sent from the mobile terminal via DR software to the reading and grading center at the hospital. All the digital images and information are graded and an opinion is relayed back to the mobile terminal in the van, with real-time consultation carried out if necessary.

Both store-and-forward and real-time modes of transfer are used for teleconsultation by Aravind. In order to make teleconsultation affordable for all eye care programs, Aravind has developed a unique teleophthalmology software solution called *eyesTalk* that uses store-and-forward technology to provide second opinions and expert advice. The software supports the integration of digital

---

[y] Formed by a group of like-minded professors at the IIT, Madras, the TeNeT Group has conducted extensive research on the issues involved in providing connections to small towns and rural areas. The huge and largely unfulfilled need in this area led to the setting up of n-Logue Communications. n-Logue was established to serve the information and communications needs of people living in the small towns and rural areas of India. To rapidly scale its operations, the company employs a three-tiered business model — three business entities involved in the operation, namely, n-Logue, the LSP, and a kiosk operator. All three must thrive for the operation to succeed.

ophthalmic imaging equipment to capture images. Referring ophthalmologists require a computer attached to the ophthalmic equipment to capture images and Internet connectivity to transfer the captured information to the experts; experts at the other end then review the images and the information and share their opinion using the same software.

While in the past a large majority of the outreach programs at Aravind have been through camps, internal research shows that the uptake of eye care services from these camps to base hospitals is a low 7%. When this is coupled with the rising cost of conducting the camps, the financial viability of this model becomes questionable. More recently, Aravind has been moving toward the establishment of a network of fixed nodes, reducing its reliance on camps and mobile units. One type of fixed node that the company has conceptualized setting up is vision centers (VCs), which are primary eye care centers equipped with slit lamps, trial sets, glucometers, lens-dispensing equipment, a computer with a digital camera (in place of a webcam), and Internet connectivity. These centers are linked to the base hospital through wireless connectivity. Patients are examined or screened at the VCs, and the medical personnel at the VCs connect to doctors at the main hospital. The patients interact directly with the doctors through video conferencing. Special software is used to compress data related to the screened eye images of patients and to send this data to the doctor at the hub hospital. The center is managed by a well-trained ophthalmic assistant but owned by Aravind.

By the end of 2007, Aravind had a total of 13 VCs, each connected to one of the five Aravind hospitals in Tamilnadu. The initial results are encouraging. Between April 2004–2006 and across five vision centers connected to Theni hospital,[z] Aravind screened 24,249 patients, 4659 of whom received corrective lenses and 1451 of whom were recommended for surgery at the base hospital. Interestingly, of the 1451 recommended for surgery, 1071 patients completed their surgery, yielding a follow-through rate of 73.8%.

A.3. *Narayana Hrudayalaya*

Narayana Hrudayalaya[a1] (NH) is a renowned cardiac care specialty hospital located in Bangalore, in the southern state of Karnataka. It was set up by Dr. Devi Prasad Shetty in 2001 under the aegis of the Asia Heart Foundation with the objective of making cardiac care accessible to the masses. Although Indians are genetically more inclined to suffer from heart disease compared to most Western nationals, the treatment options for most Indians are extremely limited. There is

---

[z] The remaining eight vision centers have only been added recently.
[a1] http://www.narayanahospitals.com/.

inadequate infrastructure (e.g., few cardiology departments or hospitals), inadequate manpower (few trained cardiologists), and the costs of treatment are typically very high, making it out of reach for most Indians. Heart disease is also unique in that it is one of the few life-threatening conditions that can be treated successfully with correct intervention by a trained professional within a limited time span (typically a few hours) after an episode. Telecardiology, therefore, has the potential to save lives through the remote treatment of such patients during an emergency, especially those who do not live within easy reach of an institution with the facilities to treat such cases.

Telecardiology operates under the basic premise that most of the time a cardiac patient does not require emergency surgery, and therefore treatment can be provided remotely by a cardiologist. For diagnosis of the disease and treatment, the cardiologist needs to see the patient's medical history, ECG, chest X-ray, and hematology reports, all of which can be digitized, compressed, and transmitted electronically. The cardiologist can also interact with the patient via teleconferencing.

Telecardiology at NH works on a standard hub-and-spoke model. Specifically, NH's Integrated Tele-cardiology and Tele-health Project (ITTP) is a network of two heart-care hubs in metro cities and 13 telecardiology nodes in remote parts of the country. In addition to NH, the other hub is the Rabindranath Tagore Institute of Cardiac Sciences (RTICS) in Kolkata. The telecardiology nodes are small, 5–10 bed coronary care units (CCUs) usually located within state-run district hospitals or charity hospitals. Curative cardiac care such as open-heart surgery is performed at the two hubs, while lifesaving emergency care is delivered through the pan-India network of CCUs. The CCUs are manned by local general practitioners, who teleconference with the hub via a VSAT connection provided by ISRO at no charge. The CCUs are equipped with a computer and telemedicine software that enables the practitioners to send digital reports to the main hospital. Online ECG machines generate a digital output, X-rays are converted into scanned images, hematology and biochemistry reports are fed into the health management system, and angiograms are converted into digital moving images, and then all of this is compressed and transmitted. The CCUs handle both inpatient telecardiology (for example, intensive care to stabilize heart attack patients under the supervision of a hub-based cardiologist) and outpatient telecardiology services, which include second opinions and patient follow-up.

NH has also taken the initiative to encourage general practitioners to purchase an echocardiogram machine, which can be used to generate an electronic ECG report that can be transmitted to one of the hub hospitals via e-mail. This technology is called Trans-Telephonic ECG (TTECG). The remote cardiologist's response is usually provided within minutes to the referrer, with a diagnosis based on the report. The system can also be used to provide second opinions to other doctors. All telemedicine services are provided free of charge to the user. The cardiologists participating in the telemedicine program gain from expanding their patient base geographically as well as improving their skill by treating more diverse cases than those that generally come to their hospital. The hospitals indirectly benefit from this service when patients from remote areas who have been treated via telecardiology in the CCUs are referred for surgery. In the last six years, more than 11,000 lives have been saved, about 1400 patients have been thrombolyzed, and over 19,000 teleconsultations have been provided.[b1]

A.4. *Apollo Hospitals*

With a vision of bringing international quality healthcare to India, Dr. Pratap C. Reddy, a practicing physician in the United States, returned to India in 1979 to set up Apollo Hospitals Enterprises Limited[c1] (AHEL). AHEL started operations in 1983 with its first 150-bed super-specialty hospital. From these modest beginnings, under the broader umbrella of the Apollo Hospitals Group, AHEL has grown to include 45 hospitals — both owned and managed — and has diversified into clinics, pharmacy retailing, hospital consulting, procurement, third-party administration, telemedicine, and education and training. By 2006, the Apollo Group had a net profit of INR673 million on total revenues of INR7.8 billion.

Apollo has been one of the pioneers in using telemedicine to deliver healthcare services in rural areas. In 2000, Apollo Group chose Aragonda, the birthplace of Apollo's chairman, to pilot the application of telemedicine in rural India. With a population of about 30,000, Aragonda is a medium-sized village in the Chittoor district of Andhra Pradesh. Until the year 2000, primary care for the residents of Aragonda and the surrounding areas was provided by one primary healthcare (PHC) center staffed by one doctor. The closest clinical and diagnostic facilities were at least 20–25 km away at the district headquarters in Chittoor. The lacunae in service providers were partially filled by about five to six registered medical practioners (RMP) serving the region. Needless to say, the needs of the region were not adequately served by this meager infrastructure.

Apollo first established a state-of-the-art 50-bed secondary care hospital in Aragonda with an investment of INR20 million (Menon, 2005). With assistance from ISRO, Apollo's Aragonda hospital was connected to Apollo's tertiary care hospitals in Chennai and Hyderabad using ISDN and VSAT, thus bringing tertiary care to the doorsteps of the villagers. The hospital was equipped with ultrasound and X-ray machines and a CT scan, and it was staffed by seven specialists, including a surgeon, a gynecologist, a pediatrician, a radiologist, an anesthesiologist, and an orthopedic specialist, supported by several additional medical

---

[b1] See http://www.rtiics.org/transteleecg.htm# (accessed December 1, 2007).
[c1] http://www.apollohospitals.com/.

personnel. Besides significantly expanding care for Aragonda and its neighboring villages, the connectivity to Apollo's tertiary care hospitals allowed Aragonda hospitals to diagnose complicated cases in cardiology, dermatology, urology, and neurology and ensure prompt follow-ups. Patients only needed to travel to the tertiary care center once for surgery. When the severe drought of 2005–2006 affecting the area brought extreme financial and emotional distress to the community, Aragonda hospital stepped up to provide psychiatric consultations using its telemedicine set-up. The telemedicine infrastructure at Aragonda has been used to provide referral services, second opinions, post-acute care, interpretation services, and health education to the general population as well as continuing medical education for the local private clinics.

Apollo Hospitals Group subsequently established Apollo Telemedicine Networking Foundation (ATNF) as a not-for-profit organization to develop and promote telemedicine and distant medical facilities in remote areas and to provide communication among members of the medical community through the dissemination of specialized medical knowledge over a technologically advanced network. Today, ATNF is the single largest turnkey telemedicine solution provider in India, with a network of 150 telemedicine centers across the globe.

The Apollo Group has ambitious plans to develop large tertiary, secondary, and primary care centers across the nation to bring quality healthcare to the masses. Several of Apollo's 45 current hospitals will form the tertiary care level. The secondary layer will consist of hospitals similar to the Apollo hospital in Aragonda. Apollo is aggressively recruiting other hospitals spread across urban and semi-urban locations in India to establish a telemedicine infrastructure that will connect to its tertiary care hospitals for specialty consultation.[d1] The next layer of the telemedicine network will consist of nodes spread across the nation that will facilitate telemedicine for expert diagnosis, second opinions, etc. These nodes fall into two categories. The first category consists of primary care centers typically staffed by general practitioners. These include Apollo Clinics in the urban areas as well as a network of primary care centers (to be developed in partnership with various corporate entities) which will expand Apollo's reach into rural areas, and also several government establishments. While the purpose of these primary care centers is to provide diagnosis and medications for the basic health needs of a family, they can also provide consultation in specialty areas of care on an as-needed basis via their connectivity to secondary and tertiary care hospitals. Each primary care center will be equipped with a pharmacy, basic medical equipment for diagnostics, and the infrastructure for

---

[d1] Apollo is recruiting hospitals that are part of the Family Health Plan Limited, a third-party administrator of insurance and a division of Apollo. There are about 4000 hospitals in the network, and a little over 800 hospitals have shown interest in telemedicine connectivity thus far (Srivastava, 2006).

telemedicine. Apollo presently has 51 such clinics[e1] with plans to expand to 250 across the country. The second category consists of kiosks that provide connectivity for telemedicine but are not staffed by a medical practitioner. These kiosks can be used to get second opinions and, as necessary, to initiate a consultation directly between a patient and an expert at a secondary or tertiary care center. Between January 2000 and June 2002, 3986 consultations were completed across all specialties, resulting in 591 patients being referred to specialty centers and the remaining patients receiving treatment at the TCCs. This highlights the costs saved by patients who avoided unnecessary travel to the specialty center (see Section 7.2.3.1).

A.5. *Byrraju Foundation*

The Byrraju Foundation[f1] is a not-for-profit organization doing developmental work in rural areas. It currently operates in 152 villages in five districts in the southern state of Andhra Pradesh. Healthcare is one focus of the foundation and is part of the overall goal of village-level transformation. In pursuit of this goal, the foundation realized that although quality healthcare was available at the district centers with the proliferation of teaching hospitals (there are 34 such hospitals in the state, each with multiple specialty departments), most villagers were either unwilling or unable to access these services. Telemedicine, therefore, was seen as a solution to this problem, to improve access as well as to lower costs for villagers.

The Byrraju Foundation follows a two-pronged approach to the delivery of health services. At the village level, they provide primary health services through their rural health clinics (RHC). A medical doctor visits an RHC every day for about two hours. The doctor is assisted by a trained auxiliary nurse midwife (ANM), who resides in the village. By June 2007, the foundation had set up 175 RHCs in Andhra Pradesh. Initially, the RHCs provided health services free of charge. Since the later part of 2006, however, they have started charging nominal user fees (e.g., INR5 per consultation, including 10 days of free medication, and INR10 per month for care of chronic illnesses such as diabetes). Interestingly, the Foundation has not experienced any drop in the demand for services, in spite of the fees.

In addition to the RHCs, the Foundation has set up several information and communication technology centers across the state to deliver a number of services, including education, health, and e-governance applications. These ICT centers are called Ashwini centers. By June 2007, there were 33 Ashwini centers spread across the West and East Godavari districts of Andhra Pradesh.

[e1] http://www.theapolloclinic.com/NewsRoom.asp (accessed on June 10, 2007).
[f1] http://www.byrrajufoundation.org/.

The Ashwini centers are connected to the Foundation headquarters in Bhimavaram through which various services are delivered. Each Ashwini center is equipped with a personal computer, printer, and video conferencing equipment such as a camcorder and television. Also, given the unreliability and poor quality of power available in the typical village, an uninterruptible power supply (UPS) with a maximum capacity of eight hours of power is provided at each center.

To provide specialty consultation via telemedicine, the Ashwini centers are also connected to the Alluri Sita Ramaraju Academy of Medical Sciences (ASRAM), a medical school located in Eluru, Andhra Pradesh. ASRAM is a private teaching hospital with the capacity to handle about 800 outpatients per day. The connection is made through wireless LAN (802.11 b/g), which requires the setting up of a tower (with dish antenna) and a direct line of sight with the district headquarters; this yields 2 Mbps connectivity. The link with ASRAM (as a TSC) provides primarily curative services through consultations with physicians, cardiologists, gynecologists, pediatricians, and other specialists. The consultation services are provided by experts from the medical school on a set schedule. The Foundation then schedules various villages for the teleconsultation. On the appointed day, villagers in need of consultations are bused to the Ashwini center. The consultation process between the expert in the medical college and the patient at the Ashwini center is mediated by the center's ANM. Depending on the diagnosis, the patient is given advice on whether he or she needs to travel to the medical school to seek specialty care. Patients who come to the medical school through such referrals are given a discount on the service charges. The Ashwini centers themselves, however, have provided teleconsultations to the patients free of charge up to this point.

In the Foundation's initial experiment with telemedicine (December 2006–June 2007), about 510 patients availed themselves of the service, of which 106 were referred to the medical college for further treatment. The demand for telemedicine is now outstripping the supply of available expertise. Plans are underway to expand the supply of expert consultation times, both through ASRAM and through links with other medical schools in Andhra Pradesh. Initially, in order to popularize the telemedicine efforts, there was no screening of the patients who came to the Ashwini centers seeking consultation. Going forward, however, the Foundation plans to initiate a referral system whereby patients will need to obtain a referral from the local medical practitioner at the Foundation's RHC or any other clinic to avail themselves of the teleconsultation.

LEVERAGING INDIA

Jayashankar M. Swaminathan

While India is a low-cost outsourcing destination for manufacturing and services, it is also a huge and growing market for various types of products and services. In 2003, the Indian retail market was estimated at USD250 billion, which put it in the top 10 countries in the world. This market is projected to reach USD400 billion by the year 2010, making India one of the world's top five retail markets. As multinationals eye opportunities in India, it is important for them to learn from failures and to adapt their approach in dealing with the Indian market. There are fortunes to be made in India — but it is critical for firms to ground their strategies in reality in order to achieve success.

In Chapter 8, entitled "Entering India's Product and Service Markets: Ten Caveats That Can Help You Tame the Asian Elephant," Prof. Sridhar Balasubramanian, Roy and Alice Richards Bicentennial Scholar and Associate Professor of Marketing at the Kenan-Flagler Business School, University of North Carolina at Chapel Hill, and Prof. Prabhudev Konana, Professor of Information, Risk and Operations Management, McCombs School of Business, University of Texas at Austin, highlight the top 10 pitfalls firms should avoid when entering India. These include underestimating tough competition, particularly from the small-scale sector; overestimating the firm's short-term growth prospects in India; expecting quick returns on investment; assuming the relevance of the firm's core competencies in India; underestimating execution challenges arising from the informal sector; failing to identify weaknesses in the value-delivery chain; employing a single scale or scope focus; not employing technology effectively; transplanting the firm's existing marketing mix; and ignoring the social aspects of business in India. This advice will serve as an invaluable "reality check" for companies that are considering entering India's growing domestic product and service markets and will help them to make an informed decision about whether the timing and circumstances are right for such a move.

CHAPTER 8

ENTERING INDIA'S PRODUCT AND SERVICE MARKETS: TEN CAVEATS THAT CAN HELP YOU TAME THE ASIAN ELEPHANT

Sridhar Balasubramanian[*] and Prabhudev Konana[†]

Introduction

Over the last decade, India — the "Asian Elephant" — has woken up from its slumber. Its young have discovered a new-found sense of optimism and eagerness. And even its seasoned managers, who have lived much of their careers within the confines of a bureaucratic, socialist-oriented economy, now recognize that there is much to be learned and much to be done to remain competitive in the country's rapidly changing marketplace. But this change has not come easily. A brief journey into the past can help place the recent developments in the appropriate perspective.

The past. In the burst of patriotism that followed independence from Great Britain in 1947, India's first Prime Minister, Jawaharlal Nehru, laid plans for an economy shaped by state planning and control over the "commanding heights of the economy" but with private participation in multiple areas. Nehru envisaged the state playing a key role in the energy, banking and insurance, transportation,

---

[*] Roy & Alice H. Richards Bicentennial Scholar, Associate Professor of Marketing, Kenan-Flagler Business School, University of North Carolina at Chapel Hill, Campus Box 3490, McColl Building, Chapel Hill NC 27599-3490, USA. E-mail: Sridhar_Balasubramanian@unc.edu

[†] Professor of Information, Risk and Operations Management & Distinguished Teaching Professor, McCombs School of Business, University of Texas at Austin, 1 University Station, #B6500, Austin TX 78712, USA. E-mail: pkonana@mail.utexas.edu

mining, fertilizer and cement, steel, defense, and other "strategic" sectors. Two of the central objectives behind this role of the state were: (a) to protect the substantial public interest in these sectors and (b) to employ the state's presence in these vital upstream sectors to moderate the private sector's role in other areas of the economy. This vision of the economy was implemented through successive Five-Year Plans designed by the Planning Commission of India, with the first such plan being launched in 1951.

The legacy of these initiatives has been mixed.[3] On the positive side, the early state investments in these sectors laid the foundation for an industrial economy in a nascent nation where capital and technology were in short supply. At the same time, the excessive interference of the state stymied growth and industrial progress over several decades. Some symptoms of this outcome are described below. These examples simply serve to highlight the broader implications of the early industrial policy for India's product and service markets.

(1) Before 1983, cars that were manufactured in the private sector in India were primarily either "Ambassadors" (variants of the 1948 Morris Oxford out of the United Kingdom) or "Premiers" (models based on old Fiat designs). For example, the Premier President, introduced in 1973, was a variant of the Fiat 1100, first produced by Fiat for the Italian market in 1937. Maruti Udyog Ltd., launched its first car in partnership with Suzuki in 1983 — but even here, the Indian government initially held a 74% stake in the venture.

(2) The involvement of the government continued beyond the "strategic" sectors of the economy. The state government of Karnataka to this day operates a company making soaps and detergents, including the well-known "Mysore Sandal" brand. Likewise, the public-sector machine tool manufacturer HMT diversified into the design, production, and marketing of wristwatches.[a]

(3) All private-sector banks were nationalized in 1969. On the positive side, this move put the might of the government treasury behind the banks. This, in turn, led to a dispersion of branch locations into underserved areas and the emergence of a banking system that could be trusted by customers who were often illiterate or unfamiliar with the workings of financial institutions. On the negative side, this led to mediocre service and the entrenchment of strong unions that initially opposed various modernization attempts, including the use of computers.

(4) Until 1990, intercity airline routes were operated solely by the government carrier Indian Airlines (now renamed "Indian"). The implications of having a monopoly in charge of civil aviation, and that too one without a clear

---

[a] See Chapter 4 of this volume for an in-depth discussion of the effect of government policies on the manufacturing sector in India.

profit-maximization objective, were inescapable — Indian flyers became fed up with poor levels of customer service, high prices, and a limited route network. Likewise, until recently, no domestic carriers were allowed to fly international routes out of India — these routes were operated by foreign airlines or by Air India. Again, the latter was controlled by the Indian government through its Ministry of Civil Aviation.[b]

The present. This situation has undergone a dramatic transformation over the past two decades. While there is some debate about who should be given the credit for these changes, there is broad agreement that the economic liberalization initiatives during the reign of Prime Minister P.V. Narasimha Rao from June 1991 to May 1996 were the turning point in India's economic trajectory. Successive governments have built on this impetus, and now the Indian economy is being steadily integrated with the global economy.[c]

These policy changes have deeply affected India's product and service markets, and the current economic situation across sectors contrasts sharply with the gloomy past described above. For example, over a dozen global automobile manufacturers have set up manufacturing and assembly plants in India, and others source parts for their vehicles out of India. The automobile market in India is now growing rapidly, and it is highly competitive. While the government remains a significant presence in a range of industries, it has tried to reduce its presence in non-core sectors through a series of disinvestments. To keep up with the private sector, banks in the public sector have ramped up their investments in technology and in the training of management and employees, and they now offer a higher level of customer service. The airline sector has been liberalized — private carriers now account for over 65% of the traffic, up from 0.4% in 1991. And most importantly, the "license raj" — the hated relic of state control that required onerous multilevel applications and approvals for any industrial initiative, regardless of size or intent — has been progressively dismantled.

Against this backdrop of growth and optimism, we analyze India's internal markets for goods and services in this chapter. We adopt two perspectives in the analysis. First, from the perspective of a firm from a developed economy that seeks to enter the Indian market and benefit from its future growth, we address the following issues: What are the key "mind-traps" that they are likely to fall into when they enter the Indian marketplace? How can these firms craft a strategy that can address many of the associated challenges? The analysis is structured as a set of recommendations that are tied back to the key challenges that the firms are

---

[b] Further details on the influence of government policies on the aviation logistics sector can be found in Chapter 6 of this volume.

[c] See the discussion of the effect of the government's economic liberalization policies in Chapter 4 of this volume.

likely to encounter. Second, from the perspective of Indian companies that are anticipating the globalization of the Indian marketplace, our analysis illuminates the other side of the coin: What are the key challenges that potential foreign entrants would face when entering the Indian market? Knowledge about these challenges can help Indian firms to correctly gauge the likelihood and implications of entry by foreign companies, and to calibrate their responses accordingly.

8.1. Caveat 1: The Indian Market Can Be Brutally Competitive

A key mistake that many firms make when they evaluate the rapidly growing Indian market is that profits are there for the taking. The assumption underlying this view is that developing economies were hitherto not well served by firms on account of their limited profit potential. In reality, many Indian markets are extremely competitive. For example, the FMCG sector has been well developed and competitive for decades, with international majors such as Unilever and P&G playing a key role in driving the sector forward. Besides these global firms, there is substantial competition from a strong local industry that has learned the tricks-of-the-trade over several decades of hardscrabble fighting for market share. Industries in which companies of Indian origin have developed world-class capabilities — on both the manufacturing and marketing fronts — include plastics, pharmaceuticals (in the area of designing and producing generic drugs), vehicle manufacturing (in the non-luxury automobile and two-wheeler segments), packaged foods and drinks, detergents, body-care products, and the software sector.

Interestingly, this is unlike the situation in many African countries that are looking forward to growth as well. In many of these countries, competition is far less of a concern. There is some profit "on the table" to be taken by firms that invest in these countries and deliver goods and services that serve the marketplace well. Not all developing economies are the same.

Recommendation: Firms planning to enter the Indian market must not mistake market growth potential for profit potential.

8.2 Caveat 2: Evaluate the Indian Market Against the Backdrop of the Company's Growth Aspirations

Before embarking on an India-focused strategy, companies must ask two questions of themselves: What are our growth aspirations? And to what extent will entering the Indian market support these aspirations?

Table 8.1.   A comparison of the sales revenues and profits of the top 15 Indian and US companies.

S.No.	Top 15 Indian companies[i]	2005–2006 sales (US$)	2005–2006 profits (US$)	Top 15 US companies[ii]	2005–2006 sales (US$)	2005–2006 profits (US$)
1	Indian Oil	$34.6 bn.	$1.1 bn.	Exxon Mobil	$340 bn.	$36.1 bn.
2	Reliance Industries	$18 bn.	$2.1 bn.	Wal-Mart Stores	$315 bn.	$11.2 bn.
3	Hindustan Petroleum	$16.9 bn.	$101 million	General Motors	$193 bn.	($10.6 bn)
4	Oil & Natural Gas (ONGC)	$15.9 bn.	$3.5 bn.	Chevron	$189.5 bn.	$14.1 bn.
5	Bharat Petroleum	$14.7 bn.	$353 million	Ford Motor	$177.2 bn.	$2 bn.
6	State Bank of India (SBI)	$13.7 bn.	$1.2 bn.	ConocoPhillips	$166.7 bn.	$13.53 bn.
7	Steel Authority of India (SAIL)	$6.8 bn.	$1.6 bn.	General Electric	$157.2 bn.	$16.4 bn.
8	National Thermal Power Corporation (NTPC)	$6.1 bn.	$1.3 bn.	Citigroup	$131 bn.	$24.6 bn.

(Continued)

Table 8.1. (*Continued*)

S.No.	Top 15 Indian companies[i]	2005–2006 sales (US$)	2005–2006 profits (US$)	Top 15 US companies[ii]	2005–2006 sales (US$)	2005–2006 profits (US$)
9	Tata Motors	$5.2 bn.	$388 million	American Intl. Group	$108.9 bn.	$10.5 bn.
10	Tata Steel	$4.5 bn.	$838 million	IBM	$91.1 bn.	$7.9 bn.
11	ICICI	$4.2 bn.	$543 million	Hewlett-Packard (HP)	$86.7 bn.	$2.4 bn.
12	Mineral and Metal Trading Corporation (MMTC)	$3.5 bn.	$34 million	Bank of America	$84 bn.	$16.5 bn.
13	Adani Exports	$3.4 bn	$28 million	Berkshire Hathaway	$81.7 bn.	$8.5 bn.
14	Larsen & Toubro (L&T)	$3.3 bn.	$240 million	Home Depot	$81.5 bn.	$5.8 bn.
15	Gas Authority of India (GAIL)	$3.2 bn.	$467 million	Valero Energy	$81.4 bn.	3.6 bn.

[i] For a history of India's economic development and the impact of post-independence economic policies, see Das (2002). India Unbound: The Social and Economic Revolution from Independence to the Global Information Age. New York: Alfred A. Knopf.
[ii] RNCOS Report (2006). Indian Food Processing.

A huge company in India is but a moderately large company by global standards. Table 8.1 compares sales and profits numbers across the top 15 Indian firms and the top 15 U.S. firms. Some of the comparisons are striking. First, the combined sales revenues of the 15 largest Indian firms equal less than 50% of the sales revenues of the world's largest firm, Exxon Mobil. Likewise, the combined profits of the 15 largest Indian firms are less than 50% of the 2005–2006 profits of Exxon Mobil. Second, of the top 15 Indian firms, nine are quasi-government entities in the fuel, finance, and metal/mineral sectors (namely, Indian Oil; Hindustan Petroleum; Oil & Natural Gas; Bharat Petroleum; State Bank of India; Steel Authority of India; National Thermal Power Corp; Mineral and Metal Trading Corp.; and Gas Authority of India). Third, the largest non-government-controlled entity in India is the Reliance Industries, with total sales of about USD18 billion. On the Fortune Global 500 list for 2006, Reliance ranks only about 120.

The lesson is that the Indian market may not serve the short-term growth needs of large companies. For example, for an existing company with USD10 billion in sales, a 10% growth rate would require an additional USD1 billion in sales over the following year. The Indian market can support only a fraction of that growth. For a large company, a more realistic time horizon for its involvement in India to have a significant impact on the bottom line is in the order of a decade or more. The situation is different for smaller companies: for them, entering the Indian market can influence the bottom line more quickly.

Recommendation: Companies planning to enter the Indian market must carefully match the potential and trajectory of that market with their growth aspirations. Even when large global companies are very successful within the Indian market, such success may have a negligible short-term impact on their global bottom line and shareholder value.

8.3. Caveat 3: Invest Today, But Do Not Expect the Returns Today

India is a palette of cultures and histories. It takes a tourist an enormous amount of time to explore India. The situation is no different in the business context. Market structures, customs, and customer preferences vary strongly across regions. Indian food manufacturer Britannia, for example, has a strong presence in the neighboring states of Tamil Nadu and Kerala, in South India. Its Marie brand of biscuits is highly popular in Tamil Nadu, but just across the border in Kerala, its Thin Arrowroot brand — which is very similar in taste and appearance but contains a slightly different set of ingredients — wears the crown.

Further, in each of these states, Britannia competes against a set of entrenched local manufacturers. These manufacturers have limited national ambitions but are highly attuned to their immediate marketplace and responsive to local tastes. Getting to know these nuances in the Indian market takes time, money, and effort.

On the cultural side, as well, there is a lot to learn about the quintessential "Indian" way of doing business. Time is a more generic, flexible concept in India than in the Western world. What is an immutable deadline for a German company can mean "somewhere around that time" for an Indian company. Indian managers tend to hesitate to say "no" in an upfront and direct fashion — the lack of acquiescence has to be read between the lines. It takes time to acquire the explicit and tacit cultural knowledge needed to compete well in the marketplace.

Recommendation: Companies planning to enter the Indian market must consider their early investments as buying them "a seat at the table." Firms that seek immediate, substantial profits are likely to be disappointed. Consider partnering with an Indian firm to leverage existing resources and knowledge.

8.4. Caveat 4: Question the Relevance of Your Core Competencies in the Indian Context

Core competencies that have served firms well in developed markets may not be highly applicable in Indian markets. For example, direct marketer L.L. Bean has strong competencies in the catalog and Internet marketing of apparel. These capabilities span multiple stages of the value chain, including: (a) understanding customer preferences, (b) designing apparel that appeals to customers, (c) marketing that apparel through catalogs and the Internet, and (d) managing the logistics related to procurement and delivery.

At first sight, there appears to be no significant hurdle to the transplanting of these competencies into the Indian market. However, at least three assumptions that anchor and support this business model in the United States and other developed economies can be seriously questioned in the Indian context. First, Indians have traditionally purchased clothes in retail stores after much touching, rubbing, feeling, and draping. Buying clothes via catalog or over the Internet is a new practice that goes against this tradition. Second, the postal services in India seriously lag their Western counterparts in terms of reliable, on-time delivery and the technological capabilities related to automated payment, package tracking, and delivery confirmation, all of which are crucial aspects of the catalog/Internet marketing business model. Third, in a land of inexpensive labor, a very large proportion of the clothes worn by Indians continue to be custom-tailored. In this process, the customer wades through collections of fabrics, chooses a few fabrics, and is custom-measured for fit. The tailored clothes are available for inspection a week or so later. The customer usually tries them on, and any final adjustments are made. The finished clothes are then ready for pick-up within a few days.

For L.L. Bean to enter and succeed in India's markets, it will first have to work at building the culture of catalog and Internet shopping for apparel. And because the company's value chain is only as strong as its weakest link, it also must carefully address infrastructural deficiencies in other parts of the value chain. Despite the attractive prospect of selling apparel to India's huge and growing population, these tasks are so formidable that for a company like L.L. Bean they may effectively forestall entry into India, at least in the short run.

Recommendation: Companies that have successfully leveraged a set of core competencies in a developed economy must not assume that these competencies can be similarly leveraged in the Indian market. They must question the extent to which each of these existing competencies is relevant in the Indian market.

8.5. Caveat 5: Do Not Take the Informal, Unorganized Sector Lightly

The unorganized sector in India consists of numerous small, labor-intensive manufacturing units. Many of these units are not officially registered. They primarily leverage low labor costs to churn out products ranging from luggage to pickles. These products are not nationally branded, but they can develop a strong local reputation. This unorganized sector has a robust presence in many industry sectors. For example, in food processing, a recent report pegs the market share of the unorganized sector at slightly over 50%.[8]

The manufacturing and marketing strategies employed by the informal sector frequently lag those employed by large companies in terms of scale and sophistication. Yet, this sector has emerged as a formidable competitor. The meager investment in manufacturing infrastructure and low administrative overhead mean that manufacturers within the informal sectors are not burdened by high barriers to profitability. Despite the lack of a strong brand, they can each command considerable influence over their local area. Within this area, they can build deep relationships with retailers that national brands, with their more diffused marketing effort, can find difficult to replicate.

Consider, for example, the market for salted snacks. Well-known national brands, including Snax and Monaco, dominate the baked-biscuit end of the category. However, fried snacks comprise a large fraction of this category. Here, the informal sector has a significant presence in the low-end retail outlets in major metropolitan areas and towns and in more rural areas. The more widely known food outlets will often run their own operations to prepare, package, and sell salted snacks under their store brand rather than sourcing them from an outside vendor. Other, smaller retail outlets often source these products from local manufacturers, who batch process these snacks using cheap labor. An operation that produces fried banana chips, for example, can comprise a simple mechanical machine that cuts bananas into thin slices, one or two large vats of heated oil in which the chips are fried, several large collection pans in which the chips are drained and salted, and a few workers who hand-package the chips with speed and dexterity. All these activities can take place in a single large room with a couple of fans to dissipate the heat and maintain ventilation. A faithful application of Adam Smith's principle of the division of labor ensures a high output-to-asset ratio for these labor-intensive operations. In addition, these manufacturers are often able to deliver fresh chips to retailers within a few hours of their being fried. This is a delivery schedule that national manufacturers, with their centralized and automated production facilities, cannot come close to matching.

The strategies of firms entering new markets are shaped by their understanding of the relevant market boundaries and their assumptions about who the key competitors are.[16] The informal sector may not be on the radar screens of foreign firms entering the Indian market, either because such a robust sector may be absent in environments that the firms are more familiar with, or because the unorganized and unsophisticated nature of the sector does not convey a sense of serious competitive capability. On entering the market though, these firms may be surprised by the size and resilience of the informal sector.

Recommendation: Companies that enter the Indian market must research the influence of the informal sector in their sphere of business and must explicitly factor the impact of the informal sector into their entry strategy.

8.6. Caveat 6: Check the Entire Value Delivery Chain for Weak Links

Designing and managing the value delivery chain that stretches from the manufacturer to the final consumer is a key challenge in many Indian markets. In developed economies, the transportation infrastructure and logistics that are responsible for the movement of the product from the manufacturer's warehouse to the retail outlets are taken for granted.[d] The usual point of resistance in the value chain in developed economies is the retailer: some combination of bargaining, persuasion, and incentives is often required to get the retailer to stock the product. In the Indian context, the value chain intermediaries *between* the manufacturer and final retailer can often present the strongest challenge.

In the late 1970s, Coca-Cola and some other foreign-owned companies exited India in the face of government actions that were not positively disposed to foreign investment. Taking advantage of the more liberal industrial policies, Pepsi entered India in 1990 under the Indianized brand name "Lehar Pepsi" and quickly established itself as a popular brand behind Thums-Up, a well-liked and widely distributed cola brand of Indian origin. Coca-Cola re-entered India shortly

---

[d] Further details on the influence of government policies on the aviation logistics sector can be found in Chapter 6 of this volume.

thereafter. Their return was eagerly awaited: awareness levels were high, and the return of the Coca-Cola brand kindled a sense of nostalgia in the market. However, in the process of setting up distribution channels to reach smaller towns and villages, a big challenge that Coca-Cola encountered was the lack of reliable local distributors of carbonated beverages. The distributors with sufficient financial resources and expertise were already stocking either Thums-Up or Pepsi. To circumvent this problem, Coca-Cola ultimately purchased the Thums-Up brand. This purchase was driven as much by the need to quickly obtain robust distribution channels as by the desire to own a strong brand.

Recommendation: Companies that enter the Indian market must carefully examine each link in the value chain for vulnerabilities. The weak links in the Indian context may differ from those that are typically problematic in a developed economy.

8.7. Caveat 7: Employ Both Economies of Scale and Economies of Flexibility

India's population in 1901 was about 240 million. At the turn of the millennium, it was about 1 billion. By 2006 it was over 1.1 billion. India's population is projected to exceed that of China by 2030. The number of Indian children below age five comfortably exceeds the entire population of France.[6] To profitably serve a value-conscious market of this size, companies must achieve strong economies of scale in sourcing and production.

These economies of scale cannot, however, be captured at lower levels of the supply chain. India's high population density, lack of robust transportation infrastructure, and poorly planned development have together led to the growth of crowded and chaotic cities. Correspondingly, the retail sector also suffers from a lack of clear zoning rules and disciplined organization. Retail stores in Indian towns and cities tend to be small and located close to each other, and to have a limited turnover. These small retailers are typically located on extremely busy streets with robust pedestrian and two-wheeler traffic. Managers are often faced with the prospect of managing distribution channels that incorporate thousands of these small retailers (see Fig. 8.1). Overall, the first impression of the visitor unfamiliar with Indian markets is one of overwhelming complexity.

The economies of scale that are highly relevant at the sourcing and manufacturing stages of the value chain break down at the street level. To keep the thousands of small retailers supplied, firms must shift from economies of production to what we term "economies of flexibility." Distribution at the level of local retailers is best accomplished by small three-wheelers carrying limited supplies that can dart in and out of the traffic and can park briefly in front of the retail storefronts without blocking the street. An 18-wheeler so commonly

Fig. 8.1. A crowded marketplace in the city of Chennai, South India.

encountered on American roads would struggle to make a few yards of progress in these areas.

Despite the inapplicability of economies of scale, what is surprising is that these small retailers are remarkably efficient when it comes to stocking and managing inventory. To understand this paradox, it must be recognized that the small size of the retailers is actually an advantage when viewed against the context of the distribution infrastructure that keeps them supplied. In the presence of cheap labor, the distribution system displays a kind of flexibility driven by its labor-intensive character. For example, stocking and monetary transactions, including the provision of credit, are managed by a distributor sales force that, using small vehicles or even bicycles with mounted carriers, is able to visit a single retailer on a daily basis, or sometimes even twice during the same day. This supply pattern comes close to the concept of "just-in-time" delivery. The resulting economies of flexibility lead to a tightly run operation at the retail level with little overstocking or waste.[14] An empirical study of small retailers in Brazil indicated that they had an annualized inventory turnover ratio of approximately 41 — i.e., their annual sales were 41 times the average inventory carried at any point in time. Studies of retail establishments in the United States indicate annualized turnover ratios of around 15 for grocery stores, 21 for gas stations, and 12 for confectionary stores.[1] Small retailers thus may be able to generate a significantly higher turnover, despite the lack of scale and the absence of automated information-processing capabilities.

Recommendation: Managers entering the Indian market must be prepared to pursue distinct objectives at various levels of the supply chain. In terms of sourcing and manufacturing, they need to establish the same economies of scale that are an enduring source of competitive advantage in developed economies. However, at the retail level, they need to harness labor-intensive efficiencies that are well suited to the disaggregated nature of the retail marketplace.

8.8. Caveat 8: Do Not Shy away from Technology — Instead, Employ Useful and Usable Technology that is Light on Infrastructure Requirements

India's booming technology sector has primarily focused on external markets. As a consequence, leading Indian manufacturers and marketers lag their Western counterparts in the application of high technology.[12] Likewise, the average Indian consumer lacks the resources to purchase the latest and greatest technological advances.

In this scenario, there nevertheless exists the potential to apply technological applications to make markets more efficient for both consumers and sellers. Specifically, markets in India stand to benefit substantially from the reduction of transaction costs and information asymmetries between the demand and supply sides of the marketplace. Sometimes these benefits can be delivered by a device as simple and ubiquitous as a cell phone. India is today the fastest growing cellular market in the world, with about 6 million cellular subscribers added in August 2006 alone.

Consider the example of fishermen sailing the seas off the southern state of Kerala, who used cell phones to improve market efficiency and profits. The market was inefficient, with prices varying as much as 50% for the landed catch across markets just 12 miles apart. With cellular coverage extending to about 15 miles off the coast, fishermen began to call around to a dozen or so potential markets to find the best price, offloading their catch at the markets that offered the most. As the result, both the wastage of fish and the price dispersion between competing markets were greatly reduced, and the average profits of the fishermen increased by 8%.[9]

The employment of appropriate technologies can also help market intermediaries who interface between service providers and customers. In Indian cities, a "travel agent" is often a person with a cellular phone who operates out of a physical space that is not much more than the proverbial hole-in-the-wall. However, these travel agents are extremely adept at using their cellular phones to access information from reservation databases to update their customers' bookings. An inquiry to one such agent regarding the availability of seats on one of the thousands of daily trains operated by the Indian railways elicits the immediate and adept use of the cellular phone. After a series of inputs, the agent is able to inform the customer within a minute about whether seats are available on that train for any class of travel, and if not, the length of the waiting list for seats. The availability and clever use of cellular phone-based technology has lowered the entry barrier into the travel sector, making it a robust and competitive arena.

The rapid deployment of cellular technology illustrates the ability of developing economies to leapfrog the intermediate technologies through which developed nations have had to gradually progress. For example, in Western Europe and the United States, there has been a gradual increase in the penetration of telephone land lines to households, and today over 90% of households in these countries have a landline connection. In India, however, tens of millions of consumers have skipped the land line phase altogether and have transitioned directly from the no-phone era to the cellular-phone era. At the same time, many of the households with cellular phones do not have access to a computer that is connected to the Internet via a broadband link. Therefore, the Internet currently plays a much weaker role in facilitating information search and transactions than in developed economies.

Recommendation: Managers planning to enter the Indian market must be prepared to employ technology in unconventional ways to lower transaction costs and enhance efficiency. These managers must focus on clever applications of simple technologies to solve pressing problems, and not on the introduction of the most sophisticated, feature-rich, or infrastructure-intensive technology.

8.9. Caveat 9: Do Not Transplant Your Existing Marketing Mix into India — Instead, Embed Your Marketing Mix in the Local and National Culture

Until the mid-1990s or thereabouts, India looked to the West for the latest trends in product design, technology, and fashion. Since then, there has been a strong rise of the sense of Indian nationality and pride. The rapid emergence of India's world-class software companies, including Infosys, HCL, and TCS, has spearheaded this newfound sense of confidence. Accompanying this is a resurgence of pride in Indian culture, with its accompanying themes and symbols. From a marketing standpoint, this implies that global marketing campaigns that are directly transported into India without adaptation to the local context are less likely to be successful. Firms that can integrate well-recognized Indian motifs into their marketing mix are better placed to make rapid inroads into the Indian marketplace. Often, this involves the leverage of themes and concepts that are already embedded in the minds of Indian consumers. For example, in a market dominated by carbonated colas, the lemon-flavored drink 7-Up was introduced as the "Uncola"; likewise, in the rental car market in the United States, Avis positioned itself against the dominant incumbent Hertz by employing the tagline "We're number two. We try harder".[18,e]

The case of computer manufacturer Lenovo's rapid growth in the Indian marketplace offers some interesting insights in this context. This company was a late entrant into the Indian market, where local brands such as HCL and other computer majors including HP/Compaq and Dell already had a strong presence. Lenovo recognized that building up a brand from scratch would be an expensive and risky proposition. Instead, it decided to leverage icons that were already embedded in the minds of Indian consumers. India's two great passions are Bollywood (a major home of the sprawling Indian movie industry) and the game of cricket. Bollywood stars and cricketers who play on the national team are well-recognized icons in India and are frequently the subject of conversation in public and private forums. Building on these interests, Lenovo first featured a prominent product placement in "Kaun banega crorepati?" — the Indian equivalent of the American quiz show "Who wants to be a millionaire?" Indian movie doyen Amitabh Bachchan was the host of the show, and he frequently consulted a Lenovo laptop to judge the correctness of the participants' answers. The company also teamed up with the Bollywood brother-sister duo of Saif Ali Khan and Soha Ali Khan in February 2006, appointing them as brand ambassadors for India. The pair starred in a number of well-received commercials that featured the brand. These campaigns increased the market awareness level about Lenovo from the single-digit percentage levels to over 70% within just two years. Established rival Compaq followed Lenovo's lead by sponsoring the next installment of "Kaun banega crorepati," further cementing Lenovo's image as a brand that was already a serious competitor in the Indian personal computer market.[15,f]

Recommendation: Managers planning to enter the Indian market must seek ways to leverage more of what is already in the minds of potential customers. To rapidly gain awareness and positive associations, managers must consider employing deeply ingrained Indian cultural traditions and national passions to help position their products in the marketplace.

---

[e] For more on positioning strategies, see Ries and Trout (2000).

[f] Beyond integrating with local culture in a marketing context, companies must also ensure that their products meet the functional requirements of the Indian consumer. For example, Ford designed the Ikon car for the Indian market with high-door apertures and wide-door openings to accommodate Indian women who wore a six-yard sari. For more details on the design of the Ikon, see Mahajan, V, K Banga and R Gunther (2006). *The 86% Solution: How to Succeed in the Biggest Market Opportunity of the 21st Century.* Upper Saddle River, NJ: Wharton School Publishing.

8.10. Caveat 10: Pursue Profit in the Indian Market, But Do Not Ignore the Social Aspects of Business

Money is no longer a dirty word in the India of today. At the same time, the unfettered pursuit of profit and the ostentatious display of wealth are likely to attract social opprobrium for two reasons. First, Indian value systems, which are anchored by millennia of religious tradition, have consistently valued knowledge and an ascetic mindset over wealth and power. Second, despite near double-digit growth rates that now rival China's, India remains a land of stark contrasts. The relevant statistics are striking. India ranks 126th out of 177 countries on the United Nations Development Program's Human Development Index. Despite the rapid growth of the ranks of the wealthy and the middle class, between 250 million and 400 million Indians fall under the poverty line, depending on the criteria applied. This constitutes the largest number of poor for any country in the world.[5] Many of the urban poor live in high-cost environments: in the absence of robust marketplaces for their daily needs, they end up paying more than affluent consumers who live in high-income areas.[2,g] India accounts for 20% of the world's children but 40% of the world's underweight children.[7]

The theme of corporate social responsibility is now resonating across the globe, but this theme is particularly salient in countries like India where there are sharp social divides in terms of education, income, and opportunity.[11,h] How must a market with such stark divides be approached by a company that places profit maximization at the core of its existence? There are three alternative strategies here. The first is to treat the poor as a market, one no different from those consisting of affluent customers. This would require that products be designed, packaged, and marketed in ways that appeal to consumers with low income levels. For example, retailers in India carry micro-packaged, individual servings of consumable goods ranging from shampoo to pickles — the poor can afford these small expenditure outlays.[19,i] At the other extreme, companies could adopt the role of the social planner. Here, the emphasis is less on considering the poor as a profitable market and more on empowering the poor in the long run by providing opportunities that increase their disposable income.[10] This approach, however, can

---

[g] See Caploritz (1963), *The Poor Pay Move*. This paradox has been sometimes described as the "poverty penalty."
[h] For a discussion.
[i] A frequently overlooked benefit of such micro-packaging is that it disciplines consumption. A consumer provided with a large bottle of shampoo is likely to waste more shampoo than a consumer who is provided with a single serving, see Wansink, B (1996).

work against the profit-maximizing firm's core objective of enhancing share-holder value, and it can blur the distinction between the role of the for-profit corporation and that of the government. The proverbial sweet spot, as is often the case, appears to lie within these extremes. It involves the development of a corporate philosophy and a market strategy that primarily focus on maximizing profits, but which also entail the pursuit of a set of closely aligned social goals that are selected with discipline.[13]

In the Indian context, Tata Steel — part of the Tata Group — has demonstrated how social initiatives and the quest for profitability can be aligned. Around its sprawling steel plant in the city of Jamshedpur, Tata Steel has consistently invested, through times good and bad, in improving accessibility to quality education, medical care, and civic services for both its employees and the broader local populace. These initiatives have, over time, built Tata Steel a credible reputation as a company that cares about its employees and society. Tata Steel has been able to leverage this reputation during difficult times. For example, this reputation served Tata Steel well when it worked to steadily downsize its workforce by more than half after 1991, and when it dismantled the company policy that guaranteed employment for an immediate relative of each retiring worker who had achieved a certain length of employment with the company. The powerful employee unions were persuaded that an inefficient company would not survive the opening of the Indian economy, and got behind the transformation. From a bloated organization that was profitable mainly on account of the barriers erected to protect the Indian steel industry, Tata Steel is today an efficient producer of high quality steel that is a formidable competitor in the global marketplace — but one that also continues to take its social charter seriously.[17,j]

Depending on the industry in which the company operates, such a tight alignment between social and profit objectives may be difficult to achieve. In such cases, a company may consider separating its socially oriented initiatives and profit-maximizing activities into separate spheres. For example, a fertilizer manufacturer might contribute financial resources to help the local government build a hospital or a school within the firm's area of operation. This separation will ensure clarity of focus in the company's strategic planning and in its tactical decision-making.

Recommendation: Managers planning to enter the Indian market must pay attention to the social realities of their operating environment. Ideally, they should find ways to naturally embed the delivery of social benefits within their profit-maximization goals.

---

[j] For details on how other companies have aligned social initiatives with shareholder value creation in the Indian context, see Prahalad (2007).

8.11. Conclusion

The Indian economy is on the path to decades of sustained, rapid growth. There is money to be made in the Indian marketplace, but the path to success is neither straight nor smooth. There are many obstacles that need to be surmounted along the way, and many traps that await the unprepared manager.

In this chapter, we have laid out 10 issues that managers must be sensitive to when crafting their strategy for entry into India. Managers who pay careful attention to these caveats and prepare to address them at strategic and tactical levels will enhance the likelihood of their firm's long-term success in the Indian marketplace.

References

1. Bermans, B and JR Evans (1989). *Retail Management*. New York: Macmillan Publishing Co.
2. Caplovitz, D (1963). *The Poor Pay More*. New York: The Free Press of Glencoe.
3. Das, G (2002). *India Unbound: The Social and Economic Revolution from Independence to the Global Information Age*. New York: Alfred A. Knopf.
4. Diamond, J and G Pintel (1997). *Retail Buying*. Englewood Cliffs, N.J.: Prentice-Hall.
5. Government of India (2006). *Towards Faster and More Inclusive Growth: Approach Paper to the 11th Five Year Plan*. New Delhi: Planning Commission.
6. Haub, C and OP Sharma (2006). India's population reality: reconciling change and tradition. *Population Bulletin*, 61(3), 1–20.
7. India Country Programme (2007). Research report prepared by UN World Food Program. Rome: Italy.
8. Indian Food Processing (2006). Research report prepared by RNCOS E-Services Pvt. Ltd. New Delhi: India.
9. Jensen, R (2007). The digital provide: information (technology), market performance and welfare in the South Indian fisheries sector. *Quarterly Journal of Economics*.
10. Karnani, AG (2007). The mirage of marketing to the bottom of the pyramid: how the private sector can help alleviate poverty. *California Management Review*, 90(4), 90–111.
11. Konana, P (2006). Towards corporate social responsibility (9 March 2006). *The Hindu*, Opinion leader page.
12. Konana, P, J Doggett and S Balasubramanian (2005). Advantage China. *Frontline*, 22(6), 12–25 (March).

13. Konana, P and S Balasubramanian (2002). India as a knowledge economy: aspirations versus reality. *Frontline*, 19(2), 65–69.
14. Lenartowicz, T and S Balasubramanian (2004). Small retailer performance in a developing economy: an empirical analysis. Working paper, University of North Carolina at Chapel Hill: Kenan-Flagler Business School.
15. Mahajan, V, K Banga and R Gunther (2006). *The 86% Solution: How to Succeed in the Biggest Market Opportunity of the 21st Century*. Upper Saddle River, NJ: Wharton School Publishing.
16. Porac, JF and H Thomas (1990). Taxonomic mental models in competitor definition. *Academy of Management Review*, 15(2), 224–240.
17. Prahalad, CK (2005). *The Fortune at the Bottom of the Pyramid*. Upper Saddle River, NJ: Wharton School Publishing.
18. Ries, A and J Trout (2000). *Positioning: The Battle for Your Mind*. New York: McGraw-Hill.
19. Wansink, B (1996). Can package size accelerate usage volume? *Journal of Marketing*, 60, 1–14.

CHAPTER 9

OBSTACLES ALONG THE WAY

Jayashankar M. Swaminathan

As we have seen in the previous chapters on the various vertical sectors in India, there is a sea change happening in the Indian business economy today. These changes have presented an immense opportunity for India to become a super-power in the 21st century. However, before this can occur, there are a number of major issues that need to be resolved.

9.1. Take Me on the Ride

For any foreigner who has visited India for either business or pleasure, one thing that is painfully striking is its disparity: the disparity between the opulence of five-star hotels and the shanty houses along the roadside at a stone's throw; the disparity between the air-conditioned coaches in which foreign groups travel and the sweaty, crowded public buses in which the lower and lower middle classes travel; the disparity between the opulence of the malls and hypermarkets and the tiny mom-and-pop retail stores that form 96% of the retail sector; the disparity between the state-of-the-art corporate office build-ings and the poor public facilities at government offices, railway stations, and airports; the disparity between the uninterrupted power supply in business offices and hotels and the hours-long power outages in lower- and middle-class residential locations; the disparity between the abundance of bottled water sold by multinationals such as Coke and Pepsi and the lack of public drinking water reported in several parts of the country; the disparity between the Western-style corporate success stories and the charges of corruption at different levels of the government; the disparity between a group of engineers who may be inventing the next greatest thing at GE or Google and the millions of people who have no better than a primary education.

While the middle and upper classes have enjoyed the benefits of the economic development over the last 15 years, there is another group of Indians who are crying for help. This we will call the "rest of India," for they have been left out of this economic development. They are the more than 700 million people who struggle for two square meals a day, and who do not have access to proper water, power, roads, or education. According to one report,[3] about 47% of Indian children under the age of five are either malnourished or stunted. The adult literacy rate is only 61% (behind Rwanda and barely ahead of Sudan). About half of the world's hungry live in India, and more than a quarter of the Indian population lives on less than a dollar a day. Many of these people live in remote villages. Some who have come to modern cities in search of their livelihood have only footpaths on the roadsides or slums to sleep in. It is clear that for India to become an economic superpower, it has to raise the standard of living of these people and bring them, at the very least, to the level of the poor in the developed world. Such a dramatic change cannot happen overnight; it will be a gradual process, and the government and the well-to-do will need to create the incentives to make this happen. As a growing number of billionaires are of Indian origin, one hopes that they will create major charitable foundations (much more so than is being done today) to help in this cause. If the economy continues to grow in such a lopsided fashion, there is greater risk for period of inflation and economic turmoil.

Another way India has been trying to improve the living conditions of those who have been left behind has been to prepare them for gainful employment through participation in the educational system as well as in government cadres of employment (a form of affirmative action in which a fixed proportion of seats in leading institutions and offices are allocated to people from the lower castes of

(a)   (b)

Fig. 9.1.   Village life.

society). This has been helpful to many from the lower classes, since it has provided them opportunities for higher education and better jobs. Since the allocation is based more on caste status at birth rather than economics, however, it has unfairly benefited rich people from the lower classes at the expense of the poor people from upper castes. Clearly, this system needs to be substantially modified if it is to benefit society in the way it was originally intended.

The other aspect of the lopsided development in the recent years is the concentration of development in the big cities. Most of India's recent economic development has been centered around large metropolitan cities such as Mumbai, Bangalore, Hyderabad, Chennai, and Delhi. It is true that smaller towns such as Chandigarh and Pune have also grown as a result of the recent economic development, but these are exceptions. Most of the growth has happened west of an imaginary vertical line that passes through Chennai. Meanwhile, rural India, where about 60% of the Indian population resides, has been largely left behind. One of the ways that the people in the rural villages have tried to catch up is by moving to the big cities. The net result is that the major cities in India are choking. According to one estimate, 31 more villagers will relocate to an Indian city every minute over the next 43 years. This translates into 16 million new people entering the big cities in India every year, further straining the infrastructure and creating serious issues for basic amenities such as power and water. Power cuts and water rationing have become commonplace in most large cities. It is evident that the country needs a plan for the development of rural India, both in the villages and in the suburbs.

One of the features of developed countries is that the majority of the population, barring unusual circumstances, have basic amenities and economic opportunities. In the age of the Internet, it is now possible to connect the people living even in the remotest regions of the country and provide them with economic and social services. As highlighted in Chapter 7, telemedicine can play an important part of providing health services to the rural poor. Other strategies related to the "bottom of the pyramid" will also facilitate the economic development of the rural segment of the population.[10] Some of the leading firms in India are developing successful business models along those lines, such as the ITC e-choupal case study discussed in Chapter 5. In the financial sector, a number of Indian firms are providing micro-financing loans to poor villagers based on social collateral. These loans enable the rural poor to create new business opportunities and thereby improve their standard of living. However, these activities are happening in bits and pieces as opposed to being part of a co-ordinated plan. The need of the hour is for some high-level creative thinking and planning for rural and suburban development so that this lopsided development can be corrected and the energy of the "rest of India" can also be channeled into the nation's overall economic development. And there is hope for this, with the support of political leaders such as the Prime Minister, Dr. Manmohan Singh, who spoke at the CII annual conference in May 2007 about the government's agenda for "inclusive growth" in upcoming decade. In personal conversations, Mr. Chandrababu Naidu, former chief minister of Andhra Pradesh, highlighted inclusive development as a make-or-break factor for India's future. It is clear that the top echelons of the government recognize the need for such growth. The question is, can they execute these plans successfully in the next decade?

9.2. Miles to Go

As you step out of the plane at the international airport in Delhi, Mumbai, or Chennai you immediately realize you are in India. The lines are long at immigration and at baggage claim counters. You think the worst is over, but as soon as you hit the roads you realize how efficient the airport was. It is not uncommon in big cities like Bangalore for travelers to spend several hours on the road from the airport to their hotel, which might be just 15–20 miles away. On a busy evening in Bangalore, it can take diners an hour to travel just one mile by bus to their restaurant. As noted by Mr. Kulkarni in Chapter 2, such congestion threatens to slow the growth of the BPO and technology sectors.

The situation is no different at India's domestic airports. One of my friends advised me last year that the best flights to take are the first ones in the

Fig. 9.2.   Traffic on the road.

Fig. 9.3. Electricity cables in an older neighborhood in Delhi.

morning, since they are the only ones that ever leave on time. And even if they depart on time, they rarely land on time due to runway and air traffic congestion. The story is no different for India's railways and ports. A manager once commented to me that his concern was not whether his local or foreign suppliers produced the needed product on time, because they were pretty good at that; it was more about how he could manage the uncertainties in delivery lead time due to transportation and customs delays. It is clear that although infrastructure projects are currently underway in several parts of the country — including new international airports, metrorails, and expressways — India is far from being at the level of a developed nation.[a]

While most agriculture- and manufacturing-based businesses rely on a good transportation and logistics network, the service industry relies extensively on power and telecommunications systems. Unfortunately, the infrastructure challenges are no different there. The shortage of power is becoming more acute day by day. It is estimated that by 2012 India will need 200 gigawatts of power generation capacity. This is nearly double the 2005 production of 115 gigawatts, or to put this in perspective, the increase is equivalent to the United Kingdom's entire power generation capacity.[2] Whether the power is generated from coal, water, gasoline, or nuclear resources, India's supply lags far behind its needs. The main reasons for such shortages on the supply side are the inability to efficiently tap existing resources, the lack of technology to identify new resources,

---

[a] For more on the transportation logistics and infrastructure challenges facing India today, see Chapters 5 and 6 of this volume.

inefficient operations, and a substandard logistics infrastructure. If the Indian economy is to take giant steps forward, the privatization of these sectors is a must.

The results of privatization are clearly visible in India's telecommunications industry. Twenty years ago, prior to deregulation, it used to take a typical Indian family in a major metropolitan city up to 10 years to get a telephone line in their home; today it happens in a couple of days. India's wireless market is growing at the fastest pace in the world. It is indeed heartening to see that the power sector is being opened up and that roadways and airports are being constructed through public-private collaborations. The Reliance Energy public issue was the biggest IPO of this year. It is also crucial for the water situation to be addressed. With the tremendous growth in Indian population, the proper collection, distribution, and reuse of water is essential. Proper water canal networks would enable India to decrease its reliance on monsoon rains for agriculture. The USD150 billion project linking the rivers of India (the Brahmaputra, Ganga, Godavari, Krishna, and Yamuna) via a system of waterways, if executed as planned, could go a long way toward improving the residential and commercial water needs across the nation. In addition, people must be educated about water conservation, particularly in the big cities. Water faucets should not be left running, with water being wasted, when the municipal water supply must be rationed during the early morning and late evening hours to households in that city.

Opening up many of the currently regulated sectors, such as retail, insurance, and banking, among others, would free up considerable resources for the government that could be channeled into these critical infrastructure projects. While India has opened up several sectors, including telecommunications, software, and certain aspects of manufacturing, there are still many sectors of the economy that are tightly controlled. The standard reason given for this is that these are sectors of national importance and cannot be privatized in a hurry. But we have seen the positive benefits of reducing bureaucracy and facilitating investments, and privatization would go a long way in furthering India's economic development. In one of my conversations with a CEO of a U.S. textile firm, he mentioned how China and India, although both growing strongly, differ in their level of hospitality toward foreign investors. While local government officials in China compete with each other to attract investment to their region and the whole process is "smooth as a cake," there is minimal competition of this nature in India. Therefore, foreign firms often experience a frustrating process from start to finish, with numerous visits to various ministries and the signing of thousands of documents and often even the need to bribe officials along the way. Edward Luce,[1] in his book on India, highlights corruption at various levels as one of the impediments to India's future success.

Further, India's organized sector (comprising firms that have more than 10 employees) has strict labor laws that make it difficult for employers to hire and fire employees freely. Although an employment-at-will policy is painful during downturns, it does provide firms the ability to be agile and flexible in the face of changes in the business environment. Conversations with managers in India's private sector indicate that this problem is not as severe as it could be, because they have been able to work out a relationship with the labor unions. Yet, these managers felt that their limited ability to lay off workers was indeed a hindrance to true workforce flexibility. The government and public sector is a different situation altogether, since post-probation period employees are permanent and for all practical purposes cannot be fired. If India is to become an economic superpower, it will need to loosen these labor laws and welcome FDI in many sectors. Further, it has to root out the rampant corruption that has become part and parcel of any kind of business dealings. Otherwise, without the additional inflow of capital from foreign investors, India will be forced to rely on the existing tax base to fund the improvement of its infrastructure.

9.3. The Flower and the Bee

Chanakya, one of the most famous ministers from the Mauryan empire who wrote the political treatise *Arthaśhāstra*[b] and who is widely believed to be responsible for ushering in the first Indian empire (the Mauryan empire in 300 BC), preached that taxes collected by the state should be like the collection of honey from the flower by the honey bee. It is a bond that should create a symbiotic relationship between the giver and the receiver. Taxes should be such that the giver is willing to give the money to the government because he or she realizes that the money will be put to the right use. The receiver is supposed to collect taxes from everyone who owes taxes, according to the economic prosperity of the giver. The poor state of India's infrastructure is often blamed on two things: (i) the insufficient government funds allocated to such efforts and (ii) the application of only a fraction of the funds to the real cost of labor and materials, the rest being siphoned off by corrupt politicians and government officials.

Let us look at the first factor. A few years ago, while I was traveling with my students in India, one of them commented that it should be no problem for India to collect money for all of the necessary infrastructure projects because of its large population and the amount of commerce that was happening around us. I had to explain to her that in India only a very few people have taxes deducted from their pay. Typically, these are government officials, employees of the public-sector companies, and employees of some of the large publicly traded firms. The rest of the population — including bollywood stars, athletes, film directors, private businessmen, privately practicing professionals such as doctors and accountants, small business owners, landlords, small- to medium-sized

---

[b] http://en.wikipedia.org/wiki/Arthasastra.

Fig. 9.4.   Typical retail stores.

manufacturers, and employees of small businesses — pay taxes only at the end of the year. Unlike in the United States, where an audit by the Internal Revenue Service can send shivers down the spine of any common man, these workers are not afraid of legal action against them. Not surprisingly, most of the populace is not interested in paying taxes on time and in the right amount. Therefore, the government does not collect enough taxes from people based on their incomes. Furthermore, with 96% of retail transactions occurring in small mom-and-pop stores, the taxes associated with the sale of items are also not being paid. Retailers commonly say, "It would cost you X if you pay by cash but it will cost you X + Y if you pay by credit card or want a real bill." This is so because retailers have to pay the sales tax on credit card transactions (for which there is a record) but can, and do, avoid paying the tax if customers pay cash and accept a handwritten receipt.[c]

Given that the government receives only a small percentage of its share in the form of taxes, it is rather hard for it to carry out significant plans for infrastructure development. In the last few years, the Indian government has instituted a card called the PAN (similar to the Social Security card in the United States) and is also issuing all citizens an I.D. card. Most of the working class, at least in the cities, have already received their cards. Not only do these I.D. cards provide identification for all people, but they also provide a mechanism by which the government can track individuals' income and transactions within the country. Another important change in large infrastructure projects is the growing number of public-private partnerships, which in my opinion will reduce the

---

[c] Most shopkeepers are very honest and will honor a piece of paper that has their stamp and a handwritten note describing the amount of the transaction and the date of purchase.

amount of inefficiency in project execution, therefore making development projects more efficient and commercially viable. As described in Chapters 5 and 6 on logistics infrastructure, projects such as the Delhi Metro and the Hyderabad International Airport have been real success stories. As these and similar projects increase in number, this may lead to a better appreciation for the need for tax money for such projects, and, hopefully, the flower will start releasing more honey to the bee.

9.4. Can I be an Instrument?

One of the fundamental indicators of India's potential to be an economic superpower is its people power. With a population of over a billion, about half of whom are under the age of 25 years, India has the opportunity to be a leading player in the world's economic symphony. However, a major issue is how many of these people have been educated and have the skills to become an instrument in the process. It is true that India possesses a large pool of technical talent. Based on the estimates of the NASSCOM, India graduates more than 2.3 million undergraduates and an additional 300,000 post-graduates each year from its 347 institutes of higher education. Of these, 495,000 are engineers. But despite this abundance of educated people for the workforce, only an estimated 10%–15% of the graduates are directly employable in a global platform (Narayanan and Swaminathan, 2007). With the projected growth in the IT industry, a shortfall of 500,000 workers is expected by the year 2010.[6] To understand the intensity of competition for labor in this industry, consider the following facts. The five largest companies in this sector in India — namely Infosys, Wipro, Tata Consulting Services, HCL, and Satyam — were planning to hire more than 80,000 employees in 2007. Add to this the plans of the global players such as IBM, EDS, and Accenture, that sums up to firms looking for more than 150,000 people. The inflow of fresh graduates is limited. Therefore, firms need to focus on how best to train and retain the personnel that they recruit. Firms such as Infosys and Wipro have extensive training programs in which they hire science graduates and teach them to be software engineers.

Once the economic growth engine in the manufacturing sector starts picking up as projected, India will have to invest heavily in technical and manufacturing programs that can provide the workforce required for this sector. The fundamental difference between the workforce requirements for the service sector and the manufacturing sector is the part of society from which the workers are likely to come. While service sector employees for industries such as software, consulting, banking, and BPO are likely to come from the urban middle- and upper-class population, the workforce for the core manufacturing sectors is more likely to come from rural or semi-urban locations, from the lower-middle and lower classes of the population. This is where the problem resides for manufacturing growth. India was ranked 101 out of 125 countries in terms of literacy by the UNESCO in 2007, and India, together with Nigeria and Pakistan, accounts for 27% of the children in the world who are not enrolled in schools. In terms of female literacy, India was only better than Bangladesh, Pakistan, Nepal, and Afghanistan.[4] These are not statistics that are typically associated with an economic superpower. Therefore, if India wants to attain this economic status, a renewed and enhanced focus on education will be a key component. As with the need for inclusive growth in the next decade, the government is now recognizing the importance of a focus on education in rural areas as well as the need for technical training to create the kind of workforce that China has been able to develop to power its manufacturing growth. There are some success stories within India, such as in the state of Kerala, where literacy rates are comparable to those in the developed world. However, it is important that the central government increase its effort to adopt best practices at the national level. The focus here needs to be on increasing the breadth of the educated population in the country through better public-private initiatives beginning as early as the primary and secondary school levels.

Another important change that is needed is related to the opening of the higher education sector to foreign investment. Based on my own experience, I believe that India's top colleges and universities such as the Indian Institute of Technology, the Indian Institute of Management, the Birla Institute of Technology, the Indian School of Business, Delhi University, Madras University, Mumbai University, and Calcutta University offer a good standard of education in comparison to global averages. However, these institutions are only a handful in number and not sufficient to meet current and future demand. Furthermore, there is a rapid drop in quality between some of these recognized institutions and the rest of India's institutions of higher education. Clearly, not everyone in the educated population needs to be a nuclear physicist or an astronomer, but, they do need to have a good level of education for furthering their career. The National Institute of Information Technology (NIIT) is a great example of an institution that has enabled dissemination of technical education to a vast majority of Indians. Started in 1981 as a small private training institute, NIIT today is one of Asia's largest training centers for computer-related courses. Many students who did not have the opportunity to attend university received their technical education from NIIT and are now working as software engineers in the IT sector. NIIT claims to have trained one-third of the software engineers in India. Why cannot this be replicated in the manufacturing sector? The privatization of skill-oriented education, along with the establishment of an accreditation body for governance and the identification of target segments for technical-skills training, would go a long way towards preparing the Indian manufacturing sector for

Fig. 9.5. Rural India needs to be a part of this growth story.

the next wave of growth. India's strength is its young population. There are millions of young boys and girls, particularly in rural India, who are eager to play a role in India's growth, and they have tremendous potential that needs to be harnessed.

9.5. Innovate for the World

Indian firms have improved their operational performance exceedingly well over the last 20 years. Despite having very poor infrastructure, Indian firms are recognized worldwide for their competitive cost and high quality of performance, both in service and in manufacturing. As discussed in Chapter 3, during the 1990s several Indian software service providers improved the level of their quality by undertaking an assessment of their quality processes based on the levels suggested by the Software Engineering Institute at the Carnegie Mellon University (SEI-CMM levels). This focus on the quality of services provided by Indian vendors has been an important element in the growth of the software industry in India. The NASSCOM website states: "As of December 2005,[7] over 400 Indian companies had acquired quality certifications, with 82 companies certified at SEI-CMM Level 5".[d] This number is the highest of any country in the world. Indian manufacturing firms have also caught up with the rest of the world in the last few years in terms of international recognition for cost and quality.

---

[d] This is the highest level of process assessment by the Software Engineering Institute.

Small- to medium-sized Indian firms, such as Intimate Clothing in the apparel industry and Sterling Tools Limited in the auto sector, are key suppliers to brand names such as Nike, Gap, Victoria's Secret, Ford, and GM. Larger manufacturing firms such as Tata Motors, Reliance Industries, Mahindras, Ranbaxy, Reliance Industries, TVS Motors, Aditya Birla Group, and Hero Honda have been recognized with many international quality awards — including the highest honor, the Japan Quality Medal from the Deming Prize Committee, which was awarded to Sundaram Clayton (part of the TVS Group of industries) in 2002. More recently, the Hazira Manufacturing Division of Reliance Industries Limited (RIL) became the first global petrochemical unit to be awarded the Deming Prize for Management.

Despite such advances in terms of cost and quality, Indian firms are behind the curve in terms of innovation. They seem to be quick and successful in adopting existing technology and in some cases adapting it to the emerging market conditions. However, very few breakthroughs have come in the manufacturing and service sectors that have had a major impact on the world. Two such innovations that stand out are iFlex solutions for the financial sector and Tata Motor's Nano car. iFlex solution's FLEXCUBE suite offers a banking platform that is highly flexible, scalable, and robust. More than 300 financial institutions in over 115 countries have selected FLEXCUBE as their technology platform, including Allied Irish Bank, Banco de Chile, Caixa Galicia, Citibank, DAB, HDFC Bank, IMF, North Carolina Department of State Treasurer, Sicredi, Shinsei Bank, Syndicate Bank, UBS, and Yes. In 2005, iFlex was acquired by Oracle for roughly USD900 million. The Tata Nano car is the other noteworthy innovation. Nano is the first India-designed car, and at a price of about USD2500, it created quite a wave when it was introduced in 2008. Tata says it will offer the Nano in other emerging markets in Latin America, Southeast Asia and Africa within four years.[5] Many more such innovations are needed if Indian businesses are to become leaders.

One of the main reasons that such innovations have been hard to come by is because Indian firms have mostly focused on "today" rather than "tomorrow." Although India is a great hub for R&D innovations for multinationals such as GE and IBM, very few Indian firms have demonstrated the commitment to invest in R&D for the future. There are exceptions, such as Ranbaxy, the largest pharmaceutical company in India. In the last few years, Ranbaxy has significantly increased its investment in research and development, and it is actively pursuing patents for new drugs. It is also collaborating with leading drug manufacturers of the world in the drug development value chain. This represents a fundamental shift from the way that drug firms from India have operated in the past — mainly focused on generic-branded drugs or on Indian versions of branded drugs. The fast copycat approach, which is practiced in both the manufacturing and service sectors, has thrived due to weak protection for intellectual property. However, in the last decade, a positive shift has been taking place in terms of respect for intellectual property. This has encouraged large firms to have the confidence to take a risk on R&D projects. Still, much remains to be done to increase the protection for intellectual property developed by small and medium-sized firms. The legal system is so archaic and backlogged that oftentimes court cases are not heard during the lifetime of the plaintiff. Therefore, most small and medium-sized firms do not even try to strive for big innovations, because they fear that the potential benefits are rather limited. Today, most of the innovation in India is coming from large firms with a lot of muscle power. This is in contrast to the high-tech culture in the United States, where most of the major innovations in the last 15 years have come from small firms such as Netscape, Google, Yahoo, or Cisco that have only subsequently become major multinationals. Rapid innovations in new technologies are more likely to come from small firms rather than larger firms because of their disruptive nature. Therefore, if Indian businesses are going to make a big splash on the world economy, there must be respect for and protection of intellectual property and innovation. This will create incentives for greater investment in R&D in all types of firms. Another important change in mindset that is required is the need to think beyond the current market, which in most cases is limited to India. Indian businesses will have to start developing products that will be attractive to people all over the world, and not just India. Once there are a number of significant, innovative, "Made in India" products, India will attain its goal of becoming a world-class economic superpower. Mr. Adi Godrej,[8] CEO of Godrej Industries, remarked to me, "You can safely forget about the fiction part of the India story. It is a question of when India will become a superpower, not if."

References

1. Edward, L (2007). *In Spite of the Gods: The Strange Rise of Modern India.* New York: Doubleday Broadway Publishing Group.
2. Gupta, R, V Tuli and S Verma (2005). Securing India's energy needs. *McKinsey Quarterly*, Special Edition, 91–101.
3. http://money.cnn.com/2007/02/08/news/international/pluggedin_murphy_india. fortune/index.htm.
4. http://portal.unesco.org/education/en/files/43366/113100877752adultyouth literacy.pdf/2adultyouthliteracy.pdf.
5. http://wheels.blogs.nytimes.com/2008/01/10/tata-nano-the-worlds-cheapest-car/?hp.
6. http://www.nasscom.in/Nasscom/templates/NormalPage.aspx?id=2584.
7. http://www.nasscom.in/Nasscom/templates/NormalPage.aspx?id=6316.
8. http://www.godrejcp.com/aboutus/godrejgrpprofile.php.

244 J. M. Swaminathan

9. Narayanan, S and JM Swaminathan (2007). Information technology offshoring to India: pitfalls, opportunities and trends. In *New Models of Firm's Restructuring after Globalization*, Prasnikar, J and A Cirman (eds.), pp. 327–345. Slovenia.
10. Prahalad, CK (2006). *The Fortune at the Bottom of the Pyramid: Eradicating Poverty Through Profits*. USA: Wharton School Publishing.

CHAPTER 10

STORM OF OPPORTUNITY

Jayashankar M. Swaminathan

As I conclude this book on the potential of Indian businesses and the Indian economy to join the world stage and become leaders, I believe the future is full of potential. Indian businesses have the scale, capability, and intellect to excel, and it is only a matter of time. Sometimes when I mention this, I am asked about the differences between India and other countries such as Thailand, the Philippines, and Mexico, which also showed a lot of promise and did develop rapidly but never reached the status of an economic superpower. Others ask me why I expect more from India than from China at this point in time. In the following passages, I will offer some thoughts on the reasons I believe we have only seen the tip of the iceberg in terms of India's economic story.

10.1. Unlike an Asian Tiger

In the 1980s and early 1990s, there was a mad rush to relocate businesses to the Far East countries such as Singapore, Thailand, and Malaysia. The primary advantage for multinationals, as in most cases, was cost. It is indeed true that by the relocation of the multinationals' manufacturing bases to these countries, both the companies and the countries benefited, since it led to economic development in these regions. So, will it be the case that many multinationals that have come to India will be departing as soon as the labor arbitrage advantage vanishes? In order to find the answer to this question, we must consider why so many foreign firms set up operations in India in the first place.

Multinationals have come primarily for four reasons. The first is obvious: it is less costly for firms to produce items or services in India than elsewhere. The second reason is market size. With a population of over a billion people and a very large economy that is growing fast, there are immense opportunities to sell products and services in India. For example, while IBM global services initially came to India for cost advantages, today it is the largest IT services provider for the Indian market. The third reason is quality. While many of the clients of firms such as HCL, Wipro, and Infosys initially chose these firms for the cost advantage, they have remained with them and are growing their businesses because of the service quality provided by these firms at the price points charged. Indian firms, whether in manufacturing or services, are constantly innovating and improving their processes and thereby staying on the cutting edge. Finally, the last reason for a large multinational presence in India is risk mitigation. Many of the multinational firms currently in India first started operations in China. Once they expanded their operations in China beyond a certain limit, they wanted to diversify their risk and as a result set up operations in India. It is clear that the political risk in China is high and is not going away in the near future, and this puts India and Indian firms at a huge advantage.

In sectors such as BPO, which have competed predominantly on cost, many of the top Indian firms have already started diversifying and expanding their operations into other countries such as the Philippines, China, and the Maldives to provide a further cost advantage to their clients. For example, Wipro BPO has offices in China, the Philippines, Poland, and Romania, and it plans to open up new facilities in Atlanta and in Monterrey, Mexico, in 2008. In the manufacturing sector, many multinationals are leveraging India not only as a low-cost production center but also as a low-cost innovation facility. Take, for example, John Deere. It set up an R&D lab in India in 2001 as a way of entering the Indian market. The facility designed a bare-bones tractor model 5103 without air conditioning or a cabin, which suited the needs of Indian farmers. These tractors were so basic that John Deere never contemplated selling them in the United States. However, when Mahindras started selling their tractor models in the United States, John Deere slightly modified the 5103 Indian model and marketed it as model 5003 in the United States at a starting price of USD14,400. This model has a 42 hp engine, compared to model 7630, which has 140 hp, and model 9630, which has 530 hp. Although 5003 is not ideal for most American farmers, who typically want a larger machine, it is a perfect fit for those farmers who want something smaller and less expensive. Today 50% of the tractors produced by John Deere in India make their way overseas.[11]

Even if the cost advantage of coming to India should begin to fade, the other reasons that firms have come to India remain as applicable today as when the multinationals first arrived. For this reason, I firmly believe that multinational investment and interest in India is for the long run and will not evaporate quickly like it did in the Asian Tigers during the last century.

10.2. Chindia Economic Coopetition

I am often surprised at how little MBA students or working executives in the United States know about Indian businesses in comparison to their knowledge about China and the business opportunities there. Perhaps, this is because China opened up its economy more than a decade before India did, and China is definitely ahead of the curve in terms of economic development. It is interesting to analyze how China has managed the process of joining the global economy, since China is similar to India in terms of population, market size, ancient history, and human intellectual capital. As the co-director of the UNC-Tsinghua Center for Logistics and Enterprise Development, our collaborative research center with Tsinghua University in Beijing, I have visited China at least once a year for the last few years. I was astonished at the level of infrastructure in cities such as Beijing and Shanghai on my first visit to China. I had expected a scenario similar to India, but what I saw was light years ahead in comparison to what was available in India at that time.

Clearly, the government in China had made a conscious decision that its entry into the global economy would be through the leveraging of low-cost manufacturing advantages that it could offer. Therefore, in addition to creating special economic zones for such investment, the government channeled money toward the country's logistics infrastructure, which now serves as a critical backbone for the global supply chain. Soon afterward, multinationals started pouring in, and along with them came investment in capital, technology, and processes that Chinese firms have exploited to become the "factory for the world." In the process, many Chinese firms such as Lenovo have moved up the value chain from low-cost manufacturers to world-class brands in the span of 20 years. It is the direct investment by multinational firms and their stake in China that is reflected in the overwhelming interest in and knowledge about China in the United States and elsewhere. The fact that most of the items that people shop for at retail stores in the United States nowadays come from China helps in this as well. While in the past the Chinese economy has grown mostly through manufacturing-related activities, over the last few years the government has made a conscious attempt to attract firms in the services and software sector. This shift is directly correlated with the level of fluency in the English language among the Chinese population. More than a decade ago, the government made plans to improve the knowledge of the English language among its people, and the first set of students from the programs that emerged from these plans are just beginning to graduate from the universities. My own experience with graduate students from China indicates that this effort has been successful. Today's students are far better in their English ability compared to the students I taught ten years ago.

While China started with a manufacturing base and has now moved to service-oriented businesses (the typical progression of development), India on the other hand is improving its manufacturing sector behind the service-led economy. Therefore, development in the manufacturing sector in India is not likely to be in very low cost, nuts-and-bolts items or toys but rather in higher-end manufacturing, which involves some degree of engineering and/or other knowledge-related activities. The high-class manufacturing in the automotive and automotive components industry is a good example. Similar to the shift away from the sole reliance on Chinese suppliers for manufacturing-related activities, we are likely to see a movement away from sole reliance on Indian suppliers in the service sector. Going forward, the friendly and mostly collaborative competition between China and India is going to provide numerous attractive opportunities for multinationals, be it in the manufacturing or the services sector. This is accurately summed up by Prof. Jagdish Sheth in his new book, *Chindia Rising*: "The rise of Chindia brings with it opportunity on a scale never before contemplated".[12] In my own opinion, India holds an advantage in the next decade or two over China because of its younger working population and the great number of Indian people who are fluent in English.

10.3. The Public Sector Wakes Up

During the post-independence period of socialistic development, India set up large government-owned firms in several core sectors such as banking, steel, coal, oil and natural gas, and power. These were called *public sector undertakings* (PSUs). These firms worked mainly on projects identified and backed by the government of India, which were essentially an extension of the government's influence on the economic development of the country. Many of these projects were highly subsidized and were in many cases loss leaders. Since the early 1990s, when the period of economic deregulation started, one by one the government started converting these PSUs into financially autonomous organizations in which private institutions and individuals could be shareholders. These moves have converted some of the better PSUs into the darlings of the financial market, since these firms have immense potential and could very well replicate what state-owned enterprises in China have been able to do over the last decade. The requirement to be answerable to the shareholder has turned many of these organizations from being internally focused to being market-focused. For example, in 2006, Oil and Natural Gas Company Videsh (ONGC) paid USD1.4 billion for Exxon Mobil's 30% stake in an oil field in Brazil's Campos Basin. It is also investing USD6 billion in a power plant and railroads in Nigeria in return for stakes in that nation's oil fields. Clearly, these kinds of entrepreneurial activities were not the norm for public sector firms. Taking their cues from such firms,

Fig. 10.1. A busy railway station.

many other Indian organizations are also innovating in their operations. Indian Railways, which for the first 50 years of independence operated mainly with a mission to sustain operations and was declared to be heading towards bankruptcy in 2001, turned itself around to become the second most profitable public sector unit in 2006.[14] The turnaround was made possible by focusing on profitable core offerings, such as freight services and upgraded services for individual customers. The Railways streamlined passenger travel, incorporating novel schemes such as e-tickets and paper tickets delivered directly to homes; availability-based upgrades for passengers; and faster non-stop service. More recently, as the retail sector was analyzing solutions for the fresh-food supply chain in the grocery industry, the Indian Railways came up with a proposal to provide storage facilities at each of its railway stations, thereby acting as a cold-storage distributor. Such novel initiatives are becoming the hallmark of the new public sector undertakings in India.

10.4. Joint Economic Family

It is not uncommon in India to find three generations living in the same household, working together while contributing in their own ways to the family. The Indian business economy today is no different. In order to understand this phenomenon, we need the perspective of history. Firms such as Tata, Birla, TVS, and Godrej have a very old legacy — some more than a 100 years — and they were in existence during the British rule in India. These firms have diversified holdings and are very successful family-run businesses, which is common in many

Indian firms. Although these firms have a family member at the top, they recruit and retain some of the best management talent in the country to run the day-to-day operations. These firms have traditionally had a significant dominance in the domestic sectors in India, and they continue to innovate, diversify, and excel in their centuries-old businesses. On a recent visit to Godrej Industries in Mumbai, it became clear to me why they are such a successful firm even after a 100 years of business. The commitment of the management to invest in their people; the passion and drive of the executive management to keep the long-term sustainability of the business in mind; and the adoption of the best management practices of the times in the organization are unparalleled. These firms are beginning to expand outside India in a significant manner and for most part, are taking the acquisition route.

The younger businesses (or perhaps not so young anymore) such as Reliance Industries, Wipro, and Ranbaxy have created a strong legacy spanning a wide variety of sectors over the last 40-odd years. These firms have had to adapt their styles as the Indian economy has gone from a strongly regulated to a more deregulated market economy. While dealing with regulated economies in a creative way, these firms have also learned how to be agile, adaptive, and highly competitive in a market economy. These firms are also expanding worldwide, some through acquisitions while others are growing organically.

The newer generation of firms such as Bharti Telecom, Suzlon Energy, Infosys, and Biocon are companies that made it big after the economic liberalization in 1990, and they are somewhat different. These firms are not content just to be national leaders: they want to be world leaders very early in their lives. For example, Bharti is the largest private provider of wireless telecom services in India and is often credited (along with Reliance Infocomm and Tata Telecom) for launching the wireless telecommunication boom in India, as a result of which India has not only the highest growth in terms of subscribers but also the lowest costs (approximately 1 cent per minute). Recently, Bharti has announced that it plans to acquire MTN in South Africa. Although this plan did not go through, as Bharti expands to other parts of the world, it will take along with it all the knowledge associated with running a wireless network in an emerging nation with limited infrastructure. Suzlon Energy is ranked fifth worldwide in the supplying of windmill turbines. It operates in 16 countries and has 7.7% of the global market share. Suzlon is growing rapidly and intends to be one of the top three providers of windmill turbines in the next few years. Biocon, the largest biotechnology firm in India, delivers innovative biopharmaceutical solutions. They have in-house R&D programs and offer custom clinical research services to international pharmaceutical and biotechnology firms. Biocon has rapidly developed a robust drug pipeline, led by monoclonal antibodies and anti-cancer drugs. Firms such as Biocon, Infosys, Bharti, and Suzlon are examples of young

Indian firms that are aiming to become leaders in young industries that could be the future of the new world. The net impact of these three generations of firms working in their respective ways is hard to exactly quantify, but it can be easily qualified as immense.

10.5. Future Growth Sectors

The growth of the Indian economy is beginning to spread further, to several new sectors. While the IT sector and in some cases manufacturing, logistics, and retail have garnered a lot of international attention, there are other sectors that are waiting behind the scenes, promising to show similar trends in the coming decades. In some ways, the lessons learned from the loosening of regulations and the experience of other foreign investors has eased the learning challenges that these industries face. Consequently, we can expect more successes and better performances by companies in these sectors in the coming years. In this section, I highlight a few of the industries that have already started on the growth curve and are showing the signs of growth and sustainability in line with the boom seen in the Indian economy overall.

10.5.1. *Biotech*

One of the emerging sectors of the future is the biotech sector, with Indian pharmaceutical and biotech companies rapidly innovating new processes and reaching out to a larger worldwide market. Some successes in this field are Dr. Reddy's Laboratories, Biocon, Transgene, Biotek, Shantha Biotechnics, and Bharat Serum and Vaccines. Mr. M.K. Bahn, secretary for the Indian government's Department of Biotechnology, highlights the importance of a conscious effort to develop this sector when he says, "The biotech industry could surge to USD25 billion in annual sales by 2015 from the current level of USD1.5 billion in 2006, if the industry and government act and invest decisively".[13] Evidence of early government support comes from the establishment of the Genome Valley[a] project at Hyderabad, in the state of Andhra Pradesh.

Ernst and Young considers India to be among the five emerging biotech leaders in the Asia Pacific Region.[b] With more than 280 biotech companies and 180 biotech suppliers, India is ranked third in the number of biotech companies in this

---

[a] Currently, this is a major earner of foreign exchange (USD1.24) from pharmaceuticals, biotech, and chemicals and allied chemicals.

[b] Others include Singapore, Taiwan, Japan, and Korea.

region. India is first in terms of growth in transgenic crops: it registered a 200% growth in transgenic crops as compared to the global average of 13%. Currently, India is the world's largest vaccine producer, as well as the largest cultivator of Bt cotton.[7]

In the light of these facts, we can expect to see a biotech trend similar to that which occurred in the IT sector, in which companies that currently conduct clinical trials for the major U.S. drug manufacturers will also move up the value chain and develop sufficient in-house capabilities to produce drugs for a world market. Some of the world's leading pharmaceutical companies, such as Eli Lilly (partnering with Jubilant Organosys), Pfizer, Merck, and Astra Zeneca (partnering with Clinigen), have been quick to recognize this advantage and have already set up research and development centers in India. With the right inputs, favorable government policies, and the large pool of untapped talent in India, this sector could witness a sustained growth pattern parallel to that of the IT sector.

10.5.2. *Real Estate*

The backbone of a booming economy lies in its infrastructure. A striking comparison between India and China today is the level and sophistication of this seen in both countries. Infrastructure development is a new area of opportunity for investment and growth in India. A study by Indicus Analytics projects demand to be over 24.3 million for self-living in urban India alone by 2015; similarly, Merrill Lynch estimates the need for an investment of over USD25 billion in urban housing to keep up with the current growth in the cities. The growth in the IT sector has also fueled the demand for commercial office space, projected to reach 150 million sq. ft. by 2010, and the up-and-coming retail industry is expected to need an additional 220 million sq. ft. by this year.

Given these huge requirements, a number of international players have already entered the market. Jones Lang LaSalle, the world's leading integrated global real estate services and money management firm, plans to invest approximately USD1 billion in the country's burgeoning property market. Dubai-based DAMAC Properties likewise plans to invest up to USD4.5 billion to develop properties in India. UAE-based real estate company Rakeen and Chennai-based mineral firm Trimex Group have formed a joint venture company, Rakindo Developers, that plans to invest over USD5 billion in the Indian real estate market over the next five years. The Indian giant in this sector, DLF, has also formed a joint venture with Limitless Holding, a part of Dubai World, to develop a USD15.23 billion township project in the state of Karnataka.[4]

Large Indian players have been branching out to other countries as well. The Embassy Group has struck a deal to construct a USD600 million IT park in

Serbia; the Puravankara Group is constructing a high-end residential complex in Sri Lanka; and the Hiranandanis are constructing five-star hotels with over 5000 rooms between Abu Dhabi and Dubai.

Recognizing the need for investment in infrastructure, the government has eased some of the regulations associated with FDI, and the real estate component is projected to grow from USD12 million (2005) to USD40–50 million in the next five years.[1] This makes India one of the top destinations in Asia for private equity investment. Real estate accounted for 26% of the total value of private equity investment in 2007, and this is only the beginning of the boom to come in this industry (Fig. 10.2). Many global real estate majors, such as Dubai World, the Trump Organization, Smart City (Dubai), Kishimoto Gordon Dalaya, Khuyool Investments, Bonyan Holding, Plus Properties, ABG Group, and Al Fara's properties, have set their sights on India, bringing in an estimated investment of USD20–25 million in the next two years.

10.5.3. *Finance and Insurance*

While the economy has growing at a frenetic pace, the stock market has followed suit, emerging as the third best performing market in the world in 2007 and generating an impressive 71.23% return on every dollar invested. Last year also public issues have raised USD11.48 billion (an 83% increase from 2006), and deals worth USD17.4 billion (compared to USD7.8 billion in 2006) were mobilized. Real estate, infrastructure, banking, and financial services were the major investment areas (55% of the total private equity investment). The mutual funds market also received a shot in the arm, with a self-feeding cycle of an increasing number of fund houses and a corresponding increase in the number of people who use mutual funds as a savings instrument, yielding a growth rate

Fig. 10.2. An office complex and a residential building in Gurgaon.

of 124.93%. The mutual fund market is expected to grow at CAGR of 30% in the next three years, becoming a strong USD241.79 billion industry by 2010. The banking industry boom is showcased in the listing of nine Indian banks among the top 50 Asian banks.[2] Similarly, seven Indian microfinance institutions were included in the Forbes list of the World's Top 50 Microfinance Institutions (http://www.forbes.com/). Yet, the potential for future growth is still immense, as India has the second largest number of financially excluded households in the world.[6]

Partial liberalization of the regulations governing market entry and foreign investment has opened up the insurance sector to rapid growth in the coming decade. Premium collections have grown by 19.9% compared to a world average of 2.9%, making India the 15th largest insurance market in the world. As this represents a penetration of only about 2% of the GDP for life and non-life insurance (as compared to a world average of 7.5%), it is apparent that this industry is only beginning to take off.[7]

A report from Goldman Sachs estimates that the growth in India's debt market will be about USD1.5 trillion by 2016, driven primarily by the insurance, mutual fund, and pension sectors. More significantly, the non-government sector is expected to grow from USD100 billion in 2006 to USD575 billion in 2016. This represents a major shift in market share from the traditionally nationalized companies (e.g., LIC) to private players, as insurers from both within India (e.g., ICICI Prudential Life, HDFC Life Insurance) and abroad (e.g., Max Life Insurance) expand their market share (Fig. 10.3).

Fig. 10.3.   National Stock Exchange building in Mumbai.

10.5.4. *Entertainment*

Although many in the West are familiar with bollywood (the local film industry) films, the amount of investment made by multinationals in this sector thus far has been quite limited. As the budgets for Indian movies as well as their revenues outside India continue to increase, however, investments are also increasing in this area. Last year, Sony produced a bollywood movie called *Saawariya* that cost USD12 million to produce. Next year, it is set to produce four films in collaboration with Eros Entertainment. Disney, Viacom, and other firms are also exploring the Indian entertainment market.[3]

10.5.5. *Education*

Another exciting opportunity in the upcoming years will be the privatization of education, particularly in the areas of technical and managerial training. Recently, Georgia Institute of Technology became the first U.S. institution to set up a campus in India in Hyderabad. It is only a matter of time before institutions of higher learning from around the world are allowed to offer technical training and bachelors- and masters-level programs throughout India. This will accelerate the ability of multinationals worldwide to leverage the immense potential that India has to offer to the world in terms of human capital and brainpower while at the same time bringing quality education to many more Indian students.

10.6. Changed Times

Every 100 years or so, a new set of countries joins the group of superpowers in the global economy. In the 18th and the 19th centuries it was France and Great Britain, while in the 20th century it was the United States, Japan, Germany, and the Soviet Union. In my opinion, this century is likely to witness the rise of India (along with China) as a world superpower. India's economy and its businesses have all the ingredients to make this happen. To achieve this goal, however, India needs to do three things: (1) maintain constant and timely inflow of capital; (2) get appropriate direction from the government for the inclusive growth of the economy; and (3) benefit from the continued enthusiasm and energy of its workforce. In conclusion, I want to share two different experiences from my most recent visit to India in March 2008 that strengthened my belief that the sea change is already deeply established in the Indian economy and that these are changed times.

By March 31st, 2008, the new airports at Bangalore and Hyderabad were scheduled to open. Since the old airports would be closed down at this point, and as a result layoffs were imminent for many airport workers, the airport union called for a strike at these and many other airports across the country starting at midnight on March 12. I was scheduled to fly on March 11 and then again on March 14 to return to the United States. I was very concerned, because I had a business engagement between March 11 and March 14 and had not planned for much time between my domestic and international connections. The memory of strikes and *bandh* closures was still fresh in my mind from the last time I had witnessed these in the 1980s, and I mentally prepared for the worst. I imagined political effigies being burned, passengers stranded all over, total chaos at the airport ... but to my surprise, the night of March 12 came and went, with no major stoppage of any kind. All of the airports operated normally. At first I thought that perhaps the unions had not gone on strike. The airport union workers indeed had gone on strike, but all the other airline employees were working, and the government had proactively deployed hundreds of trained air force personnel to manage the exigency. This, I would have expected in China, but I was delighted to see taking place in India.

The second experience occurred this year during our MBA program business visits in Mumbai, when we were invited to visit the Welingkar Institute of Management.[10] I had never been to Welingkar before and, frankly, I had not even known of the existence of this institution, since it is not among the elite schools of India (for instance, the Indian Institute of Management or the Indian School of Business).[9] However, Welingkar is a good private institution, of which there are at least 30 in India today, and I was curious to understand these Indian educational institutions in-depth. As we were walked through the multistoried building with several air-conditioned classrooms and labs, I saw students accessing the wi-fi network and browsing the Internet. The scene did not look very different from that of any college or university in the United States. We were told about several programs that the institute offers, including one in Management of Innovation. In the typical Indian style, one of the professors volunteered to let us visit his class and asked his group of students to present their project synopsis to us in real time. As the three young aspiring MBA students went through an outstanding presentation about their work on roadside auto workshops in India, they showed us an interview video clip, translated the conversation in Hindi seamlessly into English, and finally took questions from our group of MBA students with poise and confidence. I guessed that the students who were presenting were probably not among the top 2000 students in terms of their management school admission test performance; nevertheless, they were comparable to many of the students that I have seen at top 20 business schools in the United States. What I saw was far better than what I had expected from them — this was a mind-blowing experience for me. These students showed how much intellectual potential resides in India, and how, if properly nourished, India could become an economic superpower much sooner than expected in the 21st century.

References

1. Grand Thorton, Doing Business in India. http://www.wcgt.in/html/publications/publication_title?pub_id=4.
2. http://sify.com/finance/.
3. http://us.ft.com/ftgateway/superpage.ft?news_id=fto031820081631524554.
4. http://www.ibef.org/industry/biotechnology.aspx.
5. http://www.ibef.org/industry/realestate.aspx.
6. http://www.ibef.org/industry/financialservices.aspx.
7. http://www.ibef.org/industry/insurance_industry.aspx.
8. http://www.forbes.com/.
9. http://www.isb.edu/isb/index.shtml.
10. http://www.welingkar.org/Welingkar/.
11. John Deere's farm team (2008). *Fortune*, April 14, 2008.
12. Seth, J (2008). *Chindia Rising*. Tata McGraw-Hill Publishing Company Limited. New Delhi: India.
13. Smith, A (2007). India's elephant in the room: weak patent laws tenfold increase projected for India's biotech industry, but weak patent laws frustrate foreign investors, May 4 2007. http://money.cnn.com/2007/05/04/news/companies/india_biotech/index.htm.
14. Turnaround of Indian railways: a critical appraisal of strategies and processes. Working Paper No. 2007-02-03, Indian Institute of Management, Ahmedabad, February 2007.

CHAPTER 11

THE GLOBAL CREDIT TSUNAMI AND ITS IMPACT

Jayashankar M. Swaminathan

In the time between the preprint version of the book and this final version, the global economy has experienced an unprecedented turmoil. What seemed like a minor credit problem in the mortgage sector in the US has become a global financial credit tsunami.[4] The US stock market has lost more than 40% of its value from the peak, several well known financial institutions such as Lehman Brothers and Bear Stearns are no longer existent while others such as Goldman Sachs and Citibank are struggling. The big three automakers are trying hard to live through this crisis. Even gold standard firms such as GE,[7] IBM, Intel and Apple are projecting tough year(s) ahead, and there is a general consensus that the US economy may be headed for a long recessionary period.[1,10] In today's tightly coupled global economy, the impact is being felt all over the world — the bankruptcy declaration in Iceland,[5] lower growth projections in China, and negative growth predictions in England and Spain in the upcoming years. India is not an exception to this global crisis.[3] The stock market in India has fallen more than 60% from the all time high of 21000 reached earlier in the year, many foreign financial institutions are pulling money out of India,[11] the Indian rupee is at an all time low against the dollar (at Rs. 49.50 per dollar)[a] and many Indian firms are projecting lower growth, while some are downsizing in a significant manner.[8] The role of emerging economies such as China and India in enabling a solution for a global financial crisis is larger today than ever before, as reflected in the recently concluded ASEM nations summit at Beijing and the proposed summit in the US next month.[9]

So what does this financial crisis mean in terms of India's economic growth, opportunities for multinationals to leverage assets in India and opportunities for Indian firms to be leaders in the global economy? Which elements of India's

---

[a] As of October 26, 2008.

economic growth, highlighted in earlier chapters, will continue to shine? In this chapter, I will provide my views on these questions.

11.1. India as a Producer

India's biggest strength is its people. Despite the current financial crisis, India will continue to be an important contributor to the global economic activity due to its large, educated, middle class population. However, many of the current growth industries will need to adapt themselves. Take for example the BPO and IT sectors (described in Chapters 2 and 3 of this book) that have been the growth the engine for the Indian economy for many years. Most of the firms in these industries obtain a majority of the revenues through outsourcing contracts from the US and European firms.[8] As the economic growth in developed countries slows down and unemployment rises, there is going to be increased social pressure in those countries to reduce the amount of offshoring. Does this mean that we will see an end of offshoring? No. However, firms will deliberate more carefully the social and economic implications of such actions. While I do not see a major shift in direction with regard to offshoring decisions related to activities such as information technology and back office automation, I do believe that some of the offshoring had been taken to an extreme in the economic boom days. For example, the *4-Hour WorkWeek*,[2] provides several examples of highly paid working professionals, who offshored many of their daily and mundane tasks. There are several firms in the BPO sector in India who provided remote personal assistant services. These services helped investment bankers and highly paid professionals (those who were making an unrealistic amount of money before) with activities such as remote desktop management of their office computers (where the person sitting in India would remotely be cleaning up the clutter on their desktop) or managing 'to do' tasks and performing travel agent functions. There is going to be a dramatic drop in offshoring of such activities because firstly, the number of such highly paid individuals is going to be lower in the upcoming years in the US and other developed nations and secondly, if needed, the availability of local personal assistants, for the same work, is going to increase with the increase in unemployment rates in those countries. Fundamentally, we will witness a significant reduction in the low valued added offshoring activities while critical activities that have been offshored will see a lower degree of slowdown. What this implies is that Indian firms will have to move faster towards the innovation and high value added activities in the IT and the KPO sector for long-term sustainability (something that I highlighted in Chapters 9 and 10). On the positive side, as activities in the BPO and IT sectors slow down, the very high turnover that these sectors have witnessed for the past several years is likely to reduce as well. Further, with the fall of the rupee against the dollar, firms in these sectors are likely to become even more competitive in the global marketplace. Therefore, the news for Indian firms in these sectors is mixed. I believe the best of the Indian firms will emerge even stronger in these sectors.

The situation in the manufacturing sector is similar but given that Indian firms are only now beginning to become global providers (unlike Chinese manufacturing firms), in my opinion the effects of these slowdowns are only going to be marginal. In fact, I believe that Indian firms in the manufacturing sector have a tremendous opportunity to create global brands (like the Tata Nano) since many consumers in developed economies are likely to become more price conscious in these times and hence are more likely to try out less expensive (and lesser known brands). In order to bring this opportunity to fruition, firms need to think strategically about how they could innovate and adapt their existing products for the western consumer. Further, both Indian manufacturing and services sector firms could focus more on the local market in terms of developing India's basic infrastructure related to logistics, utilities and healthcare.

While so far we have talked about Indian firms as producers, multinationals also will have to change some of their strategies. If a multinational has an offshore provider in India, this might be an opportunity to renegotiate the terms of the contracts since they are likely to get better terms with the provider. If the multinational has captive operations in India (in services or manufacturing), this might be the time to take advantage of the loose employment market and tap into some of the best professionals in the industry, utilize them to develop innovative products and services in India that could be also be deployed worldwide. There will be more examples like that of John Deere tractor discussed in Chapter 10.

11.2. India as a Market

While many multinationals have gone to India with the intent of leveraging the resource base, yet others had gone to India to capture consumer market. As indicated in Chapter 7, the Indian consumer in general is quite value conscious, so the market is hard to crack to begin with. In the last few years, as India experienced tremendous growth with the boom in the BPO and ITES sectors, there was a lot of easy money *per se*. Many college graduates received greater salaries than their about-to-retire parents (as indicated in Chapter 1). With the slowdown in the economic growth, one is going to see that there will be consolidation in several industries, the job prospects are not going to be as good if one didn't have good skill sets, and, salaries and disposable income are not going to be increasing at the same levels as before. Thus, the expectation of a huge consumer market, as projected from the continued growth of the Indian middle class and targeted by many multinationals, is going to be harder to materialize. This is not to say that this opportunity is going to vanish, it is just that multinationals who for a while could sell the same consumer product (that they sold in the developed world) at similar price points in India are going to find that this not going to be easy anymore. They would have to strategically position their products in the market place as well as innovate more for the Indian market. There will be greater opportunities for the "shampoo sachet" type products in India rather than "Gucci handbags" in the near future. The early multinational entrants into the Indian market such as IBM, GE and John Deere that are focused on infrastructure-oriented businesses are going to be less affected, in my opinion. Despite the slowdown in the global economy (and its effect on India's growth), the Indian government will most likely continue to invest in projects that will lead to better infrastructure across the country. Therefore, these firms would be able to find adequate opportunities to contribute and gain from those efforts.

11.3. India as a Country

In many ways, I think the next few years of slower economic growth might be a blessing in disguise for India as a nation if the people and the government capitalize on it.

It is true that the tremendous economic growth in India brought a lot of good to many people all over the country, but the excesses were getting too concentrated in few pockets (as indicated in Chapter 9). This was causing some concerns that if things continued that way, it could lead to social unrest and turmoil. Slower growth is going to alleviate this concern considerably. The economic growth in cities had led to skyrocketing real estate prices due to speculation. In the upcoming months we will see a good correction in the real estate prices in many big cities where frankly, the valuations had gone berserk. This should help make it easier for lower middle class and middle class to afford housing in these cities and help alleviate their anxiety. Also, the slower growth in cities will reduce the massive inflow of villagers to the cities (at least temporarily) and will provide some time for the government to develop a strategic plan for the development of rural India that will lead to an all inclusive growth.

Second, in the last 15 years I saw a significant shift in the value system of the younger population (teenagers and college students). In my generation, in the eyes of parents of a middle class family, you had to be a doctor or an engineer in order to be successful (since those professions eventually led to gainful employment). Of course, this was not the best of expectations, and as a result, many teenagers were under a lot of pressure to perform well academically. However, this also had a positive impact in terms of the huge number of doctors and engineers India was able to train for the world economy. Since these are academically deep professions, it also led many to pursue higher education opportunities.

The newer generation that could find jobs as call center representatives soon after high school or any college education did not have to face the same kind of pressure at home. The positive side has been that they are happier. Many of these students are more creative and confident (as indicated in Chapter 10); however, many of them have also slackened off and have not realized their full potential since jobs for English-speaking graduates have been so easy. Fewer opportunities in easy jobs such as a call center representative is likely to create incentives for the youth to push themselves further and hopefully, create greater interest in knowledge and skill-oriented professions such as bio tech, information technology and high-skilled manufacturing rather than routine activities such as answering calls or managing remote desktops. Given that "skilled people" is India's biggest asset, this could be a welcome change for the long term.

Although the slower growth in the global economy will affect India's economic growth, the negative effects can be mitigated if the government, along with the private sector, acts in a decisive fashion.[6] India has an advantage over China in this period, due to two reasons — first, India is way behind China in terms of infrastructure and second, Indian SME have largely concentrated on the large domestic market. I believe that the current economic environment presents a unique opportunity for the government to push forward more private public partnerships for infrastructure development across the country. Many more roads, airports, dams, and power generation plants could be developed. This will improve employment, create opportunities and will be supported by world organizations. Finally, all inclusive growth plans (reducing the gap between the urban and rural India) are more likely to get the support of private sectors in this period, as outside private sector opportunities are reduced.

In closing, these are challenging times for any individual, firm or nation. It is hard to predict what might be the eventual outcome of this financial crisis on the global economy. However, it is said, crisis often brings out the best. This financial global financial crisis could be the shot in the arm for Indian firms, people and the government to work together, beyond caste, religion, language and national boundaries, to become an integral and important part of the global economy in the upcoming century.

References

1. Economic crisis of 2008 (2008). http://en.wikipedia.org/wiki/Economic_crisis_of_2008 [Retrieved 26 October 2008].
2. Ferris, T. (2007). *The 4-Hour Workweek*, New York: Crown Publishers.
3. Global financial crisis of September (2008). http://en.wikipedia.org/wiki/Global_financial_crisis_of_September%E2%80%93October_2008 [Retrieved 26 October 2008].

4. Greenspan, A (2008). U.S. in 'midst of a credit tsunami. http://edition.cnn.com/2008/BUSINESS/10/23/global.markets/index.html [Retrieved 24 October 2008].
5. Ibison, D (2008). Iceland requests $2bn bail-out from IMF, October 24 2008. http://www.ft.com/cms/s/0/9e812fb4-a1da-11dd-a32f-000077b07658, dwp_uuid=a36d4c40-fb42-11dc-8c3e-000077b07658.html.
6. India and the credit crisis (2008). From the Economist Intelligence Unit ViewsWire, October 14, 2008. http://www.economist.com/agenda/displaystory.cfm?story_id=12411151&fsrc=rss.
7. Report: GE will cut costs as it braces for 2009 (2008). Associated Press (New York), October 24, 2008. http://www.businessweek.com/ap/financial-news/D9416GIO0.htm.
8. Sheth, N and V Agarwal (2008). India's tech firms unlikely to elude global crisis lackluster profits from flagship companies suggest sector won't dodge global crisis, October 23, 2008. http://online.wsj.com/article/SB122469807147158981.html?mod=googlenews_wsj.
9. Summit leaders: Global teamwork needed to fight crunch (2008). http://edition.cnn.com/2008/WORLD/asiapcf/10/25/asia.europe/index.html.
10. U.S. financial crisis goes global Oxford Analytica (2008). http://www.forbes.com/business/2008/09/19/banks-contagion-globalization-cx_0919oxford.html.
11. Wang, T (2008). Investors continue fleeing asian equities, October 10, 2008. http://www.forbes.com/markets/2008/10/10/briefing-asia-closer-markets-equity-cx_tw_1010markets05.html?partner=whiteglove_google.

COMPANY INDEX

SUBJECT INDEX